T0300508

Career Stress
in Changing Times

The *Prevention in Human Services* series:

Career Stress
in Changing Times

James Campbell Quick
Robert E. Hess
Jared Hermalin
Jonathan D. Quick
Editors

Routledge
Taylor & Francis Group

LONDON AND NEW YORK

First Published 1990 by The Haworth Press, Inc.
Published 2013 by Routledge
711 Third Avenue, New York, NY 10017 USA
2 Park Square, Milton Park, Abingdon, Oxon OX14 4RN

Routledge is an imprint of the Taylor & Francis Group, an informa business

Career Stress in Changing Times has also been published as *Prevention in Human Services*, Volume 8, Number 1 1990.

Library of Congress Cataloging-in-Publication Data

Career stress in changing times / James Campbell Quick . . . [et al.], editors
    p. cm.
    "Has also been published as Prevention in human services, volume 8, number 1, 1990" — Verso t.p.
    Includes bibliographical references.
    ISBN 0-86656-956-1
       1. Job stress. 2. Organizational change. 3. Career changes. 4. Career development. I. Quick, James C.
HF5548.85.C37 1990
650'.01'9 —dc20
                                             90-35840
                                             CIP

ISBN 978-0-866-56956-9 (HBK)

Career Stress in Changing Times

CONTENTS

ABOUT THE EDITORS

James Campbell Quick, PhD, MBA, is a professor at the University of Texas at Arlington. He is co-author of *Organizational Stress and Preventive Management* (McGraw-Hill, 1984), published in German as *Unternehmen ohne Stress* (1986), *Stress and Challenge at the Top: The Paradox of the Successful Executive* (John Wiley & Sons, Ltd., 1990), and co-editor of *Work Stress: Health Care Systems in the Workplace* (Praeger Scientific, 1987). Dr. Quick has been the stress expert for the American Psychological Association to the United States Public Health Service and the Institute of Medicine, National Academy of Sciences on Health Objectives for the Nation—Year 2000. He visited the Peoples Republic of China in 1988 as a member of the Society of Behavioral Medicine for a scientific exchange on stress with the Chinese Association of Science and Technology. He is an editorial review board member for *The Executive*, an Academy of Management Publication, and *Stress Medicine*.

Robert E. Hess, PhD, is the Chief of the Bureau of Mental Health in Boise, Idaho. He has received several national awards for his work in prevention, has published extensively in the field, and has served on and chaired various organizations devoted to furthering the philosophy of prevention. He is past Chair of the Division of Prevention of the National Council of Community Mental Health Centers. Dr. Hess is editor of *Prevention in Human Services*.

Jared Hermalin, PhD, is a faculty member of the Department of Psychiatry, Center of Excellence in Addiction Treatment Research, University of Medicine & Dentistry of New Jersey, School of Osteopathic Medicine. He is the founder of the Philadelphia Metropolitan Area Self-Help Clearinghouse, Co-Director of a Swarthmore College urban field placement program, and Director of one of New Jersey's largest alcohol/drug counselor certification programs. Dr. Hermalin has served on a National Institute on Drug Abuse (NIDA) contract review committee and has been a consultant to the National

Council of Community Mental Health Centers. He is also the associate editor of the journal *Prevention in Human Services,* as well as a reviewer for three other journals.

Jonathan D. Quick, MD, is Director of the Drug Management Program, Management Sciences for Health (MSH), in Boston, Massachusetts. He is serving as Health Services Advisor for MSH in Peshawar, Pakistan from 1989 to 1992. Dr. Quick is board certified in preventive medicine and family practice. He currently serves on the World Health Organization (WHO) Informal Working Group on Estimating Drug Requirements. He is co-author of *Organizational Stress and Preventive Management* (McGraw-Hill, 1984), published in German as *Unternehmen ohne Stress* (1986), *Stress and Challenge at the Top: The Paradox of the Successful Executive* (John Wiley & Sons, Ltd., 1990), and co-editor of *Work Stress: Health Care Systems in the Workplace* (Praeger Scientific, 1987). He is also senior editor of *Managing Drug Supply: The Selection, Procurement, Distribution, and Use of Pharmaceuticals in Primary Health Care,* a publication printed in Spanish and French, as well as English.

Career Stress
in Changing Times

Preface

I have been fortunate to have had a rewarding career in the U.S. Navy for 32 years as a test pilot and manager of research and development organizations. I am also fortunate to currently be in a second rewarding but completely different career—a university academic career as a professor and faculty administrator. In both of these careers I have observed the importance of technology and the turbulent changes it forces both business and academic organizations to face. These change sources are complex, varied, and normally difficult to understand. Because these changes follow an apparently random course where the linkages are not only non-linear but are obscure, it is becoming increasingly difficult to cope with them. It is causing researchers and writers to begin to focus on the management of technological unpredictability and unsettling changes—the management of chaos. While many organizations are attempting to respond to these technological and environmental changes, I have found that most people in organizations—both managers and employees—are not responding well to these changes. It is most often manifested in their expectations about their careers and the career stresses these changes create.

This book addresses these timely and critical issues. It is a significant addition to our knowledge in the areas of changing environments and their impact on career stages and career stress. Each of us, during our career life cycle, will experience the changes and sources of career stress associated with the early, middle, and late career stages. This book takes a first step in analyzing these career stages and describing the elements that cause stress points and changes in one's needs, expectations, and satisfaction throughout a career. I found this particularly relevant and valuable as most adults will change jobs and/or employers as many as 5 to 8 times during their working lifetime. As each of us pass through the early, middle and late career stages and change jobs, we need to examine the

xiii

sources of stress, the stress transition points and the issues that are associated with each stage. It is only through this examination that we can cope successfully with and develop career plans for a rational approach to solving career problems and making the appropriate career decisions.

I can directly relate to these issues in my own career. I did very little planning for my initial and early career occupations and experienced the stress points and distress identified in this book for the early career stage. As I progressed through this stage and into the midcareer stage, I realized that I needed to plan for a second major career upon the completion of my professional Navy career. This meant being aware of the opportunities and threats in the changing external environment, and seeking as much knowledge and education as possible to give me the capacity to be able to venture into new areas. All of these dimensions (and others I wish I had been aware of) are provided in the framework of this book. With the 35-54 year old age group increasing dramatically and composing over one-half the total labor force by 1995, the midcareer stage (that I am currently in) will only increase in importance and create stress points and stressful decisions of greater magnitude than ever before.

It is critical for all of us to do as much career planning, extend our boundaries of knowledge, and learn what others have researched, experienced and written about as we transition from early-to middle-to late career stages and into retirement. Each of these stages will provide a set of unique stressors, expectations and restructuring for our individual careers. The best and probably most important preventive-stress mechanism available to us is our ability to predict what is ahead and to plan for it. The key is career planning, i.e., to develop a self-image of who we are, what we want to do, and be able to analyze what is happening in our environment, so that we can make less stressful and better decisions. In the last section of this book, Edgar Schein calls these self images "career anchors" and emphasizes that each person has to discover what their own career anchors are so they can make better plans and make better decisions in career choice situations.

This book addresses all these career stage issues and is an excellent contribution to the integration of our knowledge of the various fields of career stress, career planning, and preventive stress management in a chaotic environment. As individuals, each of us has the responsibility for career planning and career anchor management and cannot afford to wait and hope someone else will do it for us. As Shein states "only if the employee of the future enters the labor market psychologically prepared for the turbulence he or she will find there, can he or she cope effectively with its realities and turn stressors into opportunities for growth." Reading and understanding the concepts, ideas, and research findings in this book should be a valuable aid in preparing ourselves for this turbulent world we live and work in as we enter the 21st century.

Wayne D. Bodensteiner, PhD
Rear Admiral, U.S. Navy (Retired)

Acknowledgements

The editors would like to thank Adele E. Neupert for her helpful administrative and editorial assistance in the preparation of this volume. We would also like to thank Beverly Antilley, Beverly Gilbert, and Cecilia Weisenfels for their secretarial support in the preparation of several of the contributions to this volume. Excellent support has lightened the editors' stress.

I. INTRODUCTION

The Changing Times of Life:
Career in Context

James Campbell Quick
Jonathan D. Quick
University of Texas at Arlington

SUMMARY. This article contains four sections, the first outlines the individual needs and characteristics which are generally identified with the early, middle, and late stages of a person's career. This discussion provides the framework for the remainder of the volume. The second section presents the case of Dr. Otto A. Faust, a 100 year old pediatrician whose career spanned 64 years and had several transitions. A brief analysis of the case leads into the third section, which examines seven career stressors. The concluding section identifies the four basic social and cultural forces which will be developed throughout the volume and which will influence careers into the twenty-first century: (1) women at work, (2) the decline of blue-collar labor, (3) the changing demographic distribution, and (4) the growth of a world economy.

In terms of time, energy, concern, and money, the career is one of the more important investments that a person makes during a

Reprints may be obtained from James Campbell Quick, Department of Management, University of Texas at Arlington, Box 19467, Arlington, TX 76019.

lifetime. This volume is about careers and about career stress in a period of considerable change in the structure, content, and cultural environment in which careers exist. To place the career in the context of the life experience and its value to the individual, we will develop four major sections in this chapter.

First, we will describe the individual needs and characteristics which are generally identified with the early, middle, and late stages of a person's career. This discussion provides the framework for the remainder of the volume.

Second, we will examine the case of Otto A. Faust, a professional whose life exceeds 100 years and whose career spanned 64 years. This case will allow us to examine major career transitions (there were five in his career) and the process of career development through changing times.

Third, we will develop the notion of career stress and discuss seven sources of career stress. These will be illustrated by reference to Dr. Faust's career.

Finally, we will conclude with a discussion of four contemporary cultural and social changes which will impact careers over the next 25 to 50 years. These changes are (1) women at work, (2) the decline of blue-collar labor, (3) the changing demographic distribution, and (4) the growth of a world economy.

CAREER STAGES

Through the career cycle a person experiences changes in his or her roles, activities, abilities, and expectations. One's needs and sources of satisfaction change and the sources of career stress change. Each person's career is a unique sequence of responsibilities, experiences, attitudes, and accomplishments, yet there are features which typically characterize the early, middle, and late career stages.

Hall (1976) has identified key developmental needs in early, middle, and late career stages (Table 1). His career stages build logically on the broader context of life stages. The earliest notable work in this area is Erik Erikson's theory of eight life stages. Erikson (1950, 1963) proposed that each stage is characterized by a developmental task which the person must accomplish before moving to the next life stage. He identified four childhood stages (oral, anal, genital, and latency). Transition into adulthood begins with *adolescence*, the developmental task for which is achieving *ego identity*. The next stage is *young adulthood*, for which the task is to develop *involvements and intimacy*. Erikson's stage of young adulthood occurs during the early career period. The seventh of Erikson's life stages is *adulthood*, during which the focus is on *generativity*, that is, contributing to the next generation through productivity and creativity. Failure in this task results in stagnation. Adulthood spans from middle career into late career. Erikson's final stage is *maturity*, characterized by *ego integrity*, acceptance of one's life cycle.

Erikson's theory was built on clinical as well as historical observations and emphasized psychological development. Other work has focused on developmental stages in career behavior. Super and his colleagues (1957) identified five stages in vocational development: the growth stage (childhood, birth to age 14), the exploration stage (adolescence, ages 15 to 24), the establishment stage (young adulthood, ages 25 to 44), the maintenance stage (maturity, ages 45 to 64), and the decline stage (age 65 on).

In another early look at vocational development, Miller and Form (1951) focused on job behaviors, rather than developmental tasks. They identified five occupational stages: the preparatory work period (childhood), the initial work period (late teens), the trial work period (late twenties, early thirties), the stable work period (thirties to the sixties), and retirement. Through empirical work with AT&T managers, Hall and Nougaim (1968) found support for the concept of career stages in management similar to Miller and Form's occupational stages and the vocational development stages of Super and his associates. Hall and Nougaim's stages were pre-work (childhood), establishment (late twenties), advancement (thirties to mid-forties), maintenance (late forties to sixties), and retirement.

More recently Levinson (1978), Sheehey (1976), and Gould (1978) have described psychological and career stages through which people pass. These and earlier typologies differ among themselves with respect to emphasis, terminology, and timing of the transitions between stages, but the fundamental concept of life stages and, within one's working life, career stages, has been

clearly established by this work. Using the basic career stages identified by Hall (1976) and many others—early, middle, and late career—it is possible to synthesize common elements in the descriptions of career stages. These common elements are summarized in
Table 1.

Early Career

The early career begins for some in the teenage years and lasts
into the early to late thirties. It is a time of exploration, a trial work
period. A core objective of the early career period is to settle into an
organization and to achieve occupational security. This is done by
gaining recognition and establishing oneself within the organization. For some this establishment period may begin with the first
job; for others the first area of endeavor may prove unsatisfactory,
leading to one or two job changes before finding a position in which
the individual can become established. Task needs in the early career include the development of action skills which build on pre-
work education and training, the opportunity to exercise creativity
and innovation, and the need to develop a specialty area. Rotation
to a new area every three to five years may be necessary to prevent
early overspecialization. For some, the early career stage can be a
time of rapid, if at times unsteady, advancement.

The early career period is characterized in psychological terms by
the need to first develop ego identity and then to develop involvements and intimacy. Social and emotional needs are for a balance of
support necessary for self-confidence and autonomy necessary for
growth and learning. The need to establish oneself among other
young colleagues raises feelings of rivalry and competition which
can motivate higher performance or interfere with effective work
relations.

Several key early career issues are dealt with in this volume.
Gray and his associates discuss the role of self-help, consultant/
counselor assistance, employer-sponsored help, and courses offered
by educational organizations and professional associations in the
career planning process. The underlying notion is that good fit
through good decisions will prevent later distress. Nelson's chapter
moves to the transition into a new organization and the associated

TABLE 1. Career Stages

STAGE	CHARACTERISTICS	TASK NEEDS	SOCIO-EMOTIONAL NEEDS
Early Career	* exploration * trial period * establishment * recognition	* relevant action skills * specialty development * creativity, innovation * rotate to new area in 3-5 years	* ego identity, intimacy * support * autonomy * deal with feelings of rivalry, competition
Middle Career	* stability * achievement * growth versus maintenance versus stagnation	* skills in training & coaching younger employees * updating & integrating skills * broader view of work & the organization * rotation into new job requiring new skills	* sense of generativity, productivity * mutual support for coping with mid-career stress * expression of feelings about mid-life changes * reorganize values and self-concepts * less self-indulgence and competitiveness
Late Career	* transition out of work organization * adjustment into retirement	* shift from power role to consultation, guidance, wisdom role * establish self in more non-work activities	* ego integrity, acceptance of one's life cycle * use integrated life experiences to support & counsel others * gradual detachment from career identity

Adapted from: Hall (1976).

5

adjustments needed to prevent distress and strain. Long's chapter vividly illustrates the process of making the transition into a career. In a sense, it is a report from the firing line.

Middle Career

As an individual establishes himself or herself in a career, the individual passes into mid-career. The mid-career stage extends from the thirties into the late fifties or sixties. For many people, this is a period of stability in one's chosen occupation. For others, the established work pattern becomes a succession of unrelated jobs.

Task needs in the middle career stage include the development of skills to support and develop other, usually younger, employees; the need to continually update and integrate one's own skills; the evolution of a broader view of work and the organization; and, in many cases, rotation into jobs requiring new skills. For some people this is a period of continued growth and advancement. For others it is a period of maintenance, of continuation along established lines. For a few, mid-career is a time of stagnation and early decline.

The middle career period is characterized in Erikson's terms by the need for generativity — productivity and contribution to the next generation. It can be a time of reflection and reorganization of values and concepts about work and family. Awareness of physical aging and mortality may contribute to mid-life stress, and feelings of limited time, lack of accomplishment, restlessness, or even defeat are associated with mid-career stress. But it can also be a time of reduced self-indulgence and competitiveness, and efforts toward mutual support help in coping with mid-life and mid-career stress.

The breadth and depth of mid-career issues is reflected in the contents of the third section of this volume. Bhagat considers the stress of blending home and family life, looking at both the dilemmas and hopes for achieving a balance between these realms of living. The lack of integration between these life arenas will increase an individual's level of stress. Gerpott's contribution looks at intracompany transfers and the role of social support in contributing to the success of these transitions. Matteson and Ivancevich address the stresses associated with the merger and acquisition boom of the

1980s, generating ideas for organizational as well as individual preventive stress management. Pliner's chapter addresses the specific issue of minimizing distress in the termination process, both for those who leave and those who stay. Hurrell, McLaney, and Murphy found in their study of 6,000 postal workers that job stressors become less important in adversely affecting health during the middle years while non-work stressors become more important. In addition, social support appears to become increasingly important as a prevention strategy in the middle years. Davis and Kedela look at learning and understanding as two key elements of preventive stress management in the middle career years.

Late Career

The transition out of the work organization and adjustment into retirement usually begins in the late fifties or early sixties, although for some it begins earlier. Late career transition may lead to retirement into full-time leisure activities; to another, usually less demanding, job; to a retirement career of civic and voluntary work; or to a combination of these endeavors. A determined minority of people manage to avoid late career transition almost indefinitely.

Late career transition out of the work organization may mean a shift from a power role to a consultative, guiding, wisdom-sharing role. An individual's effectiveness in this role depends in part on his or her attitude and adjustment to the late career adjustment and in part on the receptivity of younger members of the organization. The other major late career task is to expand or, if necessary, begin establishing non-work activities.

The psychological task in late career is, in Erikson's words, "ego integrity . . . the acceptance of one's one and only life cycle" (Erikson, 1963, p. 268). While still at work, this means integrating one's career experiences to support and counsel others. The psychological task is also to undertake a gradual detachment from the organization and from one's career identity.

The final section of this volume includes a study by McGoldrick and Cooper which looks at men in the United Kingdom who retired early. A key finding was the essential role of financial resources in a successful retirement transition, though other preventive stress management resources were also found to be important. J. F. Quick's chapter is another report from the firing line, this one looking at the structuring of the retirement years through activities that draw on developed talents, abilities, and interest. The core of Quick's thesis is the prevention of undue stress through continued usefulness.

Conclusion

Schein's concluding chapter synthesizes the whole volume while introducing the notion of an internal career which emphasizes self-responsibility as a basis for preventing career distress. He stresses the importance of career anchors to enable individuals to make better decisions regarding the careers they wish to pursue. He also makes suggestions regarding how companies and educational institutions can assist individuals in making career selections and transitions but concludes that the bulk of responsibility falls on the individual.

CAREER IN CONTEXT:
THE CASE OF OTTO A. FAUST, M.D.

The progression through early, middle, and late career stages, along with the identification of the stresses associated with various transition points, is best illustrated through a case example. A particularly appropriate example is the long and rewarding career of Dr. Otto Faust, Emeritus Professor of Pediatrics at Albany Medical College, retired psychoanalytic pediatrician, retired baby food consultant, and the father of two daughters. He was born on June 20, 1887 and lives in a small retirement home at present. A timeline of his life cycle, with an emphasis on the career aspect, is presented in Figure 1.

As we see, Dr. Faust's career spanned 64 of his 100 plus years. It would not be fair to conclude that 64% of his life was devoted to his career because much time during the mid-life years was devoted to raising children, family activities, time with his grandsons, and a month of vacation in Canada each August. On the other hand, there

FIGURE 1. A Career in Context: The Lifecycle of Otto A. Faust, M.D. (1887-)

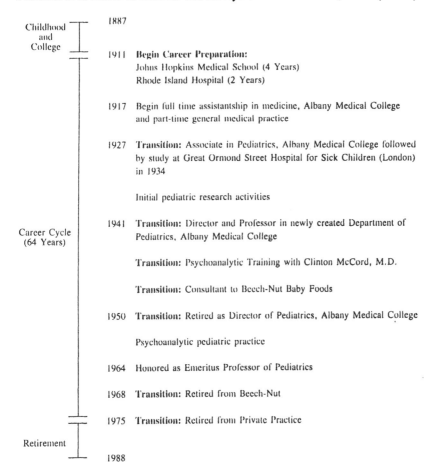

Childhood and College	1887
	1911 Begin Career Preparation: Johns Hopkins Medical School (4 Years) Rhode Island Hospital (2 Years)
	1917 Begin full time assistantship in medicine, Albany Medical College and part-time general medical practice
	1927 Transition: Associate in Pediatrics, Albany Medical College followed by study at Great Ormond Street Hospital for Sick Children (London) in 1934
	Initial pediatric research activities
Career Cycle (64 Years)	1941 Transition: Director and Professor in newly created Department of Pediatrics, Albany Medical College
	Transition: Psychoanalytic Training with Clinton McCord, M.D.
	Transition: Consultant to Beech-Nut Baby Foods
	1950 Transition: Retired as Director of Pediatrics, Albany Medical College
	Psychoanalytic pediatric practice
	1964 Honored as Emeritus Professor of Pediatrics
	1968 Transition: Retired from Beech-Nut
	1975 Transition: Retired from Private Practice
Retirement	1988

was time in the childhood and college years concerned with careers. It is at that point that we should first look.

Dr. Faust was the grandson of a German immigrant named John Faust. John Faust's trade was barrelmaking when he immigrated to America with his young wife. He was a forceful, proud man with much drive and ambition. These characteristics led him to night school in veterinary medicine and he became a "professional man" upon graduation, practicing veterinary medicine until the end of his life. John had four sons and, as was characteristic of many German homes, he largely told his sons what to do. He did give them choices in terms of the type of doctor they would become, be that veterinarian, homeopath, surgeon, or internist. Each of the four sons received a medical degree and each practiced his profession, though all were not satisfied.

It was against this willful, medically-oriented family backdrop that Otto A. Faust was raised. As a child of near 10, Otto contracted tuberculosis and was flat on his back for a year. His father, Louis, a homeopath, appeared to have doctored his son well, and the disease appeared to have little impact on Otto's long-term development. As Vaillant (1977) concludes in his longitudinal study, isolated traumatic events rarely mold individual lives. While Dr. Faust and his generation were not "told" to enter medicine as a career, it appears that his career decision was forged from the scripting of his family background.

Dr. Faust's career preparation consisted of four years of medical education at Johns Hopkins University followed by a two-year internship at the Rhode Island Hospital. This was followed by teaching and staff work for the Dean of Albany Medical College as well as general medical practice. While he was most interested in becoming an Army medical officer in World War I, his teaching skills were identified as critical to the education of medical students and he never served in the military. By 1927 he had developed a particular interest in work with children and decided to limit his practice to pediatrics. He accepted an associate position in pediatrics at the medical college and enhanced his pediatric education with hospital internships in Boston and the Great Ormond Street Hospital in London, England. Dr. Faust supported himself financially through his pediatric practice, receiving little if any compensation for his duties at Albany Medical College. (This was not uncommon for this period.)

While teaching at the medical college, Dr. Faust also initiated a limited research career which spanned a twenty year period (Faust, 1936, 1938, 1952; Faust & Stein, 1935; Hertzog & Faust, 1950). These teaching and research activities led to Dr. Faust's selection in 1941 to be Director and Professor of Pediatrics in the newly created

Department of Pediatrics at Albany Medical College. He served in the Director's position for nine years.

With the creation of the Department of Pediatrics at Albany Medical College in 1941, the United States had only six departments of pediatrics in the country. It was in this context that Dr. Faust had an opportunity to become a consultant to the Beech-Nut Baby Food Company. He maintained this relationship over a twenty-two year period, advising the company on nutritional and dietary requirements for infants. In addition to this interest in diet and nutrition for babies (Seadan & Faust, 1965), Dr. Faust evolved an increasing interest in the emotional lives of children. This eventually led to a three year study of 140 tonsillectomized children, with support from the Albany Society for the Advancement of Psychosomatic Medicine and the New York State Department of Health (Faust, 1952).

This competence had been enhanced by the successful completion of analysis with Clinton McCord, one of Freud's followers and a senior colleague to Dr. Faust (see McCord, 1940). This psychoanalytic work with Dr. McCord began in the early 1940s and extended over a four year period. Dr. Faust began further limiting his practice to hyperactive and emotionally disturbed children.

During the early 1950s, the Albany Medical College honored him with Professor Emeritus status and the Otto A. Faust Lecture Series in Pediatrics, under the auspices of which the college would bring in one eminent pediatric researcher each year for a several day period. His activities and responsibilities in the daily life of the department were minimized as he focused on developing his new specialization. The death of his wife of 40 years in 1956 was personally painful but left only a minor impact upon a very active career.

Tiring of the travel associated with his consultant relationship with Beech-Nut, Dr. Faust resigned his position in 1968 at the age of 81. He continued his private practice in psychoanalytic work with children for another six years, when he retired from his medical career at the age of 88. This concluded a remarkably evolutionary career span of 64 years beginning with his entry into medical school at the age of 24.

There are four important points to note in analyzing Dr. Faust's case. First, the structure of society and the medical profession during the twentieth century in America were enabling forces in the unfolding of Dr. Faust's career. Some in other career paths may not be nearly as fortunate. An example in this regard would be the steelworkers in America since World War II. The change in supply and demand has constricted available career opportunities, making it more challenging for steel workers and managers to be successful.

Second, we note no major points of discontinuity in the evolution of the career. Even when opportunity does not exert its stamp on the progress of a career, there may be discontinuities which occur for various reasons. For example, one of Dr. Faust's colleagues in the late career years was a man who had been an attorney and well respected judge into his late 40s. At that time, with his children raised, the judge turned a corner, went to medical school, and pursued a second career in medicine. This sort of discontinuity may result from a changing interest within the personality or delayed pursuit of early interests.

A third point to notice in Figure 1 is that there is not an extended plateau in Dr. Faust's career. Rather, there are a series of at least four developmental transitions that enhance and enrich the career. These occur through an interaction of the evolving interests of the personality with environmental opportunities. A good example would be the relationship with Beech-Nut Baby Foods, a company in close proximity to Albany Medical College and interested in retaining an authority in pediatrics. We also see two or three transitions that occur following the peak of the career which facilitate its movement to completion. This is consistent with Levison's (1978) research which focuses on the adult life transitions of men. His research and Dr. Faust's experience suggest that these transitions need not be crises. Vaillant's (1977) research also bears this out. This does not imply that there are neither difficulties nor pain. As Vaillant (1977) notes, he found not a single life in his first ten years with the Grant Study group (1967-1977) in which there were no trials or difficulties.

A fourth and final point of note is that Dr. Faust's career and life are following through to a natural close. Not all careers or lives do that, such as was the case for President Kennedy. Less severe tragedies may also intrude on one's career. For example, a highly promising young, field grade Air Force officer's father-in-law passed away suddenly in his middle life years, leaving the family business to his daughter and son-in-law. The young officer's career was able to transition into an active reserve status and he eventually attained the rank of brigadier general. While this is a highly successful career, it was reshaped dramatically in the middle years by tragic events.

From a career perspective, these are the four main points of analysis relevant to Dr. Faust's case. We will turn next to the issue of career stress, referring back at times to Figure 1 and the case presentation for purposes of illustration.

CAREER STRESS

One approach to the study of career stress would be to look at occupational comparisons. Colligan, Smith, and Hurrell (1977) take this approach in examining psychological distress symptoms. An alternative to this comparative approach, which has value from an epidemiological perspective, is to examine the stress points and/ or issues throughout the duration of the career cycle. It is this latter approach which we will use here. In this regard, we will address seven sources of stress.

1. Initial career decision
2. Career transition points
3. Changes in occupations
4. Obsolescence of skills and/or knowledge
5. Uncertainty and risk
6. Career-life fit
7. Retirement

These seven sources of stress are not the only ones experienced by those in careers, though they give us a framework to think within. It is noteworthy that in each of these issues, individual differences play an important part. For example, some will find little stress in the initial career decision while others will find it a stressful dilemma. So it is for each of these issues which we will discuss.

Initial Career Decision

The initial career decision provides the basis for an individual's first major life transition and can therefore be stressful. Many of the foundations for the decision may be laid down in childhood based upon family stories, models, and aspiration levels. In the case of Dr. Faust, the initial career decision appears quite uncomplicated and a natural extension of family history. This creates an evolutionary appearance and hence a less stressful event. High stress levels at this point will be experienced by individuals who have competing and conflicting interests within themselves. For example, a person with strong enterprising interests as well as strong artistic interests will experience stress around the gratification of these potentially competing interests.

Another source of stress concerns one's degree of reality testing. Fantasies about careers in the early and middle teenage years are an important input to career decisions. They reflect an individual's desires, hopes, and aspirations for the future. However, not all fantasies are realistic. The more reality testing a person does, the more incremental will be their experience of stress and their adaptation.

Career Transition Points

Career transition points are an inevitable feature of later stages in the career. The successful negotiation of these transition points requires adaptation, change, and adjustment on many fronts. In the case of Dr. Faust, we see three distinct, developmental transition points which are (1) the movement into pediatrics, (2) the addition of baby food consulting activities, and (3) the psychoanalytic training which led to work with emotionally disturbed and/or hyperactive children. In this case the transitions were gradual and evolutionary. Not all transitions are such. Take for example the case of Ronald Reagan. He pursued an acting career for an extended period, then turned direction and developed a political career. Engineers, accountants, and other professionals experience a key transition as they move into management responsibilities. The stress of this transition is what motivated AT&T to collaborate with Williams College in 1956 to create one of the earliest executive programs for technical experts and specialists who would be moving into management (Fitzsimmons, 1987).

Changes in Occupations

Changes in occupations occur just as do changes within individuals. For individuals who are in an occupation for an extended period of time, this becomes an important issue. Supply and demand changes for members of an occupation are just one example of this. A dramatic case of this has been seen in the American steel industry since World War II as the technology of steel production has changed dramatically and the demand for steelworkers has shrunk substantially. The old and honorable craft of the shipwright is another example of decline. As ship construction changed with the introduction of steel, fiberglass, and other materials, the shipwright no longer was in demand as in centuries past. We have seen a dramatic rise in demand, on the other hand, for computer and information specialists of all kinds in the last two decades. The occupational and professional forces driving these changes place demands on the individual to adapt and change, either effectively or ineffectively.

Obsolescence of Skills and/or Knowledge

Obsolescence of skills and/or knowledge may be an accompanying source of stress for the individual. Many professions afford their members postgraduate, continuing education and/or educational opportunities to improve the effectiveness of the individual's adaptation over time. Few occupations are so routinized that they do not grow and change. The mechanisms for accommodation need not be formal training or education, however. Informal learning activities may be equally effective in managing the stress of obsolescence. Scott (1988) makes the point that both training and education can occur in either formal or informal ways.

If we turn to the case of Dr. Faust, we see two formal and one informal learning periods which occurred subsequent to the formal medical education process and led to the avoidance of obsolescence. The first formal period was the residence in England which contributed to his developing competence in pediatrics. The second formal period was his four year psychoanalytic training that prepared him to treat hyperactive and emotionally disturbed children. The informal learning was associated with his research activities, for which he was not prepared in medical school. He developed the limited research skills he had through collaborative relationships with various faculty colleagues in the medical college.

Uncertainty and Risk

Uncertainty and risk are another important source of stress, more so in some occupations than others. Professional athletics would be a good example where this is quite relevant. The percentage of potential baseball players, football players, or basketball players who eventually have successful major league careers is quite small. The rewards for success are quite substantial as we see with current salary structures. However, failure to succeed at that level does not leave one in a very good position relevant to that career path. Minor league players may get by but do not make a very decent salary. This may be one reason why professional baseball is now encouraging young, potential players to complete college degrees as an alternative career route to success in the major leagues.

The active careerist can do much in terms of choosing the best odds and then attempting to improve them. March (1988) uses the analogy of placing a bet at the track and then bribing the bookies. This strategy improves the odds even more in one's favor.

Career-Life Fit

Career-life fit is the sixth source of career stress that one must confront. The career, albeit an important arena, is only one of several arenas in which the individual operates through the adulthood years. Family roles as spouse and parent, personal leisure time preferences, and community involvement are other arenas which compete for time and attention. The travel associated with many corporate positions and sales or consulting work may set up competitive time schedules with one's family and home life. The stress becomes one of making trade-offs and achieving integration among various demands.

Defining a comfortable balance between one's career role, one's family role, and one's role in the community may require difficult choices. Figure 2 illustrates two of many possible patterns, one a high career-involvement pattern and the other a low career-involvement pattern. Considerable stress can be generated if an individual becomes overcommitted in one or more spheres or if there is incon-

FIGURE 2. Two examples of the Career-Life Fit in Perspective

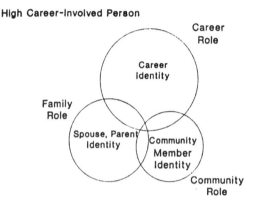

High Career-Involved Person

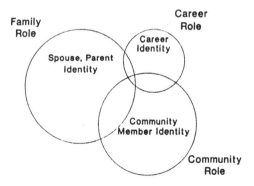

Low Career-Involved Person

Adapted from: Douglas T. Hall. (1976). *Careers in Organizations,* Goodyear Publishing, Inc., Santa Monica, CA.

gruity between a person's own sense of commitment and the expectations of others. Inability to set priorities among career, family, and community roles or inability to obtain agreement on these roles from other people can result in a chronic sense of frustration — ongoing career stress.

Individuals and organizations should also acknowledge that it is normal for the level of career involvement to wax and wane over the career cycle. While some people may maintain high career involvement throughout their working lives and others may maintain low career involvement, many people experience shifts in the career-life fit. Career involvement may be high in the early career stage; the family knowingly (sometimes unknowingly) sacrifices for the promise of future success and security. With mid-career stability and a growing family, the balance may shift away from career. In the late career stage, as children leave home, emphasis may turn back to career or possibly to greater community involvement through social, athletic, religious, or charitable activities.

With both initial definition of career-life fit and redefinition during the career cycle, the objective is not to achieve some ideal standard, but to find the fit that suits the individual and to achieve consensus on one's roles in each sphere of activity.

Another and increasingly common career-life fit issue is that of dual careers. Planning two careers as well as a life together is a complicated, stressful matter for a couple. The complications also have implications for corporate, public service, and military organizations which must incorporate dual career considerations in their personnel planning systems.

Retirement

Retirement may either be a release or a major stressor for a career person. The Cooper and MacGoldrick as well as J. F. Quick contributions to this volume address a number of key issues concerned with the transition into retirement. As we see in the case of Dr. Faust, the retirement transition may occur in several stages. His first transition occurred in 1950 (age 63) with his retirement as Director of the Department of Pediatrics, continued through his retirement from Beech-Nut in 1968 (18 years later), and finished with his retirement from private practice in 1975 (see Figure 1). The key issue for those moving into retirement is time structuring. Our social systems provide much basic structure for the structuring of large amounts of time in childhood and the developmental years (school) as well as during the career years (work). The individual must assume much greater responsibility for structuring his or her time in retirement, as illustrated in the article by J. F. Quick.

SOCIAL AND CULTURAL FORCES

There are four social and cultural forces which have been summarized in Table 2. These are demographic distribution, a world economy, women at work, and blue-collar workers. The nature of each force and its impact on careers will be discussed briefly here and elaborated on in various articles in this volume.

Demographic Distribution

The demographic distribution of American society can be expected to change markedly over the next quarter of a century. There are several elements which will contribute to this change, the most important being the change in age distribution. The average age of the population is rising, in part due to the movement of baby-boomers through the life cycle. There is also an increase due to individuals living longer. A person born in 1900 had a life expectancy of less than 50 years while one born in 1985 has a life expectancy of nearly 75 years. That is a 50% increase in life expectancy in less than a century. Mandatory retirement ages have been pushed back and may be expected to be pushed back even further, extending the career cycle for the individual who so chooses.

Age change is not the only demographic change to anticipate, though it may be the most important. Other changes are more regionalized, such as the Hispanic influx in the southwestern United States and some Asian immigration on the west coast. These changes will affect opportunities, competition, and training needs through our career management systems.

TABLE 2. Social and Cultural Forces Impacting Career Patterns

Cultural/Social Force	Nature of the Force	Impact on Careers
1. Demographic distribution	As the babyboom generation moves through the society and the following less dense generations come along, the population in America is aging.	There will be severe competition among the babyboomers and then a comparative dearth of senior talent for a period.
2. World economy	The growth of international organizations, increased inter-relations across national economies has broken down international economic barriers.	People will need to become increasingly aware of cultural differences and patterns of behavior.
3. Women at work	The proportion of women working has risen to about 40% over the past decade and appears to be stabilizing.	Women have entered traditionally male careers. Barriers and distinctions between careers are breaking down.
4. Blue-collar workers	The movement from a manufacturing based economy toward a service oriented economy has caused a decline in demand for blue-collar labor.	Large numbers of skilled blue-collar laborers will see career paths end, leaving the society with large numbers of unemployed or in-transition workers.

20

World Economy

A world economy is not imminent but it is the direction in which national economies are moving. The decreasing barriers between national economies have several effects. Events that occur within one economy are no longer isolated and cause ripple effects throughout other economies. For example, difficulties in loan repayments to American banks on the part of Latin American countries have placed substantial strains on these banks.

A second factor is the exchange and transfer of technology. For example, in becoming an exemplary company within the mini-mill steel section of the economy, Chapparal Steel company has had officers visit locations in Japan, West Germany, Scandinavia, and other parts of the world. This sort of international learning activities has become increasingly prevalent in a number of industries.

A third factor is the increasing loss of distinction between labor markets. That is, there are increasing exchanges among countries and economies of labor. For example, as Japanese companies have established subsidiaries or companies in America, they have also sent some of their managerial talent. Corporate Americans often have overseas assignments associated with international operations. Finally, the trend is reflected in business textbooks and international management programs offered in colleges of business administration.

Woman at Work

Women at work is not a new phenomenon. There were many working women during World War II. However, that was largely national necessity. The current trend toward a large percentage of women working has been of a different nature. A combination of personal career interest, efforts to improve the economic well being of the family unit, and the necessity of working for a very large proportion of divorced, single mothers have all contributed to the influx of women into the workforce.

There have been a variety of effects from the influx. Women have frequently pursued female dominated occupations in the past, such as nursing, secretarial work, or teaching. While vital occupations, the comparative financial rewards in these occupations are fewer than in others. Women have, therefore, been moving into previously male dominated occupations such as medicine, engineering, and corporate management. While not always receiving equivalent nor comparable rewards to male colleagues, females are continuing to strive in that direction.

This trend leads to some new sexual issues and dilemmas in the workplace. For example, what does an organization do when two executives of the opposite sex become involved in a romantic love relationship? (Collins, 1983). Sex and romance take on new dimensions at work.

The issue of changing health behaviors, such as smoking and alcohol consumption, becomes an important one for working women. Men have historically neither lived as long as women nor had as prevalently healthy behaviors in some areas. Women are now catching up with men. Is working truly hazardous to our health?

Blue-Collar Workers

Blue-collar workers have been hit hard in many industries as well as across the board due to the shifting nature of work in America. The shift from an agrarian to an industrial society was largely complete during this century. The shift to a service and information oriented society will not be complete until the next century. The net result of the significant decline in manufacturing's demand for labor has placed significant stresses on the blue-collar worker (Shostak, 1980).

There are both social and industrial consequences of this change, most notably the societal demand for retraining and/or reeducation of blue-collar workers left behind by changing labor demand. This has been especially true in the automotive and steel industries during the past several decades.

CONCLUSION

Individuals structure their time in six basic ways, some of which are generally constructive to the development of careers, such as activities, while others, such as games, generally are not. While these six ways of time structuring help us understand an individual's use of units of time, the large scope of time blocks in life can only be understood by looking at the broader life cycle. This was done by examining the case of Dr. Faust, whose life began in 1887 and whose career began in 1911. His career spanned the next 64 years, finally concluding in 1975 when he was 88 years old. Through this case and other case illustrations we may identify seven career demands and/or issues which place stress on the individual. These begin with the initial career decision and end with retirement. The four key social and cultural forces which are addressed in this volume were discussed in the concluding section of the chapter. These are changes in the demographics of the nation, the movement toward a world economy, the influx of women into the workplace, and the declining demand for blue-collar labor.

REFERENCES

Athos, A. G., & Cabarro, J. J. (1978). *Interpersonal behavior.* Englewood Cliffs, NJ: Prentice-Hall.

Colligan, M. J., Smith, M. J., & Hurrell, J. J. (1977). Occupational incidence rates of mental health disorders. *Journal of Human Stress, 3*(2), 34-39.

Collins, E. C. G. (1983). Managers and lovers. *Harvard Business Review, 61*(5), 142-153.

Erikson, E. H. (1950, 1963). *Childhood and society.* New York: Norton.

Faust, O. A. (1936). Primary tuberculosis, obstructive pulmonary emphysema and asthma with recovery. *American Journal of Diseases of Children, 51,* 118-122.

Faust, O. A. (1938). Chickenpox meningitis and encephalitis. *Archives of Pediatrics, 55,* 29-35.

Faust, O. A. (Ed.) (1952). *Reducing emotional trauma in hospitalized children.* Albany, NY: Albany Research Project, Albany Medical College.

Faust, O. A., & Stein, R. (1935). Influenzal meningitis treated by forced spinal drainage and transfusion. *Archives of Pediatrics, 52,* 743-748.

Fitzsimmons, E. (1987). Williams executive program offers managers of 17 companies exposure to liberal arts. *Berkshire Business Journal,* August.

Gould, R. (1978). *Growth and change in adult life.* New York: Simon and Schuster.

Hall, D. T. (1976). *Careers in organizations,* Santa Monica, CA: Goodyear.

Hall, D. T., & Nougaim, K. (1968). An examination of Maslow's need hierarchy in an organizational setting. *Organizational Behavior and Human Performance, 3,* 12-35.

Hertzog, F. V., & Faust, O. A. (1950). Edema associated with temporary idiopathic hypoproteinemia, *The Journal of Pediatrics*, *36*(5), 641-645.

House, J. (1980). *Work stress and social support*. Reading, MA: Addison-Wesley.

Levinson, D. (1978). *The seasons of a man's life*. New York: Knopf.

Levinson, H. (1981). When executives burn out. *Harvard Business Review*, *59*(3), 73-81.

March, J. G. (1988). *Learning and the taking of risks*. Third Texas Conference on Organizations. University of Texas at Austin, April 15-17.

McCord, C. P. (1940). Freud . . . the man. *The Psychiatric Quarterly*, *14*(1), 3-8.

Miller, D.C., & Form, W. H. (1951). *Industrial sociology*. New York: Harper.

Quick, J. C., Nelson, D. L., & Quick, J. D. (1987). Successful executives: How independent? *Academy of Management Executive*, *1*(2), 139-145.

Quick, J. C., & Quick, J. D. (1984). *Organizational stress and preventive management*. New York: McGraw-Hill Book Company.

Scott, R. (1988). *The organization of training*. Third Texas Conference on Organizations. University of Texas at Austin, April 15-17.

Sedam, R. N., & Faust, O. A. (1965). *Happy mealtimes for your baby*. Canajoharie, NY: Beech-Nut Baby Foods.

Sheehey, G. (1976). *Passages: Predictable crises of adult life*. New York: Dutton.

Shostak, A. B. (1980). *Blue-collar stress*. Reading, MA: Addison-Wesley.

Super, D., Crites, J., Hummel, R., Moser, H., Overstreet, P., & Warnath, C. (1957). *Vocational development: A framework for research*. New York: Teachers College Press.

Super, D. E., & Bohn, M. J. (1970). *Occupational psychology*. Belmont, CA: Wadsworth.

Vaillant, G. E. (1980). Adolf Meyer was right: Dynamic psychiatry needs the life chart. *Journal of the National Association of Private Psychiatric Hospitals*, *11*, 4-14.

Vaillant, G. E. (1977). *Adaptation to life*. Boston: Little, Brown and Company.

Career Experiences: Current and Future Themes

Kenneth G. Wheeler

University of Texas at Arlington

SUMMARY. Current and future trends in employment opportunities and the changing nature of the labor force are identified in relation to expected career experiences. The changing nature of a service based economy is explored in relation to expected changes in educational levels, demographic shifts in the age distribution, increasing participation of females in the labor force, and potential conflicts between career and family demands. Potential mismatches between employment opportunities and the requirements of the labor force are examined and organizational adaptations that might minimize potential frustration and dissatisfaction are discussed.

Current and future trends that will have major impacts on job availability in different occupations, the skills and education required for particular occupations, and career experiences can be placed in two broad categories. The first category reflects the changing employment opportunities in different industries and occupations. There is a continuing shift in employment from manufacturing to service sectors of the economy and changes in the demand for different occupations within these industries. This has major implications for the nature of the skills and type of education required, the type of work experiences, and the satisfactions and frustrations individuals will face in their careers. The continuing trend in the internationalization of business provides added requirements and opportunities for multicultural skills and experiences.

Reprints may be obtained from Kenneth G. Wheeler, Department of Management, University of Texas at Arlington, Arlington, TX 76019.

25

The second category reflects the changing nature of the population and labor force. The distribution of age groups in the labor force has major implications for the availability of workers in beginning lower level positions and competition for middle level and senior level career advancement opportunities. The level of education and training of those entering into the labor force affects the opportunities and competition for technical, professional, and managerial jobs. The increasing participation of females also has numerous implications. Role conflicts between family and career responsibilities will likely become an increasing concern for both men and women. Finally, increasing levels of immigration will affect the availability of workers as well as potential competition for many jobs. It will also require organizational and individual adaptations as workers with different first languages, cultural backgrounds, and work values become socialized into the organization.

CHANGING EMPLOYMENT OPPORTUNITIES

According to projections from the Bureau of Labor Statistics (Personick, 1985), ninety percent of the sixteen million new jobs over the next decade will be in the service industries. Nearly fifty-five percent of these new jobs will be in six specific industries: business services, retail trade, eating and drinking establishments, wholesale trade, medical services, and professional services (Table 1). This represents a continuing trend of a shift in employment from the manufacturing sector to the service sector. Employment in manufacturing declined from 25.1 percent of total jobs in 1959 to 18.5 percent in 1984 and will continue to decline to 17.1 percent in 1995, according to Bureau of Labor Statistics (BLS) predictions. During this same period, employment in the service sector increased from 14.1 percent in 1959 to 22.4 percent in 1984 to a projected 25.4 percent in 1995.

It should be noted that this change in employment levels does not represent major changes in the role of manufacturing in the total economy. Manufacturing's share of the GNP dropped less than one percent from 1959 to 1984, while the share of total employment dropped by 8.3 percent (Personick, 1985). The major factor has been in the increasing level of productivity in manufacturing, with

Table 1

Industries with Largest Changes in Employment

(Numbers in Thousands)

	1984	1995	Change	Percent Change
Business services	4,612	7,245	2,633	57.1
Retail trade	12,660	14,351	1,691	13.4
Eating and drinking places	5,733	6,936	1,203	21.0
Wholesale trade	5,897	6,985	1,088	18.5
Medical services	1,821	2,886	1,065	58.5
Professional services	1,255	2,295	1,040	82.9

Source: Bureau of Labor Statistics

relatively stable productivity in service industries. The continuing development and application of automation and robotics in the manufacturing sector will continue to reduce the number of lower skilled and semi-skilled jobs in the manufacturing sector, while many service jobs may not be easily replaced through automation and productivity increases.

The increasing number of service jobs and declining manufacturing jobs has a major impact on the type of skills and aptitudes required and the nature of the work activities and environments workers will experience. The business services industry is projected to have the largest increase in number of jobs (approximately 2.6 million) and to be second in the percent increase in employment (4.2 percent). Business services include programming and data processing, detective and protective services, janitorial and building maintenance, temporary help, public relations and advertising, consulting services, equipment rental, and consumer credit reporting and collection. Many of the services in this category, such as programming and software services, are becoming a necessary part of doing business. There is also an increasing trend toward contracting these services with outside agencies. Many individuals in the future will have temporary working relationships in a variety of organizations different from the agency that has hired them and is compensating them. The growth of the temporary help agencies will provide opportunities for an increasing portion of the labor force that is seeking part-time work and flexible work hours, including retired workers seeking supplemental income and working parents with child care responsibilities. Although the temporary help agencies employ primarily office clerks, typists, and secretaries, they also include a variety of other occupations such as service workers, technicians, and nurses. The professional service area, which includes accounting, bookkeeping, engineering, and legal services has similar characteristics to the business services area. Professional service jobs are projected to be sixth in employment growth with just over one million new jobs (Table 1).

The retail trade industry is projected to be second in job growth (1.7 million new jobs by 1995) and eating and drinking establishments is third (1.2 million new jobs). A related industry is wholesale trade, which is projected to have the fourth largest increase with about 1.1 million new jobs. The nature of the work force and characteristics of the jobs in these industries are similar. The growth of fast food restaurants has paralleled the increase in the number of families in which both spouses work, and is expected to continue. Much of the growth in the retail sector is projected to be in grocery stores and department stores (Personik, 1985). Employment in small retail stores and specialty stores is projected to decline as larger department stores provide outlets for products currently sold by these smaller stores. The work force often found in the retail and restaurant businesses tends to be lower paid and is composed of a considerable number of part-time workers. This will provide a continued demand for young workers and female workers with household responsibilities that limit them to part-time employment. However, decreasing levels of available young workers because of declining birth rates may create serious labor shortages for these industries.

The fifth largest increase in new jobs (over one million) will come from medical services. This includes jobs in hospitals, doctors' and dentists' offices, nursing homes, emergency treatment centers, and rehabilitation centers. This will result in a major increase in the demand for both registered nurses and licensed practical nurses. Doctors' and dentists' services are projected to add over a half million jobs by 1995.

Projected growth in specific occupational groups is reflected by comparing expected 1995 employment patterns with those of 1984 (Table 2). The largest increase in employment will be in service workers, with an increase of over 3.3 million new jobs. The largest job growth for a specific occupation in this category is for janitors and cleaners with a projected growth of 443,000 jobs. Food and beverage occupations, including bartenders, cooks, food preparation workers, and waiters and waitresses, will provide a total of 1.1 million new jobs. Nursing aides, orderlies, and attendants will have a projected increase of 348,000 jobs, plant guards will increase by 188,000, and cosmetologists and related workers will increase by 150,000. Similar types of jobs are found in the projected 2.2 million increase for salesworkers, primarily in retail and wholesale trades, and the food and beverage industry. The projected growth of 566,000 jobs for cashiers is not only the largest growth for a specific occupation in this category but also across all categories. Service workers and salesworkers combined are 36.5 percent of the total projected increase in the labor force through 1995. Many of these jobs are relatively low paying jobs with limited advancement

Table 2

Employment by General Occupational Grouping

(in thousands)

	1984	1995	Change	Percent Change
Total employment	106,843	122,760	15,917	14.9
Service workers	15,589	18,917	3,328	21.3
Professional workers	12,805	15,578	2,773	21.7
Executive and administrative	11,274	13,762	2,488	22.1
Salesworkers	11,173	13,393	2,220	19.9
Administrative support/clerical	18,716	20,499	1,783	9.5
Production, craft, and repair	12,176	13,601	1,425	11.7
Operators, fabricators, laborers	17,357	18,634	1,277	7.4
Technical and related	3,206	4,119	913	28.5
Farming, forestry, and fishing	3,544	3,447	- 97	- 2.7
Private household workers	993	811	- 182	-18.3

Source: Bureau of Labor Statistics

potential. The requirements for these positions generally do not include any college, although some trade school education may be needed.

The second largest increase in employment is projected to occur for professional workers, with an increase of 2.8 million jobs, and the third largest increase is for 2.5 million jobs in managerial and administrative occupations. Almost all of these new jobs are in occupations requiring a bachelor's or advanced college degree. The health field will account for a large portion of this increase, with 452,000 new jobs for registered nurses. This is followed by electrical and mechanical engineers, with a total of 287,000 new jobs, and computer systems analysis with 212,000 jobs. Kindergarten and elementary teachers are projected to increase by 281,000, reflecting the "baby boom" babies, even though the overall birth rate is down. A major projected increase of 89,000 is for service and lodging managers, reflecting the growth of the food and beverage industry.

There are also some definite negative aspects to the projections for professional and managerial occupations. Although jobs for physicians and surgeons are projected to increase by 109,000, Baldwin (1987) reports that the supply will outstrip the demand with a surplus of doctors by 1990. Jobs for lawyers are expected to increase by 174,000, but the number of law degrees awarded is expected to far exceed the demand.

The largest increase for a specific occupation in the administrative occupations category is 307,000 for accountants and auditors, but by 1990 there will be an oversupply of accountants (Odiorne, 1986). Finally, jobs for college and university faculty are projected to decline by 77,000, one of the largest drops for any specific occupation. This will be due to declining enrollments resulting from the decreasing birth rate after 1960.

Although technical and related workers have the eighth largest increase of 913,000 jobs compared to the other occupational groupings, technical jobs have the largest percentage increase of 28.7 percent. Computer programmers have the largest projected increase of 245,000, followed by electrical and electronics technicians with 202,000. A college degree is not necessary for most of these jobs, although some college or technical training is required. The technical occupations will provide good opportunities for relatively well paying positions for non-college graduates.

The growth level for administrative support and clerical personnel is projected at 1.8 million new jobs. Secretarial jobs are projected to increase by 268,000 and general office clerks by 231,000. In addition bookkeeping and accounting clerks are projected to increase by 118,000 and receptionists by 83,000. Computer and peripheral equipment operators are projected to increase by 143,000. These jobs continue to have high concentrations of females, as well as traditionally low wages and advancement potential. Career frustrations for many females in clerical occupations may increase pressures to improve wage levels relative to male-dominated jobs through comparable worth legislation.

Production, craft, and repair occupations are projected to increase by 1.4 million, with the largest increase for a specific occupation being for automotive mechanics at 185,000. Operators, fabricators, and laborers are projected to increase by 1.3 million. The largest specific occupational increase is for truck drivers with a projected increase of 428,000, nearly one-third of the total for this group. Many specific occupations in this group will have decreases in employment, as employment changes from the manufacturing to the service sector. The largest decrease will be for textile workers, including sewing machine operators, with a projected loss of 169,000 jobs.

Two occupational classifications are projected to have net decreases. Farming, forestry, and fishing occupations are projected to decrease by 97,000 jobs, reflecting major gains in productivity in the agricultural sector. Finally, private household workers are projected to decrease by 182,000 jobs, reflecting a long term decline in this category.

The opportunities for employment over the next decade will include many jobs that require a college degree. In particular, demand will be for degrees in computer sciences, engineering, retail management, hotel and restaurant management, accounting, nursing, medicine, and law. However, the proportion of workers with college degrees has increased dramatically. In 1970, 26 percent of the labor force had some college and 13 percent of these had four or more years, but in 1982, 39 percent had some college and 20 percent of these had four years or more (Bureau of Labor Statistics, 1982). Although many higher paying and rewarding jobs will continue to require a college degree, many individuals with degrees will be forced to enter into an occupation that does not make full use of their education. For example, while new college graduates found 73 percent of their jobs in professional and technical fields in the mid 1960s, only 46 percent of those graduating in the mid 1970s were able to enter into these occupations (Cotter & Dorfman, 1981). Increasing proportions of college graduates have entered into sales, clerical, and craft occupations.

One of the outcomes of the increasing availability of college graduates is "creeping credentialism" (Cotter & Dorfman, 1981). Many employers gradually increase the level of educational requirements until a college degree becomes the standard for jobs that at one time did not require a college education. As a result, a college education no longer ensures a higher paying, higher status job, but becomes a necessary requirement to attain even a moderately desirable job. This provides a great potential for frustration and violated expectations for those with college degrees that enter into occupations that do not provide the rewards and status of occupations requiring a college degree in the past.

The internationalization of many industries and the movement to a global world economy is another trend that is expected to continue through the next decade. Many organizations have major markets outside of the United States that provide for a substantial share of their total revenue. In addition, lower labor costs and greater availability of some raw materials has often been a factor in locating manufacturing facilities for U.S. based companies in other countries (Dale, 1983). This trend will be primarily in the manufacturing sector of our economy and most of the new growth in jobs in the service industries in the United States will be relatively unaffected by this trend. Many of the services serve very local markets, with consumers unable or unwilling to go beyond their neighborhood or immediate metropolitan area. Examples would be in the most rapidly expanding service industries, such as retail trades, restaurant businesses and health services. Buyers of most products that are manufactured overseas, such as automobiles, still seek repair and maintenance services locally.

The growth of the multinational organization will increase the pressure for managers to serve overseas at some point in their careers. For many organizations, overseas assignments may become a critical component for career advancement to higher management positions ("How to Land," 1985). As the baby boom generation enters into middle and upper management in the next decade creating fewer promotional opportunities and career plateauing, opportunities for advancement in overseas' assignments may become increasingly attractive. Multinationals may solve some potential shortages at management levels in the next century by training managerial talent recruited from other countries where the company has manufacturing and/or distribution facilities and relocating managers to plants in the United States.

There are indications that foreign owned subsidiaries in the United States may provide somewhat different working climates. For example, a survey of Japanese owned subsidiaries in the United States (Bowman, 1986) found that over two-thirds had some mixture of Japanese and American approaches. These organizations were more likely to avoid layoffs when possible, look for individuals with an orientation toward the group and company loyalty, and develop generalists over specialists with job duties that were somewhat broader and more ambiguous than found in most American owned organizations in the United States. This may provide an opportunity for individuals preferring this type of work environment to find a better match, resulting in more satisfactory career experiences.

CHANGES IN THE LABOR FORCE

An interesting comparison in the BLS projections is between the projected employment level of 122.8 million and the projected labor force of 129.1 million in 1995. The difference of 6.3 million would leave an approximate unemployment level of 5 percent. Of course, the employment projections are estimates and the BLS provides alternative numbers based on lower and higher trend possibilities. The potential matching of the availability of jobs with particular requirements and training to the particular nature of the labor force is particularly interesting.

Demographic shifting in the age distribution and changing participation rates in the labor force have major implications for employment and career opportunities in the future. The birth rate was relatively low through the mid 1940s, then rapidly increased and
remained high through the 1950s, to decrease and remain low after
the early 1960s. This created a demographic bulge in our society
sometimes described as resembling a "pig moving through a py-
thon." Table 3 illustrates the impact of this baby boom and the
projections for 1995. By 1995, the 35-54 year old age group will
increase by 80.4 percent from its 1975 level to compose nearly one-
half of the total labor force. During this same period, younger entry
level workers below 25 years are projected to decrease by 10.9
percent to only 15.6 percent of the labor force. At the same time,
the greatest projected increase in jobs is in the service sector, particularly lower skilled positions in the retail and food service industries. From 1984 to 1995, there is a projected decrease of 3.8 million workers below the age of 25 with a projected increase of 3.3
million new jobs for service workers. Combined with the demand
for lower skilled and entry level workers in other occupations, there
will be serious labor shortages and high demand for workers to fill

Table 3

Age Distribution of Labor Force

(Numbers in Thousands)

	Actual		Projected	Percent Change	
Age Group	1975	1984	1995	1975-1984	1984-1995
Total	93,755	113,544	129,168	21.1	13.8
16-19	8,870	7,943	7,057	-10.5	-11.2
20-24	13,750	16,045	13,106	16.7	-18.3
25-34	22,865	32,722	34,415	43.1	5.2
35-44	16,903	24,933	36,175	47.5	45.1
45-54	17,084	17,006	25,129	- 0.5	47.8
55-64	11,346	11,961	10,814	5.4	- 9.6
65 and over	2,956	2,928	2,472	- 0.9	-15.6

Source: Bureau of Labor Statistics

these positions. Many of these jobs are presently filled by part-time workers. The primary source of part-time workers are younger workers in the 16-24 age group and retired workers over 65. Two-thirds of part-time workers are women, and 27 percent of all women in the labor force are part time (Nardone, 1986). As the 16-24 age group decreases, organizations are likely to increase the employment of retired workers (Kraut, 1987) and females who have family responsibilities that limit their availability to work full time. Although retired workers may often be supplementing their incomes and have little interest in long term career opportunities, this will continue to place many females in relatively low paying part-time jobs with limited career advancement opportunities (Holden & Hansen, 1987).

The shortage of lower level workers will probably result in increased wages for these positions that will make it more attractive for females with family responsibilities to enter into the labor force. This is likely to be insufficient to fill these positions, particularly since the already increasing participation rates of females into lifetime careers will reduce the numbers available. Finally, it is possible that many of these positions will be filled by increasing levels of immigrants entering into the labor force (Briggs, 1984). It is projected that three fourths of the growth of the labor force in California through 1995 will be from immigrants, particularly Asians and Hispanics ("Shortage of Jobs," 1988). A key problem here will be in the levels of skills and the ability of these new immigrants to integrate into the organization. Current immigration policies are based primarily on political and family concerns and not on the matching of the skills of immigrants to those needed in the United States (Briggs, 1984, p. 244).

As those in the baby boom group move through their careers, they are likely to confront increasingly slow career movement. This is likely to lead to major frustrations in not reaching expected salary and advancement expectations, and possibly in boredom if trapped mid-career in a particular level and specialization. General management and administration positions are projected to increase by only 1.9 million from 1984 to 1995 (22 percent). Although this projection is not broken down by management level, the pyramidal structure of most organizations would indicate that most of these new managerial jobs will be at lower and middle level positions. During this same period, 35-44 year olds will increase by 11.3 million (45.1 percent) and 45-54 year olds will increase by 8.1 million (47.8 percent). This trend should continue well into the next century, creating continued plateauing in careers and frustration from lack of advancement.

An increasing concern has been centered on the trend for some organizations to experience substantial levels of early retirements among workers over 50, often as a result of pressure from the baby boomers (Scott & Brudney, 1987). Relatively large numbers of highly educated and highly motivated middle managers in the 35 to 54 age group with high expectations for career promotions will place increasing pressures for early retirement on those in the 55 to 70 age group (Copperman & Keast, 1983, p. 28). As members of this 35 to 54 year age group move into more senior level positions, advancement in the hierarchy will become increasingly difficult with CEOs and vice presidents almost the same age as the middle managers below them. One organizational adaptation during this time might be to copy the Japanese system of more generalized career experiences with longer periods between movements up the hierarchy. Career paths consisting of several lateral moves before a relatively small move up the hierarchy may become more common.

There will also be a growing shortage of entry level and junior level personnel at the same time as there are pressures on more senior workers to retire early because of the large numbers of managers in the 30-55 age group. To some extent, the lateral moves can create flexibility and maintain individuals at this lower level longer. But, this will not be enough in itself to cover this shortage. One possibility is to encourage retirees to return to supplement their retirement pay and develop second careers at more junior levels than those they had before they retired. Another possibility is for organizations to offer part-time positions for employees as a transition phase before full-time retirement (Copperman & Keast, 1983, p. 42).

Another major change in the labor force has been the stabilization of women's entry into the work force. The participation of females in the United States labor force has been steadily increasing since World War II. The participation jumped from 27 percent in 1940 to

32 percent in 1947. This increase represented a holdover from the war years that saw women performing many traditionally male jobs, such as riveter and machinist, for the first time. It was the beginning of a major restructuring in what were considered traditionally male and female jobs. Continued changes in values, economic pressures, family size, and federal equal employment legislation pushed the participation rate to 43 percent by 1970, and to a current rate of 56.5 percent in 1988. It is projected to increase to 59 percent in 1995 which would represent over 46 percent of the total labor force (Table 4).

The increased participation rates have also represented increasing proportions of females in higher paying and higher status occupations, such as management, accounting, law, and medicine. However, many lower and underpaid positions, such as secretaries, clerks, school teachers, and nurses, remain predominately female. Females also have disproportionate numbers in low paying, low career potential, part-time positions in retail stores and restaurants (Holden & Hansen, 1987). The high projected demand for workers in these lower paying, female dominated jobs is likely to create continued frustration and stress for many females in the work force. One possible reaction is increased pressures for wage adjustments and comparable worth for many traditionally female dominated jobs.

Conflict between career and family demands will be an increasingly difficult problem in the future. As both spouses become com-

Table 4

Civilian Labor Force Participation

	Number in Labor Force (thousands)			Participation Rate		
	1975	1984	1995	1975	1984	1995
Males	56,299	63,835	69,282	77.9	76.4	75.3
Females	37,475	49,704	59,886	46.3	53.6	58.9
Total	93,755	113,544	129,168	61.2	64.4	66.6
Percent						
Female	40.0	43.8	46.4			

Source: Bureau of Labor Statistics

mitted to their careers, the question of spouse relocation and the conflict between two careers will place serious strains on many marriages. In some cases, working wives may solve this dilemma by taking part-time and non-career jobs that are secondary to the husband's career. Although this might be a solution for some families, it is also likely to create frustration and dissatisfaction. These are relatively low paying jobs with few opportunities to satisfy either long range needs for career development or shorter range needs for growth, achievement, and recognition. Frustrations with the work situation may well spill over into resentment and conflict at home. The most frustrating situation of all might well be for women who have accepted such a secondary role and then find themselves the sole provider for a family after the divorce or death of a husband. This has placed many women in the situation of continuing to work in an unsatisfying job that does not provide an income to adequately support either themselves or a family.

Yet, the family that has both spouses in fulfilling careers will also face many difficulties. A major source of stress will come from conflicts between the two careers. As many as 75 percent of employee transfers could involve dual career couples by 1990 (Driessnack, 1987). Except in the cases where both spouses might receive simultaneous offers to make career moves to the same new location, such transfers will either require the interruption of one career to make such a move or the refusal of such a relocation offer. In any case, the decision of which spouse will make a sacrifice in their career in the interest of the other has the potential for subsequent frustration and resentment. Many organizations will provide placement programs and attempt to establish reciprocal agreements with other organizations for the employment of the spouses of transferred employees in an attempt to minimize such problems.

Work demands versus family concerns will be another source of conflict for dual career couples. Who has household responsibilities, such as grocery shopping, cleaning and cooking? Are these duties to be shared? Work versus home conflicts become particularly acute when there are children involved, which is increasingly the case. The proportion of women in the labor force with children under three increased from one-third in 1976 to over half in 1986, and 70 percent of mothers with school age children were in the labor force in 1986 (Levine, 1987). Decisions about who takes the children to the doctor, who delivers and picks them up from child care or school, and who stays home with the children when they are sick are all potential sources of conflict.

Even when these problems are resolved, the difficulty of balancing the roles required by career and family will remain. After both spouses have completed the eight and often more hours required by the job, and then shopped, cooked, taken the car in for repair, and so forth, both may well feel that they are not able to spend the time they wish with the children or with each other. Organizations will have to make numerous adjustments in order to attract and maintain the increasing proportion of the labor force that falls into this category, such as special child care leaves, on-site child care centers, flexible work schedules and job sharing (Grossman, 1982; Stautberg, 1987).

CURRENT AND FUTURE THEMES

Several themes emerge in comparing expected employment opportunities with the changing labor force. The shifts in employment from the manufacturing sector to the service sector will continue, with major growth in retail and wholesale trades, and eating and drinking establishments. Although many of the jobs in these areas may be lower paying, part-time, and limited in terms of career advancement potential, there will still be a strong demand for professional and managerial workers. However, several professional fields are likely to have an oversupply of qualified applicants. The college degree will be valuable in taking advantage of many of the excellent job opportunities that will be available, but projections indicate that increasing proportions of workers with college degrees will have to enter into sales, clerical, and craft positions that have not traditionally required a college education.

Demographic shifts in the age distribution in the labor force will make career advancement in managerial positions increasingly difficult, resulting in early career plateauing for many in the 35-54 age group. This will also place pressures on those 55 and over to retire early to make way for the "baby boom" managers waiting for a promotion. At the same time, there will be major declines in the below 24 age group, creating labor shortages for entry and junior level positions. Organizational adaptations might include more generalized career experiences with several lateral moves before a relatively small step up the hierarchy. More senior employees and retired workers might also be utilized in part-time positions at lower levels to compensate for the shortages of more junior employees.

Increased participation by females in the labor force has resulted in greater numbers of females in higher paying and higher status occupations. Yet, females still have disproportionate numbers in lower paying, low career potential occupations. The continued demand for females in clerical occupations, retail and wholesale trades, and restaurant and eating establishments is likely to continue to create career and economic frustrations for many females in the future. This may be compounded by role conflicts between career and family demands for both spouses. Such conflicts place pressures on many wives to work in secondary jobs with limited career potential. The increasing number of families where both spouses are committed to their careers is also likely to create conflicts in relocation decisions, family responsibilities, and the allocation of working and non-working time. In many cases, organizations may be able to reduce these conflicts through adaptations such as child care provisions and flexible work schedules.

Information concerning the changing nature of employment opportunities and the characteristics of the labor force is a critical part of the individual's career decision. Traditionally, individuals seek careers most likely to meet their needs and aspirations. One phase of this process is to compare needs for growth, achievement, affiliation, power, and so forth, to the reinforcers available in different possible careers. However, an important consideration in this process is the availability of jobs in the proposed career and the changing nature of the career due to economic and demographic forces. For example, those considering careers in middle management positions need to consider the increased competition, resulting in much slower career and salary progression, and those considering careers in law may wish to consider the potential availability of jobs before beginning several years of law school.

An individual also has specific organizational choices within a given career that can have major implications for future career satisfaction. Those facing the conflicts inherent in balancing family and career demands can benefit from seeking out organizations that recognize these problems and are providing appropriate programs and adaptations. Dual career couples can seek out organizations with placement programs and reciprocal agreements with other organizations to aid in meeting both spouse's career goals. Couples with child care concerns can work for organizations with flexible leave policies, flexible work schedules, and child care facilities. Individuals who would prefer particular working climates within their career may find these in foreign owned subsidiaries that have made adaptations in the organization relative to their own culture. For example, those seeking more flexible and ambiguous generalist positions with a greater emphasis on employment security and group cooperation may select Japanese subsidiaries that are more likely to possess these characteristics. In summary, current economic and demographic forces are creating a dynamic environment for career experiences in the immediate future. Careful consideration of these changes in career decision-making can help the individual avoid frustrating and stressful work experiences and maximize the probability of a satisfying and successful career.

REFERENCES

Baldwin, W, F. (1987). Proposals beginning to surface to ensure better oversight of nation's HMO industry. *Modern Healthcare, 17*, 42-44.

Bowman, J. S. (1986). The rising sun in America. *Personnel Administrator, 31*, 63-67.

Briggs, V. M., Jr. (1984). *Immigration policy and the American labor force.* Baltimore: Johns Hopkins University Press.

Bureau of Labor Statistics. (1982). *Current Population Survey* (Bulletin 2096). Washington, DC: U. S. Government Printing Office.

Copperman, L. F., & Keast, F. D. (1983). *Adjusting to an older work force.* New York: Van Nostrand Reinhold.

Cotter, W., & Dorfman, S. (1981). *Estimating educational attainment of future employment demand for states.* Albany, NY: Bureau of Labor Market Information.

Dale, R. (1983). International forces will prevail. *Personnel Administrator, 28*, 100-104.

Driessnack, C. H. (1987). Spouse relocation: A moving experience. *Personnel Administrator, 33*, 63-67.

Freidman, D. E. (1987). Work versus family: War of the worlds. *Personnel Administrator*, *33*, 36-38.

Fullerton, H. N., Jr. (1985). The 1995 labor force: BLS' latest projections. *Monthly Labor Review*, *108*, 17-25.

Grossman, A. S. (1982). More than half of all children have working mothers. *Monthly Labor Review*, *105*, 41-43.

Holden, K. C., & Hansen, W. L. (1987). Part-time work, full-time work, and occupational segregation. In C. Brown & J. A. Pechman (Eds.), *Gender in the workplace*. Washington, DC: Brookings Institution.

How to land an overseas assignment. (1985, May). *Success*.

Howe, W. J. (1986). The business services industry sets pace in employment growth. *Monthly Labor Review*, *109*, 29-36.

Kraut, A. I. (1987). Retirees: A new resource for American industries. *Personnel Administrator*, *33*, 20-28.

Levine, H. (1987). Alternative work schedules: Do they meet workforce needs? *Personnel*, *63*, 57-62.

Odiorne, G. S. (1987). The crystal ball of human resource strategy. *Personnel Administrator*, *32*, 103-106.

Nardone, N. J. (1986). Part-time workers: Who are they? *Monthly Labor Review*, *109*, 13-19.

Personick, V. A. (1985). A second look at industry output and employment trends through 1995. *Monthly Labor Review*, *108*, 26-41.

Rumberger, R. W. (1981). *Overeducation in the U.S. Labor Market*. New York: Praeger.

Scott, H., & Brudney, J. F. (1987). *Forced out: When veteran employees are driven from their careers*. New York: Simon and Schuster.

Shortage of job skills is seen for California. (1988, April 12). *Wall Street Journal*, p. 37.

Silvestri, G. T., & Luckasiewicz, J. M. (1985). Occupational employment projections: The 1984-1995 outlook. *Monthly Labor Review*, *108*, 42-57.

Stautberg, S. S. (1987). Status report: The corporation and trends in family issues. *Human Resource Management*, *26*, 277-290.

II. THE BEGINNING

Career Planning

David A. Gray
Frank M. Gault
Howard H. Meyers
James E. Walther

University of Texas at Arlington

SUMMARY. As a young adult, choice of an appropriate career can be one of life's most stressful decisions. Changing careers as an older adult may also be a very difficult transition. As previous chapters have articulated, much career choice difficulty stems from many complex and rapidly changing factors of the world of work, including the development of artificial intelligence and robotic technology (Hirschhorn, 1984; Hunt & Hunt, 1983; Majchrzak, 1988), globally driven markets (Halberstam, 1986; Hoerr, 1988; Scheuerman, 1986) where oil production decisions in Saudia Arabia quickly affect job markets in Texas, paperless information and communication systems where office employees can be separated by an office partition or by 3000 miles, and mergers, acquisitions, and other corporate restructuring (Blueston & Harrison, 1982; DeLuca, 1988; London, 1988; McCann & Gilkey, 1988; Woodard & Buchholz, 1987) that have stimulated the development of free agent and disposable managers (Hirsch, 1987).

Reprints may be obtained from David A. Gray, Department of Management, University of Texas at Arlington, Box 19467, Arlington, TX 76019.

This chapter describes how this stress and difficulty may be minimized through career planning. Accordingly, the sections that follow (1) contain definitions of career planning and career management, (2) offer an integrated, career-focused model providing multiple linkages for the individual to job, occupation, organization, and industry, (3) describe a career planning course that addresses many features of the integrative model, and (4) review the individual-organizational relationship in the context of career planning for job, occupation, and industry.

In addition to being an accumulation of role-related experiences, a *career* is a sequence of jobs occupied and performed throughout a person's working lifetime. For many people this sequence is actually a progression of positions with increasing authority and responsibility. Many have modeled careers into life stages of trial and development, advancement, stability, continued growth or decline, and disengagement-retirement (Dalton, Thompson, & Price, 1977; Feldman, 1988; Hall, 1976; Schein, 1978). *Career planning*, then, is a lifelong process that includes periodic self-assessment, information gathering, and goal setting.

Most adults will change jobs, and frequently employers, as many as five to eight times during their working lifetimes. Therefore, it is extremely important that individuals acquire career planning skills and adopt a rational approach to solving career problems and making career decisions. A career decision can be made at any point during one's life when a world of work transition becomes necessary. Making a career decision is not much different from making many other important life decisions (Mihal, Sorce, & Comte, 1984). One needs to define the problem, gather pertinent information, analyze and synthesize the data, develop potential solutions, determine which solution is most relevant, practical, and desirable, and implement the plan. In career planning this translates into realizing that a career decision must be made, carefully assessing one's self, objectively examining the world of work, deciding what career possibilities seem to match the personal assessment, determining which of these is most practical, and developing strategies to enter the chosen career. Beyond this the individual will need to learn skills to assist him or her in making adjustments to the new career situation.

While career planning (or the career plan) provides a road map of job/career options and decision points, *career development* involves the readiness activities necessary for skill and knowledge enhancement so that an individual can be more fully prepared to pursue and obtain jobs of greater authority and responsibility. Career planning and development activities are clearly essential aspects of managing one's career. Along with planning and development, the *career management* process entails execution of job tasks, self-appraisal and superior review of job performance, and job and/or career adjustments when career objectives are not being met.

AN INTEGRATED CAREER PLANNING MODEL

Although career planning is primarily an individual responsibility, others can provide much useful information for job and career decision making. It is necessary, therefore, to view career planning in the context of job, organization, occupation, and industry as represented in Figure 1.

A *job* (for this example, an auditor) is a set of tasks, duties, and responsibilities that constitute a work assignment for an individual.

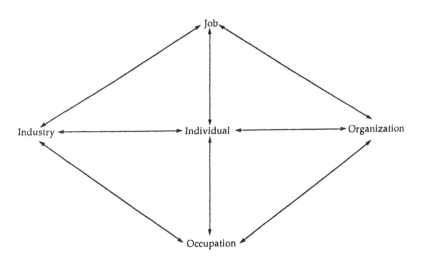

FIGURE 1. Career Planning Model

Typically, the content of a job and its relationship to other jobs is recorded in a job or position description. A collection of interdependent jobs (and the people who occupy them), resources, and technical and information processes are necessary ingredients of an *organization* (public accounting firm). The jobs or positions of an organization are frequently represented in a structural schematic (organization chart) showing the authority and responsibility relationships linking individuals at the lowest levels of the organization to those at the executive organization levels.

An *occupation* (accounting) can be viewed as a set of jobs and/or a progression of jobs based upon a specific body of knowledge and skills. An occupation provides the means through which an individual can establish professional credentials and a desired life style.

Firms that produce, distribute and/or sell the same or similar products and services comprise an *industry* (accounting, tax, and financial services). Some industries contain only a few firms; whereas, others may have firms numbered in the thousands.

The importance of this career planning framework rests with the linkage and compatibility of model elements and the timing (and sequence) of occupation, job, and career decisions. As an example, a young person may decide (occupational choice) as a high school junior to become a geologist. This occupational decision dictates one's college major and most likely narrows the college application/ enrollment decision significantly. The individual may pursue and obtain a petroleum geology degree in four years. At the time of initial college enrollment, the decision to become a petroleum geologist may have been based on very desirable occupational characteristics and strong intellectual interest with minimal consideration given to entry level job opportunities, firms, and conditions of the oil and gas industry. At graduation time, entry level job openings may not exist because of low levels of oil drilling activity, corporate reorganization and downsizing, and relatively inexpensive foreign oil. What appeared to be a good occupational choice four years ago now becomes a very poor job-organization-industry situation from a career standpoint.

The above brief example illustrates the integrated nature of the model (for other models, see London, 1983; Mihal, Sorce, & Comte, 1984; Milkovich, Anderson, & Greenhalgh, 1976; Rhodes

& Doering, 1983). As the occupational element has been extensively discussed in a previous chapter, the remainder of this chapter
will focus on the job-organization-industry connection to the individual in the career planning process, highlighting the information
gathering and analysis aspects of career planning for the individual.

ACTIVATING THE CAREER PLANNING PROCESS

As stated earlier, career planning involves self-assessment, information gathering, and goal setting. These are preparatory or formulation activities and of course precede execution or implementation
of a career plan. However, these activities may also be continuously
or periodically performed while someone is engaged in employ-
ment-related work and professional tasks. Activation of the career
plan entails job search, self-development, job performance, promotion, and mentoring behaviors (Hunt & Michael, 1983). The focus
in this chapter is on the planning-formulation side of the career
equation.

Career planning from the individual's perspective is important
for a number of reasons. It provides and allows the individual to
maintain self-determination and control over his or her intended
worklife and related experiences. It contributes to better occupa-
tion-job-organization-industry worklife decisions that may greatly
enhance job mobility and progression through successive career
stages. Additionally, career planning may significantly ease the individual through various life stages and facilitate development of
meaningful non-work roles, including church leadership and civic
and community volunteer efforts, that complement job-career roles.

To initiate and perform the career planning process, a number of
formats are available to the individual. These are (1) self-help, (2)
consultant/counselor assistance, (3) employer-sponsored help, and
(4) courses offered by educational organizations and professional
associations. Any one or combination of two or more of these formats can yield a reasonably comprehensive career plan. The formats vary, however, in terms of depth and detail of analysis, formality, cost, and career plan specificity. Table 1 provides a
comparative analysis of the four approaches in terms of the time/
cost spent by an individual, the primary focus (individual or organi-

TABLE 1. Comparison of Career Planning Approaches

Planning Approach	Time/Cost to the Person	Primary Focus	Feedback/Interactive Analysis	Degree of Model Linkage
Self-help	Significant time but may incur minimum out.of pocket expense	Individual	None or very minimal	Job/occupation may be strong, but organization/industry may be weak
Consultant	Substantial cost but may be minimal time spent	Individual	Substantial, counselor-client	Job/occupation strong but organization/industry may be weak
Employer	Minimal cost but may also be minimal time spent	Organization	Moderate, supervisor-employee-personnel specialist	Job/organization strong but occupation and industry elements less emphasized
Course	Relatively inexpensive and may require moderate time	Individual and Organization	Moderate, student-instructor-counselor-peer	Reasonably strong linkage of all elements

zation), the opportunity for feedback and interactive analysis, and the degree to which the approach creates a tight fit of elements of the career planning model. Regardless of the format or approach, the planning activities and process are likely to involve testing, interactive feedback of test results, structured exercises, individual counseling, informational and diagnostic interviewing, group-centered information exchange, data extraction from various documents, employee shadowing, and/or functioning as a paid (or nonpaid) intern.

The most limiting of the four approaches mentioned above is the self-help format in that the individual may not have the time and other resources required to secure professional feedback about test results and seek other advice and counsel. The individual also does not have the opportunity for any type of group-centered planning, analysis, and feedback. A person may, however, engage in many self-help exercises, review numerous published materials, conduct informational interviews, and participate as an employee shadow. These latter two activities may require much contact work to arrange interview appointments and to gain the cooperation necessary to shadow one or more employees for a short period of time (at least one day, but could be as long as one week). Another shortcoming of the self-help format is that an individual may not be able to obtain copies of appropriate tests and inventory instruments.

An advantage of the self-help strategy is that a person can engage in much introspective activity through structured exercises and writing. These paper and pencil activities may take the form of a career diagram or graph, autobiography, obituary, force field analysis, daily activity diary, written self-interview, and a life style inventory (for formats and samples of these items, see Kotter, Faux, & McArthur, 1978). The self-reports resulting from these self-analyses may contain lists and other indications of an individual's technical knowledge and skill, leadership potential, attitudes, values, likes, dislikes, aptitudes, work interests, and various personal strengths and weaknesses.

A second approach to individual career planning entails obtaining assistance from a career counselor or consultant. Private practice counselors charge fees for their services that may range up to

$2000. High school and college counselors provide various career services to students at minimal or no charge. Whether private practice or a student service, counselor assistance typically includes two basic data gathering and diagnostic approaches, actuarial and clinical. The actuarial approach relies heavily on testing. Some of the most widely used tests are the Strong Interest Inventory, Career Development Inventory, Kuder Occupational Interest Survey, and Adult Career Concerns Inventory. These tests focus on job, occupation, and life interests, knowledge and attitudes about career choice, and career stage and vocational maturity. Clinical assistance is provided through in depth interviewing, analysis of past behavior and career-related experiences, and qualitative appraisals of abilities and interests. Frequently, actuarial and clinical approaches are used conjunctively to generate a more holistic assessment of an individual's career preferences and prospects.

Many organizations in recent years have initiated career planning and development programs (Aplin & Gerster, 1978; Lopez, Rockmore, & Kesselman, 1980). The purpose of such efforts is to better match the individual's job and career aspirations with the organization's needs for human resource talent at future points in time; however, the outcome (result) of organization career management can lead to mismatch and employee turnover (Granrose & Portwood, 1987). Organizational career planning and programming may include special orientation and job rotation, employee-supervisor counseling, joint goal setting and mentoring, self and training needs analyses, assessment center participation, and formulation of alternative job progression charts and career paths along with managerial succession plans. Basically, these activities focus on individual-organization assessments, individual exposure to the organization, and solidification of the individual-organization relationship. These efforts are also usually linked with overall corporate personnel plans and forecasts, compensation administration, performance appraisal, and other functional areas of personnel/human resource management. Some firms have even linked organizational career management with strategic business planning (Slocum, Crow, Hansen, & Rawlings, 1985; Stumpf, 1988).

CAREER PLANNING COURSE

A fourth career planning format is a course or workshop offered by a college, professional association, or trade organization. While these are not custom designed to the individual or firm, they do focus on the individual in the context of an organized class of students. This format does, however, encourage information sharing and exchange. A college career planning course may include a text and readings (Bolles, 1986; Feldman, 1988; Hall, 1976; Kotter, Faux, & McArthur, 1978; London & Stumpf, 1982; Schein, 1978), lectures, topic discussions, career testimonials, instrumentation, structured experiences (individual and group), and cases. More specifically, the syllabus of a career planning course recently facilitated by the authors contained elements as listed in Figure 2.

This course was specifically designed for first year MBA students, many of whom worked full-time and had accumulated five or more years of technical/professional experience. Virtually all students taking the course expressed varying degrees of interest in changing careers or obtaining employment at an advanced level of authority and responsibility with their employing firm or a different organization in the same career field.

The course has been conducted as a semester long course with approximately fifteen hours of class time. With so few class hours the primary focus has necessarily been to assist the participants in studying themselves along with job, career, and industry exploration. Class time has been devoted to brief lectures, some instrumentation (testing) and exercises, general interpretation of instrument data and results, and occupational and career testimonials. Individual job and career counseling, an extensive library, and business and industry contact persons for informational interviews were made available to students so they could more effectively deal with job and career concerns.

Several semesters' experience in conducting the course leads to the conclusion that the most helpful and significant course features are the testing, informational interviews, career transition panel discussion, and career analysis paper. The mini-battery of career related tests has stimulated self-analysis and frequently provide much

FIGURE 2. Career Planning Course Syllabus

I. Lecture and Discussion Topics

    A. Career models

    B. Life planning

    C. Goal setting

    D. Testing and self-assessment

    E. Linkage of job-career-organization-industry

    F. Job search

    G. Needs and values

    H. Organizational culture

    I. Mentoring

II. Instrumentation and Testing

    A. Strong-Campbell Interest Inventory

    B. Myers-Briggs Type Indicator

    C. Hermann Survey

    D. Hall Occupational Orientation Inventory

    E. Structure of Intellect

III. Job-Organization-Industry Information Search

    A. Library orientation to corporate-industry documents and reporting

    B. Informational interviews of job incumbents

    C. Career transition panel-career change testimonials

IV. Career Analysis Paper with Focus on One or More of the Following:

    A. Life and career plans

    B. Self-assessment of interests and skills

    C. Job search

    D. Job and career transition

    E. Obstacles to job and career satisfaction

    F. Industry exploration and analysis

    G. Plans and strategies for job and career successes

V. Text -- Feldman, <u>Managing Careers in Organizations</u>

    Readings from journals in the following areas:

    A. Career and occupational choice

    B. Career planning -- individual perspective

FIGURE 2 (continued)

C. Career planning -- organization perspective
D. Career dilemmas and problems
E. Job and career mobility
F. Personal and professional career conflicts
G. Dual career problems and issues
H. Career theories and models

confirmatory data about the individual. The Strong-Campbell Interest Inventory (this and many other career planning and development instruments are described in the *CCP Catalog*, Consulting Psychologists Press, 1988) has been included in the set of tests to generate job and occupational interest profiles to help guide students along a job and career path with satisfying characteristics. Since a student's interests may not be consistent with his or her skills and abilities, ten of the twenty-six Structure of Intellect subtests have been administered to encourage the examination of personal skills and abilities.

The Hall Occupational Orientation Inventory was used to direct students to examine their needs and basic values. These inventory data led some students to realize that they may have to accept compromise. For example, a strong desire for a career that provides considerable monetary gain may not fit with an interest in social work. Personality variables (as revealed by the Myers-Briggs test) may play a similar role. A shy, introverted person with a strong interest in sales work but a low need for closure may be faced with a very difficult career decision. The Hermann Survey, an instrument assessing (brain) hemispheric dominance, plumbs for hidden motivations and may provide indications of why a person might be drawn to certain types of jobs. Research with the Hermann Survey suggests that it is no accident that left limbic dominants enjoy the planning and organizational tasks associated with the work they are performing (Schkade, Quick, & Eakin, 1986).

Along with the testing and instrumentation, students have found the informational interview to be a very helpful exercise in gathering information about jobs and careers of interest. Students are required to arrange three informational interviews. Each interview is about one half hour to one hour in length; however, sometimes a student has been able to shadow the interviewee for most, if not all, of a workday. A relatively structured interview format is followed by students in order to probe for information about (1) characteristics of the interviewee's job and aspects of the internal environment of the organization, (2) educational preparation for the person's current job and other jobs in the relevant job progression or career path, (3) job and career opportunities within the interviewee's industry, (4) job performance norms and accepted means for appraising employee performance, and (5) the importance of occupational networking, mentoring, and sponsorship. For many students one of the most interesting and revealing pieces of information uncovered through the informational interview was identification of the key entry level job that was most important for rapid job and career progression within the organization.

The career transition (Louis, 1980) panel, scheduled for the last part of the course, is composed of three persons who have experienced significant career changes; public school teacher to bank executive and naval commander to university professor are two examples of career change represented by panelists. These persons share their experiences (the sacrifices, disappointments, and benefits) in negotiating major life and career changes. They discuss career motivations, describe career transition problems and pitfalls, and offer advice and helpful hints for facilitating career change success. Through these career testimonials, panelists become role models for many of the students.

As a written course requirement, each student prepares a career paper that focuses on his/her basic purpose for taking the course. Some students desire assistance in searching for a first professional position, others are negotiating a major job and career transition, and many need help in preparing a self-assessment of occupational interests and job skills. Nearly all papers address one or more of the areas of career concern listed in Figure 2. Regardless of the paper's specific focus, this exercise has tended to be most beneficial for those students who have effectively integrated test results, informational interview data, advice from career transition panelists, and information from the career planning literature.

Two examples illustrate the positive outcomes of the career planning course. In one, a group of engineers (two male and one female) working for a highly structured aerospace firm and performing routine engineering tasks were dissatisfied with the ten-year outlook of a career track that provided more pay for similar work at only a slightly more advanced organizational level. Through the testing and self assessment process they became aware of their needs for tasks or jobs that required innovation, variety, autonomy, task identity, and some greater level of risk. These three shared information about their current job situations as well as their test results and informational interview data.

Two career alternatives were identified. One involved a transfer within the firm to a unit that served a research and development function. This was an appealing arrangement for one of the group members who had a need for the security found in a large organization. The second alternative involved a move to an engineer consulting firm with positions that provided opportunities for greater variety, innovation, autonomy, and risk. The course allowed these three individuals to better articulate and understand their job and career interests and encouraged them to explore various options together. Through this peer interaction they were plotting intermediate job and career moves by the end of the course.

The second example involves a woman in her late twenties who was a financial analyst working for a rapidly growing management consulting firm. Her work was deadline and client driven and periodically required extensive overtime. She was a wife with a desire to raise a family. She discovered through the testing process that she enjoyed tasks that were highly analytic and somewhat routine, yet provided a degree of security. She preferred work activity that focused on data as opposed to people. Through the informational interview process she became aware of the job and work environment of a financial analyst in an aerospace firm. It provided regular hours, highly analytic work that focused on large quantities of data, and a sense of job security. Fortunately, she was able to secure this position and is experiencing much job/organizational satisfaction.

As a final note to these two examples, it is of interest that in one case the person(s) became aware of a greater desire for autonomy and was able to transition from a large bureaucratic organization to a consulting firm. In the other example, the person moved in just

the opposite direction, from a consulting firm to a large, more secure bureaucratic organization.

CAREER PLANNING AND THE
INDIVIDUAL-ORGANIZATIONAL RELATIONSHIP

As previously mentioned, a crucial set of relationships for career
success are the congruent linkages of person – job – organization –
industry. This chapter has suggested career planning as a means for
establishing these connections. In the process of planning one's career and achieving job and career success, the individual will be
exposed to (as an applicant) and be a participant in (as an employee)
a number of organizational career management practices. Many of
these practices and individual career planning efforts are counter-
part activities as represented in Figure 3.

If the individual is to effectively engage in career planning, he/
she must consider organizational career management practices and
how they can facilitate (and possibly frustrate) career success. For
example, the informational interview is a means for gaining first-
hand information concerning a firm's job opportunities and personnel needs. From the organization's point of view, the realistic job
preview is a means for providing accurate information about jobs to
applicants in order to minimize selection errors. An individual's

Individual Career Planning	Organizational Career Management
Informational interview	Realistic job preview
Self-assessment	Job analysis
Self-profile of knowledge	Job description and
and skill	specification
Job search	Recruitment
Goal setting	Human resource objectives
Job and career advancement --	Succession and promotion
promotion	planning
Career planning	Personnel forecasting

FIGURE 3. Individual Organizational Career Connection

self-profile of strengths and weaknesses corresponds directly to the knowledge, skills, and abilities indicated in the job description and specification. Matching of individual career planning activities and organizational career management practices provides the individual with greater insight and perspective for career success. The individual's fit with the organization is obviously crucial for career success. Career planning provides a means for facilitating this fit and enhancing the predictability of the individual-organizational relationship and its associated experiences and outcomes. From the individual's perspective, career planning yields insight and direction and a means for coping with ambiguous role requirements and organizational demands, recognizing career opportunities, and reducing stress associated with job and career adjustments. Career planning from the organization's view provides a more structured approach to managing employee career paths and patterns. For both the individual and organization, the logic of career planning, it is hoped, allows flexibility in career plan execution (Gaertner, 1988).

REFERENCES

Aplin, J. C., & Gerster, D. K. (1978). Career development: An integration of individual and organizational needs. *Personnel*, *55*, 23-29.

Blueston, B., & Bennett, H. (1982). *The deindustrialization of America: Plant closings, community abandonment, and the dismantling of basic industry*. New York: Basic Books.

Bolles, R. N. (1986). *What color is your parachute?* Berkeley, CA: Ten Speed Press.

Consulting Psychologists Press. (1988). *1988 CPP catalog*. Palo Alto, CA: Consulting Psychologists Press.

Dalton, G. W., Thompson, Ph. D., & Price, R. (1977). The four stages of professional careers: A new look at performance by professionals. *Organizational Dynamics*, *6*, 19-41.

DeLuca, J. R. (1988). Strategic career management in non-growing, volatile business environments. *Human Resources Planning*, *11*, 49-62.

Feldman, D. C. (1988). *Managing careers in organizations*. Glenview, IL: Scott, Foresman and Company.

Gaertner, K. N. (1988). Managers' careers and organizational change. *Academy of Management Executive*, *2*, 311-318.

Granrose, C. S., & Portwood, J. D. (1987). Matching individual career plans and organizational career management. *Academy of Management Journal, 30,* 699-720.

Halberstam, D. (1986). *The reckoning.* New York: Avon Books.

Hall, D. T. (1976). *Careers in organizations.* Glenview, IL: Scott, Foresman and Company.

Hirsch, P. (1987). *Pack your own parachute.* Reading, MA: Addison-Wesley.

Hirschhorn, L. (1984). *Beyond mechanization: Work and technology in a postindustrial age.* Cambridge, MA: MIT Press.

Hoerr, J. P. (1988). *And the wolf finally came.* Pittsburgh: University of Pittsburgh Press.

Hunt, D. M., & Michael, C. (1983). Mentorship: A career training and development tool. *Academy of Management Review, 8,* 475-485.

Hunt, H. A., & Hunt, T. L. (1983). *Human resource implications of robotics.* Kalamazoo, MI: W. E. Upjohn Institute for Employment Research.

Kotter, J. P., Faux, V. A., & McArthur, C. C. (1978). *Self-assessment and career development.* Englewood Cliffs, NJ: Prentice-Hall.

London, M. (1988). Organizational support for employees' career motivation: A guide to human resource strategies in changing business conditions. *Human Resource Planning, 11,* 23-32.

London, M. (1983). Toward a theory of career motivation. *Academy of Management Review, 8,* 620-630.

London, M., & Stumpf, S. A. (1982). *Managing careers.* Reading, MA: Addison-Wesley.

Lopez, F. E., Rockmore, B. W., & Kesselman, G. A. (1988). The development of an integrated career planning program at Gulf Power Company. *Personnel Administrator, 25,* 21-29, 75-76.

Louis, M. R. (1980). Career transitions: Varieties and commonalities. *Academy of Management Review, 5,* 329-340.

Majchrzak, A. (1988). *The human side of factory automation.* San Francisco: Jossey-Bass Publishers.

McCann, J. E., & Gilkey, R. (1988). *Joining forces: Creating and managing successful mergers and acquisitions.* Englewood Cliffs, NJ: Prentice-Hall.

Mihal, W. L., Sorce, P. A., & Comte, T. E. (1984). A process model of individual career decision making. *Academy of Management Review, 9,* 95-103.

Milkovich, G. T., Anderson, J. C., & Greenhalgh, L. (1976). Organizational careers: Environmental, organizational, and individual determinants. In L. Dyer (Ed.), *Careers in organizations.* Ithaca, New York: New York State School of Industrial and Labor Relations, 17-30.

Rhodes, S. R., & Doering, M. (1983). An integrated model of career change. *Academy of Management Review, 8,* 631-639.

Schein, E. G. (1978). *Career dynamics: Matching individual and organizational needs.* Reading, MA: Addison-Wesley.

Scheuerman, W. (1986). *The steel crisis: The economics and politics of a declining industry.* New York: Praeger.

Schkade, L. L., Quick, J. C., & Eakin, M. (1986). Thinking styles, stress, and strain. *Personnel, 63,* 44-48.

Slocum, J. W., Jr., Crow, W. L., Hansen, R. W., & Rawlings, S. (1985). Business strategy and the management of plateaued employees. *Academy of Management Journal, 28,* 133-154.

Stumpf, S. A. (1988). Choosing career management practices to support your business strategy. *Human Resource Planning, 11,* 33-48.

Woodward, H., & Buchholz, S. (1987). *After-shock: Helping people through corporate change.* New York: John Wiley & Sons.

Adjusting to a New Organization: Easing the Transition from Outsider to Insider

Debra L. Nelson

Oklahoma State University

SUMMARY. Entering a new organization and assuming a new job marks a career transition common to adult life. The three stages of anticipatory socialization, encounter, and change and acquisition form a model of socialization which is used to depict what newcomers can expect to experience during the adjustment process, including stressors to be encountered. Strategies are suggested for newcomers and for organizations which can ease the transition for both parties. For newcomers, these strategies include making a realistic job choice, preparing for the experience of reality shock, and seeking out social support from others. For organizations, the recommended strategies are forming psychological contracts with integrity, providing early job challenges, flexible scheduling, and timely feedback to newcomers, and ensuring that multiple sources of social support are available for newcomers.

One of the more important transitions of adult life occurs in the form of taking a new job in a new setting. Few people would argue that this experience is not stressful, both in positive ways and in negative ways. Yet we know very little about the process of contracting with a new organization, those uncomfortable first few days at work, learning the ropes, triumphs and failures along the way, and finally settling in so that the job begins to feel like our most familiar pair of washed-out weekend blue jeans. Perhaps the

---

Reprints may be obtained from Debra L. Nelson, Department of Management, College of Business Administration, Oklahoma State University, Stillwater, OK 74078.

most memorable time when socialization experiences can be recalled is when the individual graduates from college. A colleague recalled it this way:

> We all tried to one-up each other about the jobs we had just accepted . . . bragging that we had the highest salary, the best management training program, the most desirable co-workers, the most upward mobility . . . and believed we were destined to become future corporate leaders. And so the lot of us moved to the city in the same general area. Every Friday after work we met for happy hour to visit and relate the events of the week. It is interesting to look at how the mood of those happy hours changed over the first few months . . . at first, we jockeyed for position in terms of telling stories about how great these new jobs were or how weird our bosses were. Our old school gang really hung together. Then there seemed to be cliques emerging . . . there was the big eight accounting table, the banking table . . . and people started bringing coworkers with them.
>
> Gradually, things quieted down at happy hour. The mood went from "Wow, isn't this great" to "What in the world have we gotten ourselves into?" There began to be general agreement that business wasn't all it was cracked up to be. Some of us felt we had been misled about the jobs. Happy hour turned into a real downer, a gripe session. Some people who were really disenchanted quit their jobs. It seemed like the ones who stayed with their jobs started hanging around mainly company people and formed sort of like a sorority or fraternity among themselves for each company . . . they started all dressing alike and acting alike and really began looking alike . . . you could almost identify who someone worked for by the table they sat at . . . sort of a strange cloning process.

The story raises issues concerning the successes and failures of socialization. Why do some individuals become effective, productive insiders and others leave the organization? This paper will address the question, along with other questions which arise about transitioning into a new organization. A traditional stage model of socialization which individuals go through in adjustment will provide a framework for examining the process. Within each stage, there are major variables of interest as suggested by the conceptual and empirical socialization literatures. These issues will be explored and new variables of interest will be posited. Finally, recommendations will be presented for individuals and for organizations which may make this potentially stressful process smoother for both parties. The purpose of this paper is to provide a practical tour through what we do and do not know about organizational socialization.

The model which will serve to guide this effort is presented in Figure 1. It is a traditional, three-stage model of the transition which an individual goes through in adjusting to a new job. The first stage encompasses all of the learning which occurs prior to the newcomer's first day on the job. Termed anticipatory socialization in this model, it has also been referred to as "getting in" (Feldman, 1976), "pre-arrival" (Porter, Lawler, & Hackman, 1975), and simply "entry" (Schein, 1978). Regardless of the terminology used, the basic idea is that socialization begins even before the newcomer accepts the job. Expectations of the new organization and the new job are formed during this first stage.

Encounter is the second stage in the model, also referred to as "breaking in" (Feldman, 1976) and "socialization" (Schein, 1978). The encounter stage begins the first day at work and shapes the individual's long-term view of the job and organization. During this stage, expectations meet reality, and the phenomenon called "reality shock" may occur due to disparities between lofty expectations and the realities of everyday organizational life (Dean, Ferris, & Konstans, 1985). The demands of the job become apparent during this stage, and the newcomer must devise strategies for dealing with these stressors (Nelson, 1987; 1988). While the length of the various stages has not been empirically determined, encounter is thought to span the first six to nine months on the new job (Louis, 1980).

The third and final stage of the socialization process is change and acquisition, also called "settling in" (Feldman, 1976) or "mutual acceptance" (Schein, 1978). It is during this stage that the newcomer masters the demands of the job (Nelson, 1987; 1988).

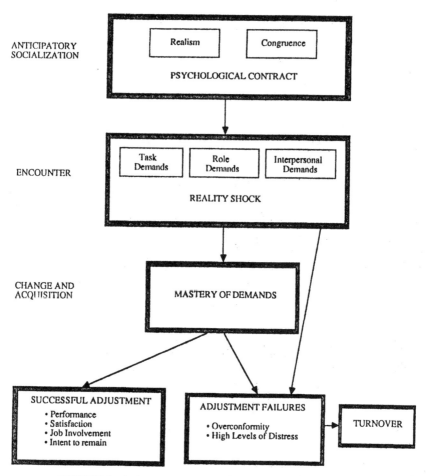

FIGURE 1. A three-stage model of newcomer socialization.

Tasks are performed dependably, role clarity is achieved, and the newcomer is integrated into the social network of the organization (Greenhaus, 1987). In terms of timing, the distinction between stage two (encounter) and stage three (change and acquisition) is not clearcut; however, it is assumed that the newcomer makes the passage somewhere in the six to nine month range, and that the total socialization process is of nine to twelve months duration.

Within each of three stages of socialization, there are important variables for consideration. Each stage will be discussed in turn, highlighting the variables of interest and the experiences which the newcomer can expect to face.

ANTICIPATORY SOCIALIZATION
(THIS NEW JOB IS GOING TO BE TERRIFIC!)

During anticipatory socialization, the newcomer gathers information about the job and organization from a variety of sources including recruiting materials, the pre-employment interview, and onsite visits. In addition, the newcomer receives cues from other individuals from both inside of and outside of the organization. Expectations are thus developed from information which is, to a great extent, uncontrollable by the organization. The newcomer fantasizes about what he/she will do in the job and forms opinions about what is achievable in the new position (Frese, 1982). There are three variables of interest in this early socialization stage.

Realism

A realistic set of expectations, developed in anticipatory socialization, can prove valuable for the newcomer's subsequent adjustment. Two forms of realism are important. Realism about the job is the degree to which a complete and accurate view of new job responsibilities is held by the newcomer. Realism about the organization is the degree to which a complete and accurate view of organizational goals, climate, and philosophy is held by the newcomer.

A realistic assessment of the new job allows the newcomer to more easily discover what is expected of him/her by role senders and can help the newcomer to pre-plan strategies for dealing with the demands of the job. Realistic portrayal of the job has been found of benefit to the newcomer in terms of anxiety reduction (Gomersall & Myers, 1966), enhanced ability to cope (Suszko & Breaugh, 1986), and increased job survival (Premack & Wanous, 1985).

Realistic expectations of the organization can help the newcomer discover the system of norms, beliefs, and values inherent in culture (Schein, 1985). Such an appreciation of culture provides a way for the individual to interpret new experiences. Organizational realism conveys such crucial factors as knowledge base, strategy, and mission (Van Maanen & Schein, 1979).

One strategy for developing realistic expectations is the use of realistic job previews by organizations. RJPs are thought to result in more realism on the part of newcomers by a variety of methods. The met expectations view holds that RJPs deflate newcomers' expectations to more realistic levels; hence, these expectations are more likely to be met by the job. A second explanation contends that RJPs have an innoculation effect; that is, they help newcomers develop coping strategies for dealing with job reality. A third explanation is that RJPs convey an air of straightforwardness and honesty to newcomers (Breaugh, 1983). Whatever the explanation, there is evidence that RJPs are valuable tools in helping newcomers achieve a more realistic portrait of the job.

Kramer (1974) developed an anticipatory socialization program to reduce the incidence of burnout among nurses. The idea behind this program was to induce reality shock before the individual is actually on the new job. Kramer's data indicated that reduced turnover and absenteeism along with increased job satisfaction were associated with the program. Jackson (1984), in analyzing such programs, cautions that the reality of the job is not altered by the programs; rather, participants are exposed to it in order to smooth their transition into the organization.

Realism regarding both the job and the new organization are thus potentially valuable factors in the first stage of socialization. This is attributable in part to their effect in helping to assure good matches between individuals and organizations. When realistic information is exchanged by both parties, better selection decisions can result. This leads to the second important factor in anticipatory socialization.

Person-Environment Fit

Wanous (1980) articulated two matches essential to good selection decisions. One match is between the skills and abilities of the newcomer and the demands of the job. The other match is between the needs and values of the individual and the organization's ability to meet these needs with the provision of valued rewards. Congruence in both of these individual-organizational matches is thought to be related to successful socialization of newcomers (Nelson, 1985).

The stress literature addresses this issue as person-environment fit (Harrison, Moss, Dielman, Horvath, & Harlan, 1987). P-E fit addresses the individual's perception of the job, the individual's perception of self, and the relationship of these perceptions to individual strain. Strain occurs when a newcomer perceives abilities to be exceeded by job demands. This individual strain is translated into organizational strain.

Congruence between the newcomer's skills and abilities and the demands of the job should allow a newcomer to proceed into the encounter stage with a sense of being well-suited to the job and therefore a sense of efficacy (Bandura, 1982). Congruence between the newcomer's needs and values and the rewards provided by the organization can be expected to perform a similarly beneficial function, especially in terms of interpersonal demands. Within a particular occupation, people tend to share certain values, attitudes, and interests (Vroom, 1964). The newcomer who perceives his new organizational colleagues to share in these feelings should be a step ahead in terms of building good working relationships.

Strategies aimed at achieving a fundamental congruence or match between individuals and organizations involve effective recruiting and selection procedures (Brousseau, 1983). Dean (1985) suggests that one workable strategy to enhance matching efforts would be to hire only those job candidates with realistic expectations. To accomplish this, organizations would need to develop a profile of those newcomers whose expectations most closely approximate organizational reality. The profile could then be used to screen out those individuals with highly unrealistic expectations who would most likely experience reality shock at encounter.

The Psychological Contract

The anticipatory socialization stage signals the preliminary development of the psychological contract between the newcomer and the organization. The psychological contract is an implicit, unwritten agreement which specifies what each party to the exchange will provide the other and in turn receive from the other (Levinson, 1962). The newcomer, for example, brings knowledge, abilities, skills, and potential to the new organization, in order to meet the organization's goals and mission. The organization contributes salaries, benefits, career opportunities, and status to fulfill the basic needs of the individual (Quick & Quick, 1984). The underlying agreement delineating the responsibilities of each party is known as the psychological contract. It is essential that this implicit agreement be entered into by both parties with "both eyes wide open"; that is, both parties should recognize their obligation to each other and hold up their end of the bargain.

The psychological contract is thus a pervasive concept which impinges upon both realistic expectations and person-environment fit, because both of these factors are preconditions to an effective agreement between the newcomer and the organization. Schein (1978) contends that one indicator of successful adjustment is mutual acceptance. This is signaled in a number of ways including conferring a promotion, giving a raise, etc. The point is that mutual acceptance is simply a ratification of the original contract which was formed in anticipatory socialization (Greenhaus, 1987). A violation of the psychological contract, such as the "surprise" (Louis, 1980) of reality shock from the organization or misrepresentation of biographical data from the newcomer will result maladjustment or eventual turnover.

Realistic expectations, optimum fit between the individual and the organization, and a sound psychological contract are important factors for getting off to a good start in the adjustment process. The newcomer's arrival for the first day of work on the new job signals the beginning of the second stage of socialization.

ENCOUNTER
(WHAT HAVE I GOTTEN MYSELF INTO?)

A new job poses multiple challenges for the newcomer in terms of tasks to master, relationships to develop, and roles to assume. In addition, this is the stage at which reality shock may occur when expectations clash with the realities of the job. Faced with unfamiliar settings with no map to guide them, newcomers experience discomfort and anxiety as they try to learn the ropes and become assimilated into the organizational culture. This is perhaps the most stressful period of adjustment, as emotional responses to the task are developed and social norms are discovered and adopted. The newcomer can thus expect two broad experiences in encounter: reality shock and the demands of the new job.

Reality Shock: Wake Up and Smell the Coffee

Most newcomers experience a very predictable "surprise" reaction when confronted with the demands of the new job. The degree to which this reaction is manifested is dependent on the realism of the expectations developed in anticipatory socialization. Having formed attitudes about the new job from the recruitment process, the interview, word of mouth, and prior work experience, the newcomer measures the novel experience against these standards, and more often than not, finds that the new job does not measure up. Newcomers often delude themselves into thinking the job meets their values; they expect a positive experience during the new job and fantasize about the job with wishful thinking (Louis, 1980). Candidates often aggrandize the job after the decision to accept it, convincing themselves that they have made the right decision (Festinger, 1957).

The newcomer is not entirely responsible for unrealistic or unmet expectations, however. Often organizations, anxious to recruit desirable candidates, distort the realities of the job and conspicuously neglect to relate the possible negative side of the job. Fearing that good recruits will be frightened off, they build up the job to attract the candidate. Whatever the source of the incongruence between expectations and reality, the newcomer may experience dissatisfaction, depression, tension, feelings of having been deceived, or feelings of inadequacy in the period of reality shock. These attitudes may be translated into behaviors as drastic as leaving the organization.

Part of managing reality shock is careful management of the anticipatory socialization stage by both the individual and the organization so that highly unrealistic expectations either do not develop or are brought quickly in line with reality. Another method for managing reality shock is to realize its inevitability and to recognize the experience of this phenomenon is simply part of the adjustment to a new job. Should this affect the individual in a severe way, it should be an obvious signal that expectations are not meshing with reality and some action should be taken to better align these two elements.

Work Demands

The encounter stage of socialization is characterized by the basic activities in which the newcomer engages (Katz, 1985). The newcomer must deal with demands emanating from these three basic activities, which are the task, the role, and the interpersonal relationships in the new job.

Task demands. The first of set of demands stems from learning to perform the tasks necessary for the new job. New skills are learned, new procedures are introduced, and often new equipment is presented to be dealt with. Even the newcomer who arrives with considerable training and preparation must adapt this knowledge for use in the new environment.

There are several demands which arise from the work which the newcomer performs. *Overload* is a stressor which may be quantitative (too much to do) or qualitative in nature (work is too difficult). Related to this is the demand of *time pressure*. This demand stems from attempts to meet work deadlines, quotas, and goals, and can result in significant distress (Lakein, 1973). *Job scope* can place demands on a newcomer. A job lacking in variety, autonomy, significance, identity and feedback may prove deficient in motivation potential (Hackman & Lawler, 1971). Katz (1985) reports that the job dimension of autonomy may be responded to in a negative manner by newcomers. They are concerned primarily with establishing their identities through social interaction and may not be ready to accept autonomy.

Rewards may also prove a source of stress for newcomers. A perceived inequity between the individual's contribution and the rewards of the organization may be distressful (Lawler, 1971). Similarly, if the distribution of rewards is seen as unfair, distress may result. *Career progress* in a new job occurs when the newcomer must cope with career development and is especially demanding for the individual who lacks career maturity. A new job may result in opportunity or conversely in a lack of challenge; either situation creates stress for the newcomer.

Task-related demands are important because they influence the ·newcomer's perceptions of the job and must be managed in order for successful adjustment to occur. These demands, however, are not the sole source of stress for newcomers. A second category of demands arises from the multiple expectations placed upon the newcomer from others both within and outside of the new organization.

Role demands. Role theory has a long and rich history in management thought and research, beginning with the work of Kahn and his associates (1964) who identified two prevalent forms of role stress. *Role conflict* occurs when the newcomer receives incompatible and conflicting expectations from others. Stress arising from role conflict occurs due to the newcomer's inability to respond effectively to these various expectations (Van Sell, Brief, & Schuler, 1981).

Role ambiguity occurs when the newcomer simply does not know what is expected of him/her by others. This can result from confusing information provided by others, a lack of information from others, or confusion about the consequences of expected behavior (Van Sell, Brief, & Schuler, 1981).

A third, more recently identified role demand is that of *work/ home conflict*. This occurs when the newcomer's work role and home role clash. Although some individuals are able to compartmentalize their lives, there is potential for the newcomer to experience stress from assuming central roles both at work and at home (Hall & Hall, 1980). Stresses from a newcomer's personal life affect performance at work, and stresses from work have a spillover effect on home life. The dual career couple is particularly prone to this demand.

An examination of the above-described stressors may lead to the mistaken assumption that role stressors arise strictly from the expectations of others. This is not so; newcomers engage in role defining and role making in a two-way process of negotiated role definition. The newcomer does not passively accept the role; rather, he/she attempts to modify the role by stamping a unique identity upon it. Nicholson (1984) has referred to the process whereby newcomers proactively alter the role in order to meet their needs as role development. Role stressors thus arise from the reciprocal negotiations which occur between newcomers and their various role send-. ers. Related to the issue of a newcomer's role is the third category of demands faced in encounter.

Interpersonal demands. Social, personal, and work relationships can be sources of stress in and of themselves. These interpersonal demands are somewhat similar to role demands, but differ in that they are not based upon expectations of others. One interpersonal stressor which newcomers often face is *organizational politics*. The new member is not often privy to the intricacies of power and influence which are part of organizations. While he/she may be exposed to the organization chart right away, the subtleties of politics arise from the informal system which is revealed to newcomers much more slowly. Politics may be a particularly stressful part of a new job for women (Nelson & Quick, 1988).

Another interpersonal demand originates from the newcomer's relationship with the new boss. *Supervisory style* has long been regarded as a potential stressor (Quick & Quick, 1984). If the style of leadership exhibited by the boss does not meet the newcomer's needs, it may be a source of demands. Individuals who consider themselves competent and experienced may resent authoritarian behavior by their superior. Newcomers who feel somewhat insecure and have high needs for affiliation may prefer a supportive supervisor. The point to be made is that individuals have different preferences for supervisory styles, and if their preferences are not fulfilled, distress may result.

Responsibility for people makes managerial work stressful. In a study conducted by the National Institute of Occupational Safety and Health, managerial jobs were listed twice in a compilation of the twelve most stressful occupations (French, Caplan, & Harrison, 1982). Responsibility for people has been found to be more stressful than responsibility for budgets or property (Cooper & Payne, 1978). Many factors contribute to the stressful nature of managerial

work. Newcomers who are in managerial positions without decision-making latitude are especially prone to stress (Karasek, 1979).
The new work group is also a source of stress. *Group pressure* is
placed on individuals when they do not adhere to the norms of
group behavior. Group members will tend to enforce these norms
very strictly if the norms ensure group survival, increase the predictability of member behavior, or reflect the group's central values
(Feldman, 1984).

The newcomer thus faces demands during the encounter stage
from the task, role, and interpersonal relationships inherent in the
new job. It is important to recognize that every newcomer experiences a different combination of demands. Individual differences
make the process of adjustment unique; however, this discussion of
demands highlights the major ones which newcomers face. To illustrate this idea, two profiles of newcomers with very different adjustment experiences will be presented. These profiles were excerpted
from a longitudinal study of newcomers to three organizations (for
additional details please see Nelson, 1985, and Quick, Nelson, &
Eakin, 1988a). The measurement instrument used to assess demands was the Stress Diagnostic Survey (Ivancevich & Matteson,
1980). The subjects of the profiles responded to the questionnaire in
their sixth month on their new jobs.

Figure 2 depicts the demands reported by a 37 year old geologist
who assumed a new job with a major oil company. She holds a
bachelor's degree and had eight years of prior work experience. The
task demands which she views as most stressful are job scope and
career progress. This may be a reflection of the economic downturn
of the energy industry in which she is employed. Role ambiguity is
a source of moderate stress for her, and she reported a lack of communication of expectations to be a particular problem. Work/home
conflicts were also reported to be stressful. As a female in a dual
career family, she is expected to fulfill the job of running the household. In the interpersonal stressor category, politics are reported to
be very stressful. Again, this may reflect jockeying for position by
individuals in an industry where positions are scarce and promotions are few.

Figure 3 presents the stress diagnostic profile of a 40 year old

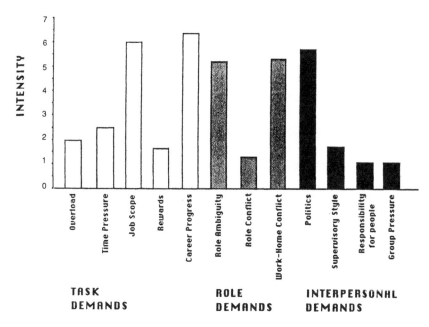

FIGURE 2. Newcomer stress profile for geologist.

male who entered a new job with a major electronics firm which is a defense contractor with the federal government. A managerial-level employee, he supervises a group of computer engineers who produce and test high technology hardware. The task demands of work overload and time pressure plague him. He reports never having enough hours in the day to get everything done. Related to the time issue, the role demand of work/home conflict is a source of stress. Long hours at work detract from his home life. The interpersonal demand of responsibility for people is high; in fact, it is the greatest source of stress he reports.

In these two contrasting profiles we can see that the process of adjusting to a new job is a demanding one which varies from newcomer to newcomer. By knowing the possible demands which one might face, the newcomer can be forewarned about potential stressors and forearmed with prevention strategies for dealing with such stressors. Managing these stressors well is part of the third and final stage of socialization.

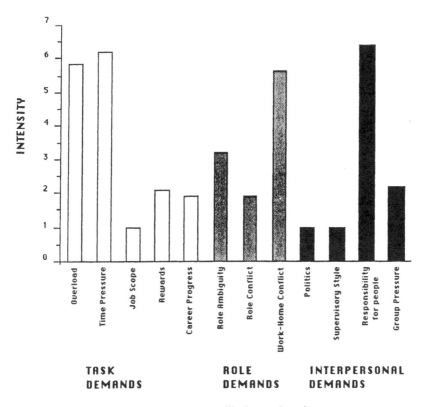

INTENSITY

Overload | Time Pressure | Job Scope | Rewards | Career Progress | Role Ambiguity | Role Conflict | Work-Home Conflict | Politics | Supervisory Style | Responsibility for people | Group Pressure

TASK DEMANDS   ROLE DEMANDS   INTERPERSONAL DEMANDS

FIGURE 3. Newcomer stress profile for engineering manager.

CHANGE AND ACQUISITION
(I'VE LEARNED THE ROPES AROUND HERE)

When newcomers are faced with demands, they direct their energy toward resolving the demands. Socialization models depict this effort toward resolution as being part of the change and acquisition stage, which is the last stage of the transition process. During this time, the newcomer begins to master the task, role, and interpersonal demands that are present in the new job (Nelson, 1985). Being able to cope with or manage these demands is a crucial accomplishment, because they are recurring or chronic demands. The stress literature has indicated that chronic, everyday demands are highly related to psychological and physiological symptoms of distress (Billings & Moos, 1984; Nelson, Quick, & Eakin, 1988).

Part of the process of mastering the demands involves the issue of control. Newcomers utilize a host of different coping techniques to master the demands, including social support, problem-focused coping, situation appraisal (Nelson & Sutton, 1988). These techniques, along with other coping mechanisms, have one thing in common: they all produce a perception of control over demands (Folkman, 1984). Creating and maintaining a sense that the newcomer can control the demands of the new job is therefore an important part of the mastery process.

It is important to note that during change and acquisition, we often assume that the demand level for the newcomer is high. This may not be so in all cases. Some newcomers may in fact find that their new positions are not challenging enough, and this is stressful too. The process of mastery thus involves resolving both types of demand levels.

This final stage is thought to complete the newcomer's transition into the organization from outsider to insider. The natural issue which arises next is how successful socialization is accomplished. There are certain outcomes which are associated with effective transitions, and others which mark unsuccessful socialization.

SUCCESSFUL ADJUSTMENT

The socialization period is a time of transition for the newcomer and the organization. The preferred outcome of this adjustment process is a ratification of the psychological contract which was formed during entry. Schein (1978) calls this outcome mutual acceptance; that is, both the individual and the organization, having negotiated the three stages of socialization, now accept the other party by deciding to continue in the psychological contract.

Other positive indicators of adjustment are performance (Berlew & Hall, 1966), satisfaction (Feldman, 1976; Nelson, Quick, & Eakin, 1988), job involvement and intention to remain with the organization (Nelson, 1985). A newcomer who has completed a successful transition may thus be expected to have good performance, a high level of satisfaction with the job, a high degree of job involvement, and intend to stay in the new job.

Greenhaus (1987) poses five questions which should be asked to ascertain whether the socialization process has been successful.

1. Has the employee learned the job?
2. Has the employee been integrated into the work group?
3. Has the employee achieved an acceptable level of role clarity?
4. Has the employee learned how to work within the system?
5. Does the employee understand and accept the organization's values?

Affirmative answers to these questions indicate the success of the transition. Note that these first three questions correspond roughly to the mastery of the three demands of encounter: task, role and interpersonal.

Just as there are positive indicators of adjustment, there are also indicators that socialization has not been effective. One such outcome is over-conformity on the part of the newcomer. The newcomer who blindly accepts the role and the values of the organization may lack the capacity to change when the job requires innovation. A more desirable outcome is a more reciprocal, negotiated compromise between the individual and the organization such that some expectations and values are accepted, but others are refined or not accepted (Schein, 1968; Jones, 1983).

Another indicator of less than successful adjustment is a high level of distress symptoms experienced by the newcomer (Nelson, 1987). Nelson, Quick and Eakin, (1988) found that the newcomer's inability to master role demands produces both psychological and physiological manifestations of distress. Psychological symptoms which may be experienced by newcomers are family problems, insomnia, depression, anxiety, and burnout (Nelson, 1987). Physiological problems related to distress include heart disease, musculoskeletal ailments, ulcers, headaches, skin diseases, and some forms of cancer (Quick & Quick, 1984). The symptoms of distress may be behavioral as well, including smoking, alcohol and drug abuse, and accidents (Quick & Quick, 1984). Distress symptoms which newcomers experience thus occur in a variety of forms. These symptoms are indicative of poor adjustment, as the newcomer who adjust well enjoys fewer work-stress related disorders.

The indicators discussed above are important because they may lead to turnover. Failure to adjust leaves the newcomer with feelings of alienation, discomfort, and may negatively effect performance (Schein, 1985). This affective state, combined with distress symptoms, may cause the newcomer to leave (Nelson, 1987). Losses such as this are costly for both the newcomer and the organization. The ultimate success of the transition is shown in individual and organizational health and well-being. Both parties reinforce the psychological contract and a good match has been made for each. There are proactive steps which individuals and organizations can take to ensure the success of the socialization process.

What Newcomers Can Do

Fundamental success in adjusting to a new job means making a good job choice, getting through the inevitable reality shock, and mastering work demands. Individuals can help ensure a smooth transition by taking steps to prepare for the adjustment period they will go through. In the anticipatory socialization stage, newcomers should seek out all available information about the job and the organization. Realizing that organizations present themselves in their best light in order to attract candidates, newcomers should ask for the negative aspects of a job if this information is not provided. The newcomer may obtain more accurate negative information if the question is posed in an objective, non-threatening manner. Multiple sources of information may help the newcomer gain insight into a realistic portrayal of the future job.

The other half of the individual-organizational equation in terms of realism is that the newcomer should be honest in presenting himself/herself to the organization. Newcomers also tend to present themselves in the best manner when job-seeking; naturally, they want to emphasize their strengths. The danger in overstating one's qualifications is that a bad match may result. Both parties must, therefore, keep honesty in mind when evaluating the possible fit between the two.

Both of the above ingredients are essential in a realistic job choice. The newcomer must perform a thorough self-assessment and organizational assessment, carefully weighing the compatability of self-interest and the interest of the organization. The recognition that it is possible to "impress and assess simultaneously" can aid the newcomer in this early socialization stage (Greenhaus, 1987).

During the encounter stage, the newcomer must prepare for the experience of reality shock. This is not to say that he/she should wait anxiously for this to occur; rather, just knowing that a slight depression a few months into a new job is natural may alleviate the distressful effects of reality shock. Another action which newcomers should take during encounter is to pre-plan strategies for dealing with job demands. Work-home conflicts which may arise can be prepared for. Dual-career families will want to have a battle plan, for example, for handling situations such as children's illnesses. Planning for demands rather than responding reactively will allow the newcomer to respond to demands with a sense of self-efficacy rather than panic (Bandura, 1982). In addition, newcomers must accept that adjustment to a new job is a stressful activity. They should periodically monitor their own stress levels and not immerse themselves so totally in the transition that they lose sight of other aspects of life.

A final strategy which newcomers can use in the encounter stage is to seek out assistance from others. Social support has been found to be an effective means by which newcomers can cope with demands (Nelson & Sutton, 1988). This support can come in several forms and from several sources. Whether informational, appraisal, instrumental, or emotional, the newcomer must admit the need for the support of others and reach out for it during this adjustment period.

During change and acquisition, the newcomer begins to "see the light at the end of the tunnel" in the new job. The comfort level of the new job increases as the newcomer begins to manage the demands of organizational life. Actions can be taken during this stage to more quickly negotiate the transition. One thing which a newcomer can do is to set realistic goals. Expecting to master the task, interpersonal, and role demands of the job at once is not realistic; rather, the newcomer should set challenging yet attainable goals and progress one step at a time. It is also important that the new-comer take credit for the small successes earned along the way. Too often, the newcomer focuses on the end state and fails to allow himself to experience the positive feelings associated with incremental successes in the adjustment process.

Feedback is extremely helpful during this stage. The newcomer will need to be aware of how well he/she is progressing in each of the demand areas. It is not safe to presume that the organization will provide this feedback along the way. Newcomers must seek out feedback, especially from the immediate supervisor, to monitor their progress. Networking with other newcomers may also be beneficial in this regard. Other newcomers can provide information on what works and what doesn't in terms of coping techniques.

There are therefore many things which newcomers can do to make the adjustment process easier for themselves. Although the transition into a new organization is stressful, it need not be traumatic if managed properly. The second essential ingredient for successful socialization is the action taken by the organization.

What Organizations Can Do

Socialization occurs regardless of formalization; that is, even if an organization does not have a formal orientation program, the informal organization will work to socialize the individual. It is in the best interest of the organization, therefore, to assist newcomers in the adjustment process and help make the transition smoother.

During the anticipatory socialization stage, organizations must form psychological contracts with newcomers which are reciprocal and characterized by fundamental integrity. Since the psychological contract negotiated at this juncture sets the tone for the entire relationship, it becomes incumbent on the organization to make honesty the theme of the contract. To ensure that the contract takes on this property, realism and congruence are priority factors.

Realistic job previews, in which both positive and negative information is provided to the newcomer, are powerful tools through which organizations can help newcomers adjust. A recent study suggests that individuals exposed to a RJP were more likely to perceive the organization as honest, have the ability to cope with job demands, be satisfied with the job, and remain in their job (Suszko & Breaugh, 1986). RJPs also serve a crucial purpose in reducing the uncertainty inherent in the adjustment process (Jones, 1986).

Congruence or person-job fit is another important factor in the early socialization stage as it has been found to be strongly related to job satisfaction and distress symptoms (Harrison et al., 1987). Organizations can facilitate congruence through effective recruiting and selection practices which are characterized by careful candidate assessment and organization needs assessment.

The second socialization stage, encounter, finds the new recruit faced with the reality of the new job. Organizations can help newcomers deal with this stressful experience by providing early job challenges which present opportunities for success. Early job challenge has been found to be related to subsequent high performance (Arnold, 1986). Success, experienced early on in the transition, can allow newcomers to proceed with a sense of self-efficacy and confidence (Bandura, 1982). Another activity which organizations can use to help newcomers adjust is to provide mechanisms for dealing with demands (Matteson & Ivancevich, 1987). Training and counseling services are two such mechanisms which can transmit information to newcomers regarding mastery strategies. Another mechanism which would help newcomers is flexible scheduling, which would allow the newcomer to resolve the work-home conflicts which emerge during adjustment.

The provision of social support to newcomers during this stage is crucial. Newcomers need support in many forms from many sources. The immediate supervisor, peers, other newcomers, and support staff are sources of support important to newcomers (Nelson & Quick, 1988). Such relationships are most effective when established within a framework of trust and mutual reliance (Arnold, 1986). Reichers (1987) argues that the rates of interaction between the newcomer and organizational insiders are major determinants of the speed with which the newcomer adjusts. Katz (1988) contends that the "social" elements of adjustment are the most important; that is, interactions with others are preferable to written media in terms of communicating with newcomers. He states further that those individuals who interact with newcomers should be chosen carefully for their effectiveness.

Mentors perform an essential role in social support. They not only provide support but also serve as role models whose behavior the newcomer imitates (Bandura, 1977). Pascale (1985), in discussing companies famous for shaping behavior through socialization, states that too often organizations leave the emergence of mentors to chance. It may be more productive, then, for organizations to provide mentors which will reinforce the corporate culture and therefore effectively shape the transition.

In the final stage of socialization, change and acquisition, organizations have two potent tools for easing the newcomer's adjustment: rewards and feedback. Pascale (1985) cites the attention given to rewarding individual performance as a key to effective socialization efforts. Particularly important in this regard are that the rewards be conspicuously tied to performance and that the reward system be consistent. The second important tool at this stage is feedback. Colarelli, Dean, and Konstans (1987) found that job performance is not ensured solely through selection; rather, it requires constant monitoring and effective management systems. In the case of newcomer adjustment, one such system is the feedback mechanism. In the helping professions, performance is often communicated de facto by dissatisfied clients or by clients who end their treatment; virtually no positive feedback is given. Performance feedback is very important in these service professions. Consistent feedback on a day-to-day basis demonstrates to the newcomer that the organization is concerned about progress and adjustment. It allows the newcomer to learn more quickly the ropes of the new job. Feedback systems for newcomers should be positive and growth-oriented as opposed to judgmental (Matteson & Ivancevich, 1987).

Adjusting to a new job is a transition experience common to all but it is usually reactively managed rather than proactively managed. Admittedly stressful, it need not be distressful or unsuccessful. Socialization failures leave individuals feeling traumatized and deceived and organizations feeling that their selection process is the culprit. Both the individual and the organization should take an active role in managing the adjustment process so that both parties reap the benefits of successful socialization: long-term, productive employment relationships resulting in organizational and individual well-being.

Implications for Researchers

Researchers can find many avenues for investigation in examining the transition experiences of organizational newcomers. Previous research on the stress of socialization provides suggestions both in terms of process and content of future studies.

First, a longitudinal design is essential if we are to truly understand adjustment to work. The transition from outsider to insider occurs gradually over time. The subtle changes which accompany this transition cannot be ascertained by cross-sectional designs. Second, perhaps it is appropriate that we rethink our conceptualization of the timing of the socialization stages. Most studies assume the traditional nine to twelve month model without empirically determining that the stages have been negotiated, or, that adjustment has in fact occurred. It stands to reason that different individuals adjust at different rates, and that some jobs require longer adjustment periods than others. Studies which empirically examine this timing issue are needed.

Third, researchers should look for differences between those newcomers who adjust well and those newcomers who have problems in adjustment. Specifically, we need to focus on what the successfully adjusted newcomers do to ease their transition, and the organization's role in facilitating their adjustment.

Finally, the theme of social support in newcomer adjustment should be explored. Many unanswered research questions arise from this theme. Do successful newcomers seek out support, or is it readily provided to them by the organization? What sources of support are most useful to newcomers? What types of social support are most helpful?

Joint efforts between the research and practitioner communities can contribute much to our understanding of newcomer socialization and adjustment.

REFERENCES

Arnold, J. (1985). Getting started: How graduates adjust to employment. *Personnel Review*, *15*, 16-20.

Bandura, A. (1982). Self-efficacy mechanism in human agency. *American Psychologist*, *37*, 122-147.

Bandura, A. (1977). *Social learning theory*. Englewood Cliffs, NJ: Prentice-Hall.

Billings, A.G., & Moos, R.H. (1984). Coping stress, and social resources among adults with bipolar depression. *Journal of Personality and Social Psychology, 46*, 877-891.

Breaugh, J.A. (1983). Realistic job previews: A critical appraisal and future research directions. *Academy of Management Review, 8*, 612-619.

Brousseau, K.R. (1983). Toward a dynamic model of job-person relationships: Findings, research questions, and implications for work systems design. *Academy of Management Journal, 8*, 33-45.

Cooper, C.L. & Payne, R.P. (Eds.) (1978). *Stress at work*. New York: Wiley.

Dean, R.A., Ferris, K.R., & Konstans, C. (1985). Reality shock: Reducing the organizational commitment of professionals. *Personnel Administrator*, 139-148.

Feldman, D.C. (1976). A contingency theory of socialization. *Administrative Science Ouarterly, 21*, 433-452.

Feldman, D.C. (1984). The development and enforcement of group norms. *Academy of Management Review, 9*, 47-53.

Festinger, L. (1957). *A theory of cognitive dissonance*. Evanston, IL: Row, Peterson.

Folkman, S. (1984). Personal control and stress and coping processes: A theoretical analysis. *Journal of Personality and Social Psychology, 46*, 839-852.

French, J.R.P., Caplan, R.B., & Harrison, R.V. (1982). *The mechanisms of job stress and strain*. London: John Wiley.

Greenhaus, J.H. (1987). *Career management*. New York: Dryden Press.

Frese, M. (1982). Occupational socialization and psychological development: An under-emphasized research perspective in industrial psychology. *Journal of Occupational Psychology, 55*, 209-224.

Gomersall, E.R., & Myers, M.S. (1966). Breakthrough in on-the-job training. *Harvard Business Review, 44*, 62-72.

Hall, D.T., & Hall, F.S. (1980). Stress and the two career couple. In C.L. Cooper and R. Payne (Eds), *Current concerns in occupational stress*. New York: Wiley.

Hackman, J.R., & Lawler, E.E. (1971). Employee reactions to job characteristics. *Journal of Applied Psychology, 55*, 259-286.

Harrison, R.V., Moss, G.E., Dielman, T.E., Horvath, W.J., and Harlan, W.R. (1987). Person-environment fit, Type A behavior, and work strain: The complexity of the process. In J.C. Quick, R.S. Bhagat, J.E. Dalton, & J.D. Quick (Eds.) *Work stress: Health care systems in the workplace*. New York: Praeger.

Ivancevich, J.M. & Matteson, M.T. (1980). *Stress and work: A managerial perspective*. Glenview, IL: Scott, Foresman and Co.

Jackson, S.E. (1984). Organizational practices for preventing burnout. In A.S. Sethi & R.S. Schuler (Eds), *Handbook of organizational stress coping strategies*. Cambridge, MA: Ballinger.

Jones, G.R. (1983). Psychological orientation and the process of organizational socialization: An interactionist perspective *Academy of Management Review*, *8*, 464-474.

Jones, G.R. (1986). Socialization tactics, self-efficacy, and newcomers' adjustment to organizations. *Academy of Management Journal, 29*, 262-279.

Kahn, R.L:, Wolfe, D.M., Quinn, R.P., Snoek, J.D., & Rosenthal, R.A. (1964). *Organizational stress: Studies in role conflict and ambiguity*. New York: Wiley.

Karasek, R.A., Jr. (1979). Job demands, job decision latitude, and mental strain: Implications for job redesign. *Administrative Science Quarterly, 24*, 285-308.

Katz, R. (1985). Organizational stress and early socialization expenses. In T.A. Beehr & R.S. Bhagat, (Eds), *Human stress and cognition in organizations*. New York: Wiley.

Kramer, M. (1974). *Reality shock: Why nurses leave nursing*. St. Louis, MO: Mosley Press.

Lakein, A. (1973). *How to get control of your time and your life*. New York: Peter H. Wyden.

Lawler, E.E. (1971). *Pay and organizational effectiveness: A psychological view*. New York: McGraw-Hill.

Levinson, H. (1962). *Men, management, and mental health*. Cambridge, MA: Harvard University Press.

Louis, M.R. (1980). Surprise and sense-making: What newcomers experience in entering unfamiliar organizational settings. *Administrative Science Quarterly, 25*, 226-251.

Nelson, D.L. (1985). *Organizational socialization: A demands perspective*. Unpublished Doctoral Dissertation, University of Texas at Arlington.

Nelson, D.L. (1987). Organizational socialization: A stress perspective. *Journal of Occupational Behavior, 8*, 311-324.

Nelson, D.L., & Quick, J.C. (1988). *Men and women of the personnel profession: Some differences and similarities in their experience of work stress*. Paper presented at Academy of Management National Meetings, Anaheim, CA.

Nelson, D.L., & Quick, J.C. (1988). *Newcomer adjustment: Social support and socialization*. Paper presented at Academy of Management Southwest Meetings, San Antonio, Texas.

Nelson, D.L., Quick, J.C., & Eakin, M. (1988). A longitudinal study of newcomer role adjustment in organizations. *Work and Stress*, forthcoming.

Nelson, D.L., & Sutton, C. (1988). *The effects of coping strategy on psychological, physiological, and work performance outcomes*. Working paper, Oklahoma State University.

Nicholson, N. (1984). A theory of work role transitions. *Administrative Science Quarterly, 29*, 172-191.

Quick, J.C., & Quick, J.D. (1984). *Organizational stress and preventive management*. New York: McGraw-Hill.

Pascale, R. (1985). The paradox of "corporate culture": Reconciling ourselves to socialization. *California Management Review, 27*, 27-41.

Premack, S.L., & Wanous, J.P. (1985). A meta-analysis of realistic job preview experiments. *Journal of Applied Psychology, 70,* 706-719.

Reichers, A.E. (1987). An interactionist perspective on newcomer socialization rates. *Academy of Management Review, 12,* 278-287.

Schein, E.H. (1975). *Career dynamics: Matching individual and organizational needs.* Reading MA: Addison-Wesley.

Schein, E.H. (1985). *Organizational culture and leadership.* San Francisco: Jossey Bass.

Schein, E.H. (1968). Organizational socialization and the profession of management. *Industrial Management Review, 9,* 1-16.

Suszko, M.K., & Breaugh, J.A. (1986). The effects of realistic job previews on applicant self-selection and employee turnover, satisfaction, and coping ability. *Journal of Management, 12,* 513-523.

Van Maanen, J., & Schein, E.H. (1979). Toward a theory of organizational socialization. In B.M. Staw (Ed.), *Research in organizational behavior.* Greenwich, CN: JAI Press.

Van Sell, M., Brief, A.P., & Schuler, R.S. (1981). Role conflict and role ambiguity: Integration of the literature and directions for future research. *Human Relations, 34,* 43-71.

Vroom, V. (1964). *Work and motivation.* New York: Wiley.

Wanous, J.P. (1980). *Organizational entry.* Reading, MA: Addison-Wesley.

Transition from School to Work

Therese M. Long

Johnson & Johnson Medical, Inc.

SUMMARY. Many students do not devote enough time to properly map out a career search strategy that is consistent with their values and goals. Consequently, graduation heralds a stressful transition into the work world. Without a good job search strategy, the first job after college or graduate school can be a frustrating experience that can negatively impact motivation and ambition. The first job never should be considered the final career choice. However, it is important that the job choice be a positive experience that will serve as a foundation for continued career success.

This chapter examines the difference between well thought out career choices and a choice that was made by default. As would be expected, the former produced much less stress and turmoil than the latter. Interestingly, the successful transition had more at stake but still was a smoother, more motivating experience that continues to have a positive impact seven years later.

Transitioning from the pursuit of grades to life after graduation often is characterized by the contradictory emotions of eager anticipation and extreme dread. Some move to the real world in a smooth and orderly fashion. Many do not.

The experience I will relate suggests that relatively successful school-to-work transitions are possible if planning and active decision making are strategically employed. I was among the lucky ones who, upon receiving a Master of Business Administration degree (MBA), sought and found a challenging, rewarding job that met my expectations. The company at which I worked offered a competitive salary, an excellent training program and a mentor of

Reprints may be obtained from Therese M. Long, Johnson & Johnson Medical, Inc. (formerly SURGIKOS), P.O. Box 130, Arlington, TX 76004-0130.

the highest level in the company. I was the first participant in an experimental program to fast track MBAs into the managerial ranks. This may sound ideal, and it was. However, this positive experience only came after I had learned first hand what *not* to do when leaving school to pursue meaningful employment.

EARLY TRANSITIONS

Perhaps it was my early upbringing as an Air Force brat, too many moves too soon. Whatever the reason, major life changes or transitions have always been difficult.

One example of a negative transition was related to starting college. While my high school record was sufficient to gain acceptance at many colleges, I exerted little effort to pursue specific institutions that might meet my values, interests and goals. In fact, I made no attempt to examine any internal questions. The safest course in pursuing higher education was to attend a known entity, in this case the same university my sister was attending. Subconsciously, I believed she might protect me from the adversities I anticipated. Side benefits included a savings in time and effort by not having to explore other institutions and avoiding the necessity of making a decision.

I managed to gain acceptance to and stay in college. After acclimating myself, I really did well. I loved school and avidly pursued both academics and extracurricular activities. So immersed was I in the university, however, that by the time graduation drew near, I panicked and accepted the first job offered. Actually, it was the only job offered.

Throughout my senior year, I rather unrealistically had been pursuing a tour director's job at a nationally recognized corporate incentives company. I felt certain I would get the job and did not bother to address myself to others. When the company informed me that I would be a candidate — after I had gotten a few years under my belt — I got the message. Unfortunately, all of my proverbial eggs were in that basket. Consequently, I readily accepted the job at the university public relations department in which I had completed a successful senior year internship.

It was far too easy to take the path of least resistance and continue working for the university. I didn't have to go out of my way in any respect. No letters to send canvassing potential employers. No interviews to arrange. No questions about strengths, weaknesses, goals, or objectives. I didn't even have to purchase a business suit. The result—I worked for approximately six months with abysmal pay, training on the job, no position for which to aspire and no mentor to guide whatever progression I could eke out. It was a very frustrating experience.

In retrospect, such decision-making by default is not so unusual. I see it today when, for example, employees make decisions by not making decisions . . . ultimately something happens and, good or bad, change is affected.

By not thinking through my values and goals, by not examining alternatives, the starting salary that sounded sufficient to my inexperienced, student-oriented ears proved unmanageable. After paying rent, utilities, and other living expenses, there was nothing left. I was unpleasantly stuck on Level One of Maslow's Hierarchy; that is, I was struggling on a regular basis to meet my fundamental physiological needs.

After a few months, I made the decision to quit work, move to another state and start graduate school. A confidant who worked in the field of higher education had suggested that if I was unhappy in academic public relations, there was always graduate school . . . and everybody knew that those with the MBA degrees could secure good jobs with generous salaries. In 1979, MBAs were not quite as prodigious as they are today, so there was some truth to that popularly espoused belief.

Once again, however, I approached change with skepticism. I had enrolled in a state institution much larger than my undergraduate university. Most of my classmates were employed full-time. These part-time students seemed better able to assimilate the information, provide pertinent examples and relate to the material taught. Again, despite a successful undergraduate career, I did not at first speak up in class or otherwise contribute.

Gradually, however, I began to overcome my trepidations and became an active participant. Graduate school became a fascinating experience and I enjoyed learning about business. The program also took me beyond theory. Through many of the courses I took and the professors, students and others to whom I was exposed, my eyes were opened to a multitude of career and corresponding lifestyle possibilities available to those who knew what they wanted.

STRATEGIC CHANGE

For the first time, I began to seriously explore my internal values and motivations. One of the most important alterations I made was to change my passivity in decision-making. I continued to enjoy academic and social pursuits as before, but this time, I kept my ears and eyes open for interesting careers, industries and companies. I formed alliances with students, professors and the business world and helped rekindle a graduate business students' association to enhance networking. Research of different industries relating to class assignments were personally interesting as a means of gaining additional insights. I read business publications, asked questions of my professors and fellow students, and talked to everyone I knew about career options. Based upon the input of those working in or with various industries, I began to visualize myself in a variety of career tracks.

I began to formulate a strategy for my job hunt. The strategy was to explore several issues that related to my values, needs, and ambitions. In particular, there were eight issues or areas of concern on which I focused. I did not order the issues in any particular way or weight any one of them substantially more heavily than any other. These eight issues were:

1. Monetary Compensation
2. Industry Type
3. Company Personality
4. Training Program
5. Mentor Availability
6. Work Environment
7. Future Opportunities
8. Total Career Package

Monetary Compensation

From my experiences as a student and university employee, I gained a real appreciation for money. Any future job to which I aspired had to offer reasonable monetary rewards. During graduate school, I tried to leave nothing to chance. I read all the articles discussing MBA starting salaries. I talked as diplomatically as I could to graduating MBAs who were getting jobs to determine their wages. I read the classifieds and studied the placement office listings in an attempt to better inform myself of what was available and what I, as a fairly marketable commodity, could expect to command.

Industry Type

The economy was fairly healthy in the early 1980s. However, steel, the automotive industry, and some other industries previously suffered downturns and appeared vulnerable to the vagaries of recessions and business cycles. Because it is generally recognized that employees last hired are the first to go, these industries appeared somewhat risky to me. Consequently, I surveyed the marketplace for an industry that was relatively recession proof. I was cognizant of the need for careful industry selection. The banking industry, seemingly healthy at that point, was not particularly appealing in terms of the type of jobs offered. In addition, friends who were accepting management training programs for banks were not making much money. While the oil industry was attractive, offering lucrative salaries and benefits, I recalled the oil embargos of the 1970s with their associated traumas. I examined the retailing industry and, while it was interesting, the salaries for at least several levels did not meet my requirements. Furthermore, I found the working hours were poor. I wanted decent work hours, weekends and major holidays off, and sufficient monetary rewards.

The two industries that were particularly appealing included the healthcare and computer/information systems industries. First, the computer industry seemed to have almost unlimited growth opportunities. Additionally, IBM, Xerox and others offered excellent training programs, competitive salaries and a challenging environment. Therefore, the computer/information systems industry seemed a viable option for me. Second, healthcare companies also had many pluses. The industry afforded an excellent opportunity to assist mankind. Additionally, the industry seemed to be stable through economic downturns. No matter what the GNP, people would get sick, seek treatment and use a pharmaceutical or other type of healthcare product. Of course, this was before the advent of Diagnostic Related Groups (DRGs) a government-mandated program that revolutionized healthcare spending and changed the complexion of this "stable" industry.

The implications of this industry analysis are not that the best careers are in healthcare or computers. Rather, each person must do a similar industry review in relation to their specific wants, needs, and circumstances so as to arrive at a good decision for oneself.

Company Personality

Company personality, or philosophy, and level of formality was another aspect I considered in preparing for the school-to-work transition. In my case, I wanted to work for a company with high ethics. I did not want to feel pressured to overlook incidents or actions. I did not even want to have to feel in the least bit apologetic about a decision made or policy adopted by a company. Not only the fact but also the appearance and perception of high ethical values was important to me.

In addition, I sought a company that employed people I could respect and with whom I would enjoy working. I previously had worked for decent people and appreciated the camaraderie that afforded. Consequently, with every company in which I was interested, I talked to as many of its employees as possible. This was achieved by seeking interviews with people from different departments. In addition, when possible, I spoke with personal friends and acquaintances employed by these companies.

A final aspect of the corporate personality that was important to me concerned the leadership styles of management. In particular, the degree of formality was a consideration. The companies that were extremely rigid and exhibited authoritarian leadership styles did not hold much appeal for me. I preferred a more relaxed, democratic type of organization in which people related to each other more informally and on a first name basis.

Training

Since I had been a student for most of my life and had little actual work experience, I was particularly keen for a company that offered an extensive training program. Quite frankly, I was nervous about the prospect of a "real" job. Many of the people that participated in the same graduate program as I were full-time employees who were pursuing advanced education part-time. They related to on-the-job examples better than I. I was not about to make this major a life change without preparing myself "on the job." A solid training program designed to familiarize new recruits with the job, company, and expectations was the logical choice for me to pursue.

Mentor Program

In graduate school readings, I learned that it was a necessity to have a mentor if one wanted to climb the corporate ladder with any efficiency. Consequently, mentorship availability became one of my standard questions during interviews. I tried to find out if mentoring was a possibility in the companies in which I was interested.

In particular, I was concerned about whether new hires could approach senior managers as possible mentors *or* if senior managers took initiative in guiding new employees. I was most interested in a mentor as a source of information, advice, and counsel during the first couple of years with the company. I saw that mentor as critical to getting off on the right foot.

Work Environment

In summer and part-time jobs through the years, I had worked in fast food establishments, factories, airline terminals, pleasant and down-right unpleasant offices alike. While it matters little to some, I was interested in a nice workplace. I wanted to feel proud of the environment in which I spent the majority of my waking hours.

Future Opportunities

One of the problems with my short-tenured job out of undergraduate school was the lack of advancement opportunities. I was ambitious and did not want to be in a position with little chance of getting ahead. I wanted responsibility, recognition, and a competitive salary. It had not been available at my first post-college job, so in this job search, I insured that the companies I pursued offered at least a reasonable chance of advancement, and I let them know I would relocate to get it.

Total Career Package

Success begets success. While there are never guarantees, I wanted to begin a career in which immediate successes were dependent upon *my* input as well as that of the company. That is, I did not want to start a job in which I was totally dependent on a person or situation. If I made the right choice and all my considerations were met and if the rest were up to me, I knew that personal determination would make the job work. While new employees generally are supervised and evaluated more carefully than senior employees, companies vary with regard to how quickly a person may have real input into their work environment. So, as part of the total package consideration, I was looking for the potential to have relatively early input and influence.

JOB SEARCH STRATEGY

As I had made a personal commitment that the transition from graduate school to the workplace would be different than the previous poorly planned transitions, I mapped out a strategy that included preparation and risk taking. I completed a resume and determined what my answers would be to the standard interview questions. I signed up for as many interviews as possible and thoroughly prepared for each one. It mattered little *initially* what the company did or made. My motivations were to experiment with and perfect my interviewing skills and to research as many companies and employment opportunities as possible.

I interviewed with computer and tire companies. I talked to accounting firms, healthcare companies, telecommunications companies and airlines. I always had a long list of questions to ask the interviewer including information cited in recent articles, news about stock fluctuations, profit margins, and competitors. I tried to make myself stand out by being definitive about my goals and what I could contribute to that organization. Finally, I followed up with letters to the interviewer and, in some cases, to others in the organization.

In short, my strategy was to do everything I had not done before. What I began to experience was unexpected. Instead of dreading the interviews and having a trying time with this more logical and strategic method of job hunting, I actually was having fun. The stress that was present in every other significant life change was for the most part absent. I began to feel comfortable with my decisive self. I enjoyed learning more about different companies and career paths and in determining which would be the best fit according to the criteria I had established.

I was extremely lucky in the early 1980s. Many corporations still were experiencing a big push to hire more females. I was definitely in the right place at the right time with the right attitude and qualifications . . . and took full advantage of it. I finally narrowed down my options to three companies with whom I had offers. I reviewed my criteria and surmised that all would be excellent companies with which to begin my career. All were large corporations in relatively recession-proof industries. All had extensive training programs. All offered competitive salaries, a pleasant work environment and future opportunities. Only mentor availability and an elusive component to the total package offering more than an average chance of success were not included in the two companies I eventually turned down.

The company whose offer I accepted did offer a mentor program that met my exact specifications. I since have learned that the most successful of mentoring relationships are those that are not forced, i.e., the natural "watching out for" or "pulling along" that is less contrived and more sincere. However, I was lucky and, even though my mentor relationship was arranged, it suited me well and helped me progress.

The other quality that made my company stand out from the others was that the position offered was a pilot program. I would be the only participant in this carefully crafted arrangement. While I am a competitive person, this test program seemed ideal in enhancing my chances of success. I knew I would work very hard to be successful and the company would assist me in every way to ensure both I and the program met expectations. I accepted the job and began my career.

REAL BEGINNINGS

Orientation to the company included a week-long series of meetings at which I met and interviewed a variety of people to gain a better perspective of the organization. A move to a different state immediately followed, where I spent the next several months learning about the business, the product and customer from a sales perspective. Stints in the Marketing and Finance Divisions also were part of the agenda with projects in Marketing Research, Product Management, Accounting and Administration. All assignments were designed to provide broad exposure to the business.

A personal commitment to achieving success made me very cognizant of attitude. I actively pursued my interpretation of the proper attitude or demeanor. I had read enough to know that most companies did not appreciate "cocky MBAs who anticipate chairmanship by the time they are 30." Consequently, my modus operandi when starting my new job was to work hard and try to learn as much as possible before attempting to make a mark. As it turned out, I did myself a favor. There were many in the company who did not appreciate this program and possibly felt threatened. Certainly, there were those who thought I had not paid my dues. Consequently, I kept my mouth shut, listened, learned, and gradually began to build my reputation.

There were several individuals who helped ease my transition from school to work. Two of the most valuable included my mentors. While not in contact on a frequent basis, the mentor who oversaw my program made his support known. Additionally, I gained an informal mentor who took me under his wing and helped me learn more about the business, its intricacies and politics. Both provided inspiration and helped me believe in my abilities.

Despite all the positives, I still suffered occasional pangs of the concerns that have dogged every one of my life changes. However, the preparation spent in making this career decision stood me in good stead. When beset by old fears, I mentally reviewed my rationale for selecting this company and regained my confidence. It helped just knowing I had been an active rather than passive decision maker and had completed a major life transition to the very best of my ability. I could not castigate myself for not considering every angle or for taking the easy way out. For once I had done everything in my ability to make a logical, well thought out change.

Upon reflection, my transition from school to work was not so unusual. It simply took me a few years longer than most to realize that successful and less stressful transitions require a lot of preparation—preparation initially to determine direction, preparation to work out the logistics and mechanisms inherent in change making, and the emotional and mental preparation to make the change and live with it. Adequate preparation forming the right kinds of relationship and possessing the right attitude were crucial for me during that transition and remain so today.

CONCLUSION

I have had both positive and disappointing experiences in moving from school to work. The central issue which made the difference in my experiences was the extent to which I accepted responsibility for the process and the decisions made. As an undergraduate, the decisions were made by default and I had a negative and unrewarding experience as a result.

My experience following graduate school was dramatically different because of the initiative I took and the responsibility I accepted. From this, I developed a much greater self-awareness and knew what my needs, values, and desires were before entering the marketplace. In addition and related to this, I gathered a wealth of information concerning eight issues that were of professional interest to me. With this information, I was able to make a better decision, certainly one of better quality than a decision by default. Because I had accepted responsibility for the whole process, I was also more prepared to do the follow-through work needed to make my decision a success once it was made.

One of the trickiest issues for me in accepting responsibility and taking initiative was knowing what the limits were. Each company with which I interviewed was also in control of its actions in the decision process. Finding a negotiated balance in which I had a sense of control without being totally in control was not always easy. However, that balance was found in my relationship with my company and has led to a successful, long-term relationship to date.

III. THE MID-CAREER ISSUES

Work and Non-Work Issues in the Management of Occupational Careers in the 1990s

Rabi S. Bhagat
Memphis State University

David L. Ford, Jr.
University of Texas at Dallas

SUMMARY. Western culture has traditionally separated work and non-work roles with the belief that personal issues are not relevant to the work environment or career. Recent research challenges this belief, identifying important intersections between work and non-work roles. Findings suggest that personal stressors may affect work performance and career progress as well as health and well-being. Three organizational strategies for preventing distress associated with work/non-work interactions are to create options for home-based workers, to train workers in effective coping skills, and to initiate changes in the organizational culture to provide for greater work/non-work role integration.

Reprints may be obtained from Rabi S. Bhagat, Department of Management, Memphis State University, Memphis, TN 38152.

In modern society, work and non-work roles are becoming increasingly interdependent. Given the importance of these two roles, it is not surprising that considerable research attention has been directed to their behavioral and organizational aspects. However, while considerable knowledge exists concerning the effects of variables specific to each of these roles on the psychological well-being of individuals, relatively little research attention has been directed to the nature of the interactions that exist between them. It is only in the past decade that researchers have become interested in the relationship between work and such non-work related issues as family interaction patterns and child rearing.

Perhaps the major reason why the interaction between work and non-work issues has received little attention is that managers of work organizations have generally attempted to separate the two domains. A common belief is that events in the personal lives of employees should not effect their job performance.

Academic researchers have also contributed to the perception of the separate worlds of work and non-work. Organizational psychologists, industrial sociologists, and industrial relations specialists have focused on work and organization-specific effects on employees while family-oriented specialists from fields such as clinical psychology and social work have tended to focus on processes that originate primarily from the domain of family and non-work related sources. Few scholars have concerned themselves with both family and work related variables in terms of their conjoint effects on both work and non-work related outcomes.

Still another reason as to why the separation of work from non-work exists lies in the value systems of employees themselves. Bartoleme and Evans (1979), for example, have found that most male managers uphold the view that professional and private lives ought to be kept both separate and independent. Similar findings are reported by Piotrkowski (1978), Dyer (1964), and Renshaw (1974). Respondents in these studies denied linkages between work and family and preferred to act in one domain as if the influences from the other domain did not matter.

Kanter (1977) has advanced the intriguing notion that the continuation of the perception of the separate worlds of work and non-work fits the interests of modern corporations. However, this view is gradually changing and it is becoming increasingly clear that the work and non-work lives of individuals interact in significant ways. In addition, it is also being recognized that these interactions have important bearings on experiences in each of these domains.

Effects of Work on Family

Work has a significant impact on the family lives of employees. Hoffman (1986) has reviewed the research in this area and provided a comprehensive overview of the effects of work on the family.

1. Work provides financial and material resources that affect the family's economic well-being.
2. The status of being employed or not employed and the occupational prestige associated with one's work affects the family's status in the community, the worker's status in the family, and the worker's own self-concept.
3. Behaviors learned in the work role are likely to be repeated in the home. For example, patterns of authority associated with the work role are likely to affect the pattern of authority in the worker's family.
4. Work has a significant impact on the worker's personality and intellectual functioning. Such effects influence the worker's behavior in the family.
5. There is a spillover of both positive and negative experiences associated with work to the family.
6. An individual's family can often be a complementary source for the satisfaction of various work related needs. Some workers may attempt to satisfy those needs which remain unsatisfied in the context of their work role by making them more salient in the context of their non-work role.
7. Involvement with work and excessive involvement with one's work role can lead to a significant amount of role overload and inter-role conflicts. This issue is particularly salient for working women with strong familial responsibilities such as child care.
8. One's work can be either dangerous in terms of safety or intrinsically unfulfilling and thus can be a source of ongoing stress.

It is clear that an employee's work related experiences can and do significantly affect non-work behaviors in the context of the family. It is important to also examine the other side of the equation, the effects of non-work and family related factors on work, to begin to gain a more complete understanding of the interaction between work and non-work roles.

Effects of Family on Work

The family of the worker can affect his or her work role in a number of different ways.

1. Satisfaction with one's work role is often a function of familial demands and conflicts as well as the adjustment of the family members, particularly one's spouse, to the demands of the work role (Nieva, 1979). In overseas assignments the adjustment of one's spouse to the demands of the foreign setting is especially important in sustaining both satisfaction and performance in one's work role.
2. Satisfaction with the family role can be an important predictor of progress in an occupational career. How one will eventually perform in one's occupational career and the extent to which one's career will be a continued source of satisfaction depends largely on the nature of the social support offered by the one's family.
3. Behaviors learned in the family can also spill over into the domain of work. In the case of educational spillover, something learned at home is used to improve some aspect of functioning in the work or organizational domain. In the case of psychological spillover, involvement with family-related roles affects the employee's moods, feelings, and involvement at work. (Crouter, 1984)

There are other ways in which the family influences the affective reactions and performance of employees in their work roles. Of particular importance are the effects of stressful personal life events on work.

**Stressful Life Events and Experiences
at Work**

All employees experience a variety of events or life changes in the course of daily living. This list includes such diverse events as the death of one's spouse, separation and divorce, additions to the family, and serious illness in the family. These events are stressful because they often require significant social adjustments and adaptations. They can have major effects on an employees work in both a psychological and physical sense.

An especially significant study of the effects of stressful life events on illness was conducted by Holmes and Rahe (1967). They showed that significant life changes are associated with the onset of illness and various symptoms of illness. Life stress precipitated by a combination of several stressful events has been found to be predictive of sudden cardiac death (Rahe & Lind, 1971), myocardial infarction (Edwards, 1971; Theorell & Rahe, 1971), menstrual discomfort and pregnancy and birth-related complications (Siegel, Johnson, & Sarason, 1979), as well as other major health problems such as tuberculosis, multiple sclerosis, diabetes, and a variety of other minor physical conditions (Rabkin & Struening, 1976). Life stress has also been found to be correlated with various indices of psychiatric disorders, anxiety, and depression (Dekker & Webb, 1974; Vinokur & Slezer, 1975).

Given the etiologic significance of life stress, it is important to focus on the significance of stressful life events on work and careers. Systematic information in this area has only recently emerged. Vincino and Bass (1978) found, for example, that life stability, as measured by low life stress scores on an abridged version of Holmes and Rahe's social readjustment scale, significantly correlated with managerial success and the experience of task-challenge in the careers of a sample of Exxon-affiliate managers. Managers, who reported higher life stability also scored higher on assessment batteries forecasting job success. Life stress has also been found to be negatively correlated with indices of academic performance (Harris, 1972) and with measures of teaching effectiveness (Carranza, 1972).

These studies clearly indicate that stressful life events can not only affect the physical and emotional well-being of an individual, but also his or her performance and related indicators of success in the occupational role. Bhagat (1980, 1985) has used the results of these studies to develop a model which links the effects of stressful life events to various organizationally valued outcomes. In his model, he presents a series of linkages between stressful life events and the development of personal life stress. Personal life stress is hypothesized to cause a series of impairments in one's work role via emotional, cognitive, and behavioral effects.

Perhaps the most important linkage in Bhagat's model in regard to occupational careers is between life strains and the involvement that one experiences in the work role. Several moderating variables are introduced which are hypothesized to either strengthen or weaken the effects of such life strains on behavioral outcomes. Figure I provides a simpler version of the model showing that coping and adaptation skills, social support mechanisms, type of organizational control systems and culture, and job/organizational based stresses can moderate the direct effects of life stresses on such valued organizational outcomes as job involvement, performance effectiveness, job satisfaction, absenteeism, and turnover intention.

Empirical research demonstrating the efficacy of these moderating variables is not yet reported in the literature; however, support for the existence of a construct called the "total life stress" (a combination of work and non-work related stresses) is found in the work of Bhagat and his colleagues (Bhagat, McQuaid, Lindholm, & Segovis, 1985). They report significant negative relationships between negative personal life stress (measured in terms of the total number of negative stressful life events in a span of three years) and a series of work outcomes. These outcomes include job satisfaction, organizational commitment, absenteeism, and turnover intention. In addition, they report that when the effect of total life stress is considered, these relationships become even stronger. They conclude that individuals do not separate their personal lives from their job lives and that there is a spillover of non-work related stress to work related outcomes.

Earlier research findings by Sarason and Johnson (1979) provide additional support for the notion that personal life stress has an effect on important work outcomes. However, additional research on the role of moderating influences, as shown in Figure I, would be

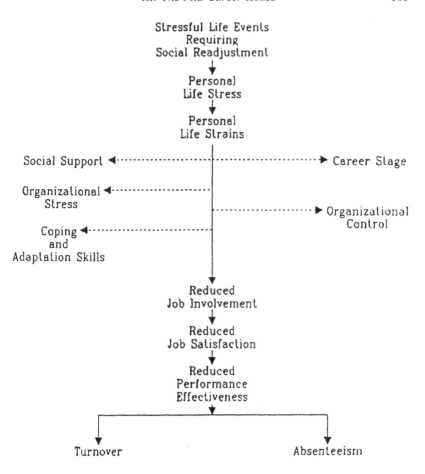

FIGURE I

helpful in the development of theory in this area. Especially in need of understanding are the effects of one's career stage on such linkages.

Work, Non-Work, and Career Decision-Making

It was noted earlier that individuals can cope better with work related demands if they feel that they are well supported by the people around them (Schuler, 1980). The presence of effective social support systems in one's work and non-work lives enhances career-related decision making processes.

Kahn and Antonucci (1980) conceptualize social support to include the following key elements: affect, affirmation, and aid. Affect is the expression of linking, admiration, respect, or love; affirmation is the expression of agreement or acknowledgement of the other person as an individual in terms of his or her rights; and aid is assisting the other person with tangible and intangible assets such as money, time, labor, and information.

Caplan (1976) describes a number of ways in which families function as effective social support mechanisms. His description of the types of resources provided by families lays the groundwork for understanding the relevance of these resources for coping with various difficulties as well as in enhancing career effectiveness.

1. The family can function as a collector and disseminator of valued information which is needed for effective functioning in one's work role.
2. The family can act as a guidance system by providing non-threatening feedback to its members when they experience distress and ambiguities in their organizational and occupational lives.
3. The family can serve as source of ideology by providing values which can greatly aid its members during confusing times in their careers.
4. The family can aid in solving problems by providing much needed resources such as money and other valuable concrete resources. In addition, some of these resources may be given without any strings attached.
5. The family provides the most effective setting for rest, recuperation, and emotional mastery. It can replenish the energies that are lost in the process of coping with ongoing as well as sudden encounters with stressful events in one's work and occupational life.
6. The family can also act as an effective reference and control group. It can assist in disentangling the real significance of some of the episodes and encounters which could otherwise remain imperfectly understood and appraised. In doing so, the

family can also act as a control group in terms of either enhancing or suppressing the significance of the various cues and events that one encounters in one's work and organizational life.

The role of the family and, in particular, the role of one's husband has considerable influence in enhancing the effectiveness of women's careers (Brett, 1980; Farmer & Bohn, 1970; Steers & Rhodes, 1978; Winter, Stewart, & McClelland, 1977). These studies show that in the case of married women, the decision to pursue a career is often a function of the quality of support she receives from her husband. Data reported by Burke and Weir (1975, 1977) suggest that women are generally more effective than their husbands in terms of being able to recognize as well as respond to their spouse's emotional states resulting from pressures at work.

The nurturing tendency of wives could decline with the assumption of work roles outside the family. Heckman, Bryson, and Bryson (1977), in a content analysis of the problems of professional couples, found, for example, that the added pressure of supporting a husband's career in addition to their own often contributed to the experience of stress in working wives. Women are socialized to be the main providers of emotional and social support in their family roles. When women are put in the position of having to devote energies to the two roles of family and work, severe role conflicts result which affect the well-being of the family (Hoffman, 1986).

What is important to note is the relative absorption of an individual with an occupation, i.e., the extent to which an occupation extends its influence over the activities that are performed in the family domain (Kanter, 1977), as increasing absorption in the work role inevitably leads to family stress. Gender differences do not seem to make much difference in how the relative absorption in one's occupation might affect the well-being of the family. Negative spillover in the family would be most common for individuals who, by virtue of their occupational demands, remain highly preoccupied with thoughts and feelings related to their work.

A new line of work on daily transition styles by Hall and Richter (1988) indicates that home boundaries are in general more permeable than work boundaries for both men and women whose work demands excessive involvement with the occupational role. However, the difference lies in the fact that while for women home boundaries are cognitively permeable (i.e., they think of work more often in their homes than do men), for men such boundaries are more behaviorally permeable (i.e., they do more actual job-related work in their homes than do women).

It seems clear that transitions between work and non-work affect women more than men since the demands for adequate role performance are almost equally salient in both of these roles. It appears that while men have sequential work and non-work roles, i.e., they assume the non-work role after the work role is no longer salient, women have simultaneous roles, i.e., they often are required to pursue excellence in two roles simultaneously. This, of course, can create considerable stress for women in managing their occupational careers.

Strategies for Prevention

Training home-based workers. Although modern technology has made it possible for many people to do their work at home, a majority of home-based workers might not be especially suited to the level of skill or training that is necessary to be effective performers in their homes. For this group of workers, it is particularly important to match skills and tasks carefully since any performance deficiencies are difficult to remedy quickly because of a lack of immediate supervisory attention. Simplification of work assignments to reduce task difficulty and quality control could aid in this regard.

Professional workers whose training and past experience make them well suited for completing complex work assignments in their non-work role need a different form of training. These workers need to manage their daily styles of transitions between work and non-work more smoothly. Many professional workers who are quite competent in their work roles, however, have considerable difficulty in managing this daily transition between work and non-work effectively. Training programs are needed to prevent the excessive demands of work from affecting the well-being of the family of the home-based workers.

Professionals should be given training in the appropriate management of their role-related demands. It is important to involve the supervisor of the home-based professional workers in such training so that he or she can aid in effective planning and monitoring of work which is being done in the worker's home. Obviously, the social support systems of the work organization is drawn in to great extent in making the outcomes of this training more effective.

Helping individuals develop effective coping styles throughout the occupational career. Hall and Ritcher (1988) emphasize the need for helping individuals develop effective coping styles throughout their career. Individuals should be given appropriate training in recognizing the danger signals of excessive role encroachment. As has been shown earlier, excessive demands can have severe short and long term effects on a career and on a family.

Using the resources of employee assistance programs, individuals should be trained to manage the adverse effects of stress from either of the domains on the other domain. Emphasis should be placed on developing effective social support systems at home and at work. Encouragement should be given in terms of planning personal time for individuals who report high levels of absorption in their work roles.

Designing appropriate organizational cultures. Work organizations in the western world do not easily recognize the separation of work and non-work roles. The belief in work being the most important element in one's life is of paramount importance and non-work roles are often relegated to secondary importance. However, as we begin to better understand the nature of the organizational cultures of other nations, it becomes reasonably clear that such an orientation might not be effective in enhancing organizational effectiveness in the long term. Non-work roles have their own distinctive influences in enhancing the quality of life at work and inadequate attention to these roles in designing an organization's culture can decrease productivity and employee satisfaction.

Western organizations need to actively encourage activities which can help in improving the nourishing aspects of various non-work roles. Recognizing the value of the transition from work to non-work, making flexible working hours more effectively integrated with human resource planning systems, providing adequate child care facilities in the work premises, and scheduling work in accordance with the natural work habits of employees are important steps in this direction.

CONCLUSION

The most effective way to understand the effects of work and non-work on careers is to focus on the continuous interpenetrations of these two domains. Work does not exist apart from non-work. Excessive demands, whether created due to unavoidable stressful life events or by the ongoing demands of one role on another, can make these daily interpenetrations or transitions difficult. While some preventive measures can be taken by the employees them-selves, this article has highlighted some of the steps that work orga-nizations should take in order to make role demands in both do-mains manageable. Strategies aimed at removing some of the adverse effects of organizational culture on work-non-work transi-tion should be a high priority in the management of occupational careers.

REFERENCES

Bartoleme F., & Evans, P. L. (1979). Professional lives versus private lives—shifting patterns of managerial commitment. *Organizational Dynamics, 3,* 3-29.

Bhagat, R. S. (1980). *Effects of stressful life events upon individual performance effectiveness and work adjustment process within organizational settings: A research model.* James McKeen Cattell Invited Address presented at the Amer-ican Psychological Association Meeting, Montreal, August.

Bhagat, R. S. (1985). The role of stressful life events in organizational behavior and human performance. In T. A. Beehr & R. S. Bhagat (Eds.), *Human stress and cognition in organizations.* New York: John Wiley.

Bhagat, R. S., McQuaid, S. J., Lindholm, S., & Segovis, J. (1985). Total life stress: A multimethod validation of the construct and its effect on organization-ally valued outcomes and withdrawal behaviors. *Journal of Applied Psychol-ogy, 70,* 202-214.

Brett, J. M. (1980). The effect of job transfer on employees and their families. In C. L. Cooper & R. Payne (Eds.), *Current concern in occupational stress.* New York: John Wiley.

Burke, R. J., & Weir, T. (1975). Receiving and giving help with work and non-work-related problems. *Journal of Business Administration, 6,* 59-78.

Burke, R. J., & Weir, T. (1977). Working men as fathers of adolescents. *School Guidance Worker*, *33*, 4-9.

Caplan, G. (1976). The family as a support system. In G. Caplan & M. Killilia (Eds.), *Support systems and mutual help*. New York: Grune and Stratton.

Carranza, E. (1972). *A study of the impact of life changes on high school teacher performance in Lansing School District as measured by the Holmes and Rahe Schedule of Recent Experiences*. Unpublished doctoral dissertation, Michigan State University.

Crouter, A. C. (1984). Spillover from family to work: The neglected side of the work-family interface. *Human Relations*, *37*, 425-442.

Dekker, D. J., & Webb, J. T. (1974). Relationships of the social readjustment rating scale to psychiatric patient status, anxiety, and social desirability. *Journal of Psychosomatic Research*, *18*, 125-130.

Dyer, W. G. (1964). Family reactions to the father's job. In A. Shostak & W. Gomberg (Eds.), *Blue-collar world: Studies of the American worker*. Englewood Cliffs, New Jersey: Prentice-Hall.

Edwards, M. K. (1971). *Life crises and myocardial infarction*. Unpublished master's thesis, University of Washington.

Farmer, H. S., & Bohn, M. J. (1970). Home-career conflict reduction and the level of career interest for women. *Journal of Counseling Psychology*, *17*, 228-232.

Hall, D. T., & Ritcher, J. (1988). Balancing work life and home life: What can organizations do to help. *Academy of Management Executive*, *II*(3), 213-224.

Harris, P. W. (1972). *The relationship of life change to academic performance among selected college freshmen to varying levels of college readiness*. Unpublished Ph.d. dissertation, East Texas State University.

Heckman, N. A., Bryson, R., & Bryson, J. B. (1977). Problems of professional couples: A content analysis. *Journal of Marriage and the Family*, *39*, 323-330.

Hoffman, L. W. (1986). Work, family and the child. In M. S. Pallak & R. O. Perloff (Eds.), *Psychology and work: Productivity, change, and employment*. Washington, DC: American Psychological Association.

Holmes, T. H., & Rahe, R. H. (1967). The social readjustment rating scale. *Journal of Psychosomatic Research*, *11*, 213-218.

Kahn, R. L., & Antonucci, T. (1980). Convoys over the life course: Attachment roles and social support. In P. B. Baltes & O. Brim (Eds.), *Life-span development and behavior* (Vol. 3). Boston, MA: Lexington Press.

Kanter, R. M. (1977). *Work and family in the United States: A critical review and agenda for research and policy*. New York: Russell Sage.

Nieva, V. F. (1979). *The family's impact on job-related attitudes of men and women: Report of work in progress*. Presented at the American Psychological Association Annual Meeting, New York, August.

Piotrkowski, C. S. (1978). *Work and the Family System*. New York: Free Press.

Rabkin, J. G., & Struening, E. L. (1976). Life events, stress, and illness. *Science*, *194*, 1013-1020.

Rahe, R. H., & Lind, E. (1971). Psychological factors and sudden cardiac death: A pilot study. *Journal of Psychosomatic Research, 15*, 19-24.

Renshaw, J. R. (1974). *Explorations and the boundaries of work and family life.* Unpublished doctoral dissertation, University of California at Los Angeles.

Rousseau, D. M. (1988). Human resource planning for the future. In J. Hage (Ed.), *Futures of organizations.* Lexington, MA: Heath.

Sarason, I., & Johnson, J. (1979). Life stress, organizational stress and job satisfaction. *Psychological Reports, 44*, 75-79.

Schuler, R. (1980). Definition and conceptualization of stress in organizations. *Organizational Behavior and Human Performance, 25*, 184-215.

Siegel, J., Johnson, J. H., & Sarason, I.G. (1979). Life changes and menstrual discomfort. *Journal of Human Stress, 5*(1), 41-46.

Steers, R. M., & Rhodes, S. R. (1978). Major influences on employee attendance: A process model. *Journal of Applied Psychology, 63*(4), 391-407.

Theorell, T., & Rahe, R. H. (1971). Psychosocial factors and myocardial infraction: An inpatient study in Sweden. *Journal of Psychosomatic Research, 15*, 25-31.

Vicino, F. L., & Bass, B. M. (1978). Life space variables and managerial success: Their relationship to stress and mental distress. *Journal of Applied Psychology, 63*(1), 81-88.

Vinokur, A., & Slezer, M. L. (1975). Desirable versus undesirable life events: Their relationship to stress and mental distress. *Journal of Personality and Social Psychology, 32*, 329-337.

Winter, D. G., Stewart, A.J., & McClelland, D. C. (1977). Husband's motives and wife's career level. *Journal of Personality and Social Psychology, 35*, 159-166.

Intracompany Job Transfers:
An Exploratory Two-Sample Study
of the Buffering Effects
# of Interpersonal Support

Torsten J. Gerpott

Booz, Allen and Hamilton, Inc.

SUMMARY. This study explored the interaction effects of stressful intraorganizational transfer and collaborative interpersonal support (CIS) on work-related outcomes in an R&D environment. Questionnaire data were gathered from 161 British/American and 266 West German scientific and engineering professionals employed in R&D units of large industrial companies. In the British/American sample, moderated regression analyses revealed significantly stronger effects of CIS on job involvement, intention to leave, and career satisfaction for transferees than for a comparison group. The buffering effects of CIS were stronger for lateral than for promoted transferees. Because similar results were not found in the West German sample, the results suggest that British/American R&D professionals benefit more from CIS in times of career stress. Findings are discussed in terms of future cross-cultural stress research needs and preventive interventions for engendering CIS among technical professionals.

Several recent reviews reveal an increasing interest among organizational researchers in employee job transfers in general and intracompany career transitions in particular (Brett, 1984; Fisher,

The author would like to thank Michel Domsch, Robert T. Keller, and Alan W. Pearson for their support in the data collection for this research. Thanks also go to the R&D Management journal and the British council for providing funds for parts of the research that resulted in this paper. This research was completed while the author was at The Institute of Personnel Management, University of German Federal Armed Forces, West Germany.

Reprints may be obtained from Torsten J. Gerpott, Booz, Allen and Hamilton, Inc., 98A Königsallee, D-4000 Düsseldorf 1, West Germany.

113

Wilkins, & Eulberg, 1982; Greenhaus 1987; London & Mone, 1987; Nicolson, in press; Pinder & Walter, 1984). While the theoretical views which have been developed to portray resocialization processes associated with job transfers differ in detail, the literature generally hypothesizes that collaborative interpersonal support (CIS) is of crucial importance in making a successful job transfer.

A closer look at the stress literature and social support reveals that the mechanisms through which support functions are more complex than commonly thought. Specifically, this literature suggests that support may not only have a direct (main) effect on individual work-related responses to organizational stressors, but that interpersonal support interacts with other career/work stressors in affecting work-related outcome variables (Cobb, 1976; Gerpott, 1988; House, 1981; Moss, 1981; Quick & Quick, 1984). As suggested by House (1981, p. 35), Rook and Dooley (1985, p. 14), and Russell, Altmaier, and Van Velzen (1987, pp. 272-273), an important implication is that scarce supportive resources should be targeted to those employees experiencing stressful job situations.

A particular limitation of existing work is that nearly all investigations were conducted with American or British samples, leaving open the question of whether support plays a similar role in stressful career transitions in non-Anglosaxon cultures. For example, Pines (1983) and Etzion (1984) have speculated that the extent to which interpersonal support acts as a buffer against the adverse effects of stressors may be culturally different. Obviously, as more and more companies become global in their operations, stress research with a comparative focus across cultural or national boundaries becomes increasingly urgent. The purpose of the present chapter is to conduct a crosscultural study (i.e., British/American versus West German) to explore the interactions between interpersonal support and stressful work-related outcomes for those engaged in intracompany transfers.

LITERATURE REVIEW

For the purpose of the present analysis, a job transfer is defined as the relatively permanent reassignment of an employee to another job within the same organization, regardless of whether the move was lateral (no increase in organizational rank) or promotional. Note that this definition implies that a transfer does not necessarily entail geographic relocation.

Job transfer has been classified as a stressful work event or organizational stressor because it disrupts ongoing work routines, creates uncertainties, puts new demands upon the transferee, and forces social readjustments (Bateman, Karwan, & Kazee, 1983; Latack, 1984; Pinder & Schroeder, 1987; Sykes & Eden, 1985). For example, Greenhaus (1987, p. 197) has argued that "a recently transferred . . . employee has many adjustments to make: a new job, a new boss, a new group of colleagues, a new office, maybe even new work norms and expectations." In fact, prior studies of the impacts of various critical life events on personal well-being (e.g., Dohrenwend, Krasnoff, Askenasy, & Dohrenwend, 1978; Holmes & Rahe, 1967) have found that people generally perceive a job transfer and the events often accompanying a transfer (e.g., change in financial state) as requiring a substantial amount of readjustment which may tax or exceed an individual's adaptive capacities.

If job transfer is an episodic (or acute) stressor, then the identification of preventive management strategies minimizing the destructive outcomes of individual stress responses (i.e., *distress*) and constructively channeling unavoidable demands associated with a job transfer to benefit both the individual and the organization (i.e., *eustress*) are of crucial importance (Quick & Quick, 1984). Most of the literature in the field of personnel management has focused on financial assistance and formal orientation activities as means to ease an employee's geographic relocation from one of an organization's operating sites to another (e.g., Cooper & Makin, 1985; Gelb & Hyman, 1987). However, theoretical and empirical work by Katz (1980) and Louis, Posner, and Powell (1983) clearly suggests that informal supportive daily interactions of transferees with co-workers and supervisors should be of greater importance in assimilating the transferred employee into the new job than formal on-site and off-site orientation sessions. Collaborative interpersonal support enables the transferee to reduce feelings of anxiety, loneliness, and helplessness. In addition, Bhagat (1983) and Greenhaus (1987) predict that social support will moderate the relationship between stressful life events or career transitions such as intracompany job transfers and various outcomes (e.g., job satisfaction, withdrawal from work).

The question of whether collaborative interpersonal support is directly related to outcome variables or has an interaction effect with job stressors, or both, is of special relevance in work environments which require close interpersonal collaboration as a necessary prerequisite for successful task completion. One such work context with high levels of reciprocal task interdependence among individuals collaborating on a certain task or project is industrial research & development (R&D) (Bodensteiner, Gerloff, & Quick, 1989; Keller, 1986). Various studies conducted in industrial R&D settings have related measures of supportive interpersonal relationships among R&D professionals to such outcome variables as job satisfaction, group performance, and self-actualization (Aram, Morgan, & Esbeck, 1971; Dailey, 1978; Kegan & Rubenstein, 1973). In general, these studies have found significant positive relationships between attitudinal or performance outcome variables and measures of collaborative interpersonal support. However, neither job transfer studies nor the group cohesiveness literature have empirically assessed the effects of collaborative interpersonal support on R&D professionals exposed to intracompany job transfers.

The literature contains a large variety of definitions of social support in general and of support types, forms, or functions in particular (for reviews see Cohen & Wills, 1985, pp. 313-315; House, 1981, pp. 13-30; Turner, 1983, pp. 107-117). It characterizes relationships between individuals in terms of frequent interactions, by strong and positive feelings, and by an ability and willingness to give and take emotional and/or practical assistance in times of need (Moss, 1981, p. 200). Sources of support may be found at work (coworkers, supervisor) or off the job (spouse, friends, counselors, etc.). From an organizational-level preventive stress management perspective, work-related support provided by coworkers is of particular interest in such work contexts as industrial R&D because high levels of interpersonal collaboration are regularly required to ensure effective mission accomplishment (cf. Bodensteiner, Gerloff, & Quick, 1989). Since the focus of the remaining portion of this article is upon colleague support for R&D professionals, the terms social support and collaborative interpersonal support (CIS) are treated as interchangeable.

It is now possible to turn to the buffering effects of CIS in the case of stressful job events. The essential idea of the buffering hypothesis is that support is significantly more important in avoiding negative outcomes (e.g., withdrawal from work) or promoting positive consequences (e.g., work satisfaction) for people experiencing high levels of episodic or chronic demands (Cobb, 1976; House, 1981; Turner, 1983). Put succinctly, the concept of buffering implies ". . . that support will have its strongest beneficial effect . . . among people under stress and may have little or no beneficial effect for people not under stress" (House, 1981, p. 32).

RESEARCH HYPOTHESES

The primary purpose of the present study is to extend previous research by investigating whether the experience of an intracompany job transfer not entailing geographic relocation interacts with perceived CIS among R&D professionals in affecting work-related outcome variables previously found to be consequences of stress. Based on the preceding literature review the following hypothesis is proposed:

H_1: Collaborative interpersonal support will be more significantly related to job involvement, career satisfaction, and work satisfaction for R&D professionals who were recently transferred within their company than for a comparison group of individuals who were not transferred.

Parenthetically, it should be noted that although the focus of this study is on transfers not requiring geographic relocation, it appears reasonable to expect that the arguments discussed earlier may also pertain to geographic relocations (cf. Pinder & Walter, 1984, p. 188).

There is further evidence suggesting that lateral and promotional transfers differ in their negative and positive qualities and that these two types of job transfer should be distinguished when examining the dynamics of transfer processes and social support (Brett, 1984;

Pinder & Schroeder, 1987; Werbel, 1983). A review of the theoretical frameworks of Payne (1980), Brief, Schuler, and Van Sell (1981), and Schuler (1984) indicates that both types of transfer can be characterized in terms of their opportunities (potential for need fulfillment), constraints (potential for preventing need fulfillment), and demands (potential for losing need fulfillment) in order to highlight the differing qualities of lateral and promotional transfers. Their theoretical and empirical work suggests a second hypothesis:

H_2: Interaction effects between job transfer and collaborative interpersonal support will be found significantly more frequently among laterally transferred individuals than among promoted individuals.

A third focus of this study was to assess whether the hypotheses would be found not only among British/American professionals but also among West German professionals. Some studies have suggested differences among these different cultural groups may exist. Specifically, Hofstede (1980, p. 165) found that the German culture favors avoidance of uncertainty more than the British/American culture. A consequence of this difference is that work roles tend to be more formalized and less ambiguous in West German work organizations than in their British or American counterparts. Thus, it may be concluded that West German employees could have a relatively lower need for CIS. Further, according to Hofstede (1980, p. 176), West German employees appear to have a stronger preference for clear hierarchical structures and lines of authority. This suggests that West Germans may be less inclined to accept support from colleagues as a legitimate means for dealing with the adaptational demands of a job transfer. The resulting third theme of this study was formulated as a general research question:

Q: Is greater support for the above research hypotheses found in the British/American experience than in the West German experience?

METHOD

Respondents and Procedure

Respondents were drawn from R&D units of 16 large industrial firms representing a wide range of different industries and applied R&D activities. Eleven were located in West Germany, three in the United Kingdom, and two in the United States.

A total of 2,164 questionnaires were distributed via company mail to the graduate technical staff of the R&D units of the sampled firms. Usable questionnaires were returned by 729 West German, 134 British, and 124 American respondents for response rates of 42, 67, and 55 percent, respectively. All responses were anonymous. Out of the 987 respondents, the responding 427 R&D professionals comprised the respondents for this study. As no significant differences were found between British and American respondents, their responses were combined to form an overall British/American sample (N = 161).

British/American respondents had an average age of 38 years, their mean company tenure was 11 years, and 96 percent held at least a bachelor's degree. West German respondents (N = 266) reported similar demographic characteristics: their average age was 41 years, mean tenure in the employing company was 11 years, and 97 percent held at least a qualification roughly equivalent to a bachelor's degree (i.e., a *Fachhochschule* diploma).

Variables

All variables were included in a 20-page questionnaire developed in German, put into English, and then back-translated into German following typical translation procedures used in cross-cultural research. To minimize possible response bias, variable items were (1) placed in separate parts of the questionnaire, and (2) interspersed with items designed to tap other constructs which were not of interest in this investigation.

Job transfer. Self-reported data about each respondent's career history in his or her present company and each individual's job tenure were used to assign respondents to a "transferred" experimental group or a "no transfer" comparison group. The experimental group was defined as those R&D professionals who had been transferred within the past eighteen months and the comparison group was defined as those who had been transferred between eighteen months and five years ago. Eighteen months was used to define the groups as the literature suggests that after eighteen months, the adjustment process to a transfer will be largely finished while those who have been in the same job for over five years are likely to have plateaued. First-job holders were excluded because of the complicating stress of socialization, which is treated elsewhere in this volume by Nelson (also see Nelson, 1987).

Using the above criteria, 76 British/American and 94 West German professionals were included in the job transfer group. Eighty-five British/American and 172 West German respondents who had a job tenure of at least 18 months made up the comparison group. Based on the self-reported hierarchical direction of their last job change, the job transfer group was further split into those respondents who were promoted (British/American = 34; Germans = 46) and those with lateral transfers (British/American = 31; Germans = 36).

A validity check of the self-reported transfer data was conducted by comparing the numbers of subordinates for the two transfer group categories. In each sample, respondents in the promotional transfer group had a significantly higher mean number of subordinates (British/American: $p < .001$; Germans: $p < .020$) than respondents in the lateral transfer group, thus supporting the self-report results.

Collaborative interpersonal support (CIS). To operationalize the concept of CIS, a five-item index was constructed based on instruments successfully used by Aram, Morgan, and Esbeck (1971) and Dailey (1978). As shown in Table 1, the items deal with noncompetitive, supportive problem solving among collaborating R&D professionals and with trust and openness in their interactions. The items tap both instrumental and emotional facets of support from colleagues.

In line with a recent R&D study of Bodensteiner, Gerloff, and Quick (1989) and the conceptual work of House (1981), a multidimensional measure was not attempted. The results of the confirmatory factor analysis in Table 1 lend support to the use of a one dimensional scale. And, to compare the similarity of this factor across the two samples, a factor congruence coefficient was computed according to Harman (1976, p. 344). A coefficient of .96 indicated that the CIS dimension had similar meaning and construct validity for British/American and West German respondents; therefore, a score for CIS was computed for each individual in both samples by averaging his or her unit weighted responses to all five items. In each sample, scale reliabilities were satisfactory (cf. Table 1).

Work-related outcomes. Four measures of adjustment to work were chosen for this study based on their previously demonstrated or hypothesized relationship to objective job stressors, perceived stress, and social support (cf. Bhagat, 1983; Burke, 1974; Greenhaus, 1987, p. 192). These are:

1. Job involvement (the degree to which an employee is identi- fied psychologically with his or her job) was measured by the average of two items derived from Lodahl and Kejner (1965). (Alphas coefficients were .74 and .68 for British/American and West German respondents, respectively.)
2. Intention to leave (an affective measure of employee with- drawal) was measured by a 6-point Likert-type scale asking respondents to indicate the likelihood that they would volun- tarily leave their present company to move to another firm during the next 3 to 5 years (0 = "not likely at all" to 5 = "very likely"). The efficacy of a 1-item measure of turnover intentions is supported by the findings of Ferris and Rowland. (1987)
3. Overall career satisfaction was assessed by a single item re- quiring respondents to indicate on a 7-point faces scale their feelings toward their personal career development in their present company.
4. Overall work satisfaction was measured by a global facet-free item using the same 7-point Kunin faces scale. For both satis- faction scales and the involvement measure, higher scores in- dicate more satisfaction and involvement, respectively.

TABLE 1. Factor Loadings of Items Comprising the Collaborative Interpersonal Support Scale for Anglosaxon (N = 155) and West German (N = 265) Respondents[a]

Items[b]	Factor Loadings[c]	Communalities
1. R&D professionals are generally willing to give other colleagues the support they need to do a good job.	.634 (.654)	.401 (.428)
2. In carrying out every day operations R&D professionals try to keep their thoughts and reactions to themselves and do NOT really reveal as to what they think and feel.	−.429 (−.617)	.184 (.381)
3. In R&D group meetings group members tend to build on each other's ideas and do NOT compete for acceptance on personal ideas.	.648 (.428)	.419 (.183)
4. In carrying out assignments R&D professionals tend to act as consultant to each other and do NOT let each man look out for himself.	.738 (.663)	.545 (.440)
5. R&D professionals working in groups for solutions to task-related problems seem to be more concerned with the question of whose solution is accepted and NOT so much with efforts to find the best solution.	−.686 (−.415)	.470 (.172)
Eigenvalue	2.585 (2.247)	
Percent of total variable variance	51.7 (44.9)	

a. Loadings and communalities for West German respondents are shown in parentheses.

b. For each item, subjects rated on a 5-point scale (ranging from 1 = disagree strongly to 5 = agree strongly) how much they agreed or disagreed that a statement accurately portrayed their present conditions of collaboration at work. The scoring on items 2 and 5 was reversed in the support scale.

c. Principal-/common-factor model. The PA2 option of the SPSS subroutine FACTOR was used as method of estimating initial communalities (Nie et al. 1975: 473-480).

RESULTS

For each sample, Table 2 contains summary statistics, reliabilities, and a zero-order correlation matrix for all variables of concern. The data show that for British/Americans, CIS is significantly related to three of the four work-related outcomes while for the West Germans, CIS is significantly related to all four outcomes. While job transfer was not significantly correlated with any of the work-related outcomes in the British/American sample, it was significantly related to the four work-related outcomes in the West German sample.

Preliminary to addressing the research hypotheses, an attempt was made to explore the study's internal validity by comparing the transfer and no-transfer groups with regard to potentially contaminating background variables in order to preclude that a moderating influence of the job transfer variable could be solely attributed to selection effects. In the British/American and West German samples, respectively, no significant ($p < .10$) differences between both groups were found in terms of education, number of subordinates, and number of employers prior to entry in the present company. In contrast, the no-transfer group differed significantly ($p < .05$) from the transfer group in terms of age (British/American sample: 40.9 vs. 35.8; German sample: 41.3 vs. 39.5) and company tenure (British/American sample: 12.6 vs. 9.9 years; German sample: 12.1 vs. 9.3 years). Because long-term, older employees are expected to benefit more from CIS (Doering, Rhodes, & Schuster, 1983) and the comparison group in this study is characterized more that way than the experimental group, tests of the interaction effect hypothesis in this study may be considered conservative.

Consistent with the buffering notion, both hypotheses in this study assert that there is a significant interaction between CIS and the experience of a recent intracompany job transfer such that the effects of CIS on outcomes will be more pronounced for individuals in the job transfer group as compared to individuals in the no-transfer reference group. Moderated multiple regression analysis is the appropriate analytical method for examining the hypothesized interactions (Cohen & Cohen, 1983, pp. 311-317; House, 1981, pp. 131-135). Accordingly, for each of the three pairs of career groups

TABLE 2. Summary Statistics on and Intercorrelations Among Study Variables for Anglosaxon and West German Respondents[a]

Variables	Means	s.d.	N	Intercorrelations[b]				
				1	2	3	4	5
1. Job involvement	3.74 (3.37)	.91 (.86)	160 (262)	74 (58)				
2. Intention to leave	1.46 (1.37)	1.46 (1.10)	160 (263)	- 03 (- 08)	—			
3. Overall career satisfaction	4.63 (4.20)	1.53 (1.51)	159 (265)	05 (13**)	- 30*** (- 26***)	—		
4. Overall work satisfaction	5.17 (4.83)	1.41 (1.29)	161 (266)	16+ (14*)	- 26*** (- 24***)	61*** (60***)	—	
5. Collaborative interpersonal support	3.43 (3.40)	.64 (.61)	155 (265)	- 02 (13*)	- 12+ (- 14**)	28*** (30***)	42*** (24***)	76 (74)
6. Intracompany job transfer[c]	.47 (.35)	.50 (.48)	161 (266)	- 06 (09+)	04 (- 08+)	02 (12*)	- 08 (12*)	- 02 (06)

a. Statistics and correlations for West German respondents are shown in parentheses.
b. Decimal points are omitted from correlation and reliability coefficients. Due to missing data, correlations are based on varying N's ranging from 153 to 161 and from 259 to 265 for Anglosaxon and West German respondents, respectively. For multi-item-scales, reliabilities (Cronbach's α) are on the diagonal.
c. Dummy coded with 0 = no job transfer, 1 = job transfer. + p< .10 * p< .05 **p< .01 ***p< .001 (one-tailed t-test)

addressed in the hypotheses, each outcome variable was regressed on CIS and a 0,1 dummy variable reflecting the job transfer group and the no transfer group included in a comparison (main effects model). Then a (support × transfer) group interaction term was added (full model). If the *b*-weight associated with a product term was statistically significant, an interaction of the predictor variables in affecting an outcome criterion could be identified. Since both hypotheses were directional, one-tailed tests were performed to investigate the significance of the partial interaction coefficients. Following arguments of Cramer and Appelbaum (1980) and Cohen and Wills (1985), main effects tests were computed only when no significant ($p > .10$) interaction was found. In this case the interaction term was deleted from the regression equation. From the viewpoint of substantive theory, a significant product term between CIS and the stressful event job transfer can be interpreted as having provided preliminary evidence for the buffering hypothesis that CIS is more beneficial for employees under career stress than for other employees.

Hypothesis 1 predicts significant interactions in a comparison of the overall job transfer group and the no-transfer group. For both the British/American and the West German sample, Table 3 reports the results of a series of moderated regression analyses relevant to this hypothesis.

Focusing on the first regression reported for each outcome variable, it can be seen that significant CIS × transfer interaction effects were obtained for job involvement, intention to leave, and overall career satisfaction in the British/American sample but not for West German respondents. In the case of overall work satisfaction the interaction term was not significant in either of the two samples.

CIS had significant positive effects on work satisfaction in both samples. However, for British/American respondents it was significantly ($p < .023$) more positively related to work satisfaction than for West German respondents.

To make sure that the interactions detected in the Anglosaxon sample were consistent with the buffering pattern predicted by the first hypothesis, regression equations were computed from the raw regression coefficients found to be statistically significant. These equations are presented and graphed in Figure 1. While the values reflect the specific measurement systems employed, the comparative slope differences (reflecting the hypothesized buffering effect) are meaningful. In the British/American sample, the three regression lines based on full model equations were consistent with the buffering hypothesis. For example, Figure 1 shows that, as predicted, high levels of CIS lead to low intention to leave in the transfer group but not in the no-transfer comparison group. Thus, results support the first hypothesis with regard to three out of four outcome variables in the British/American sample. For West German respondents, however, results offered no support for the first hypothesis.

To address Hypothesis 2, two additional sets of moderated regressions were run for the four work-related outcomes in each of the two samples. However, the no-transfer group was now compared to the lateral transfer group and the promotional transfer group, respectively. Table 3 shows that the hypothesized significant interaction between CIS and the dichotomously coded dummy variables for career status is found for all outcome criteria in the British/American but not in the West German sample when the lateral transfer group was compared to the no-transfer group. Further, for British/American respondents, the four full model regression equations are all consistent with the buffering hypothesis. To wit, CIS had significantly more beneficial effects for laterally transferred British/American R&D professionals than for their colleagues in the no-transfer comparison group. In contrast, only the two regressions for job involvement and career satisfaction reveal marginally significant buffering effects in the predicted direction when the British/American promotional transfer group is compared to the British/American no-transfer group. Again, in the West German sample, the (CIS × promotional job transfer) interaction term does not even approach statistical significance. Thus, in light of the overall results pattern it may be said that the second hypothesis is generally supported for British/American respondents but not for West German respondents. Based on the rejection of both hypotheses in the West German sample, the answer to the general research question asking if the study hypotheses would hold equally in two culturally different samples might be stated as a clear "no."

FIGURE 1. Graphic Illustrations and Regression Equations of Collaborative Impersonal Support for Work-Related Outcome Variables as Moderated by Job Transfer for the Anglosaxon Sample[a]

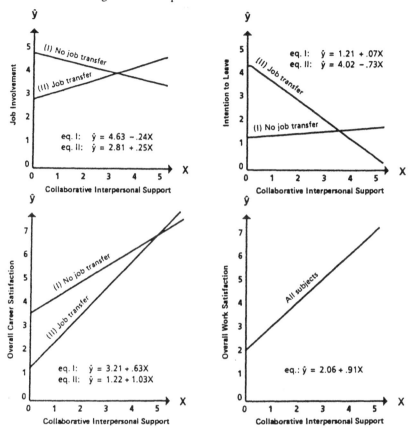

a. When the regression coefficient of an interaction term is found to be statistically significant (see Table 3) the b weights of the two main effects variables and the interaction term are used to compute intercept and slope values for the collaborative interpersonal support-outcome relationship. When no significant interaction is found significant (p > .10) main effects (simultaneous variable inclusion) are reported. Job transfer is coded as follows: 0 = no transfer (N = 85); 1 = transfer (N = 76).

TABLE 3. Tests of Buffering Effects of Collaborative Interpersonal Support on Work-Related Outcomes for Anglosaxon and West German Respondents Assigned to Various Transfer Groups[a]

Dependent Variables	Sample[c]	N	Compared Groups[d]	Main Effects (A+B)[b]			Two-Way Interaction (AxB)		
				ΔR^2	F-statistic	p <	ΔR^2	t-statistic	p <
1. Job involvement	AS	154	NT vs T	.01	—	—	.03	2.12	.018
	AS	110	NT vs LT	.02	—	—	.03	1.97	.026
	AS	114	NT vs PT	.02	—	—	.02	1.31	.097
	WG	261	NT vs T	.02	3.20	.042	.00	−.61	.272
	WG	204	NT vs LT	.02	2.49	.086	.00	−.25	.403
	WG	214	NT vs PT	.05	5.17	.006	.00	−.84	.201
2. Intention to leave	AS	154	NT vs T	.02	—	—	.03	−2.17	.016
	AS	110	NT vs LT	.01	—	—	.04	−2.08	.020
	AS	114	NT vs PT	.01	.72	.491	.01	−.91	.181
	WG	266	NT vs T	.03	3.53	.031	.00	.22	.414
	WG	204	NT vs LT	.02	2.48	.086	.00	.11	.458
	WG	214	NT vs PT	.05	5.09	.007	.00	−.90	.186
3. Overall career satisfaction	AS	153	NT vs T	.08	—	—	.02	1.69	.046
	AS	110	NT vs LT	.08	—	—	.03	1.81	.036
	AS	113	NT vs PT	.11	—	—	.02	1.39	.084
	WG	264	NT vs T	.10	14.67	.001	.00	.01	.496
	WG	207	NT vs LT	.09	10.36	.001	.00	.02	.493
	WG	217	NT vs PT	.14	17.33	.001	.00	−.15	.440
4. Overall work satisfaction	AS	155	NT vs T	.18	16.46	.001	.01	1.27	.103
	AS	111	NT vs LT	.20	—	—	.01	1.42	.079
	AS	115	NT vs PT	.17	11.14	.001	.00	.48	.316
	WG	265	NT vs T	.07	10.00	.001	.00	.62	.267
	WG	207	NT vs LT	.04	4.21	.016	.00	.01	.498
	WG	217	NT vs PT	.09	10.95	.001	.00	.41	.340

a. Following Cramer & Appelbaum (1980), the significance of main effects is tested and reported only when the 2-way interaction term is not significant ($p > .10$; one-tailed test). In each regression, the main effects are entered first, then the interaction term is added and the significance of its partial coefficient is tested according to Cohen & Cohen (1983: 107 [eq. 3.6.7]).

b. A = Collaborative interpersonal support; B = 0,1 dummy variable reflecting job transfer groups as specified in column 4.

c. AS = Anglosaxon; WG = West German.

d. NT = no job transfer group; T = job transfer group; PT = promotional transfer group.

Additional exploratory correlation analysis reveals that correlations between CIS and the work-related outcomes are consistently larger for British/American lateral transferees than for West German laterally transferred respondents; the same is true for British/American vs. West German promotional transferees. For example, for laterally transferred British/American R&D professionals, the correlation between CIS and overall work satisfaction is .59, for West German lateral transferees it is .23. While only four of the eight cross-cultural differences between pairs of correlation coefficients is statistically significant ($p < .10$), results as a set seem to suggest that CIS may be more effective in protecting British/American R&D professionals from tensions and demands associated with a job transfer than for their West German counterparts.

DISCUSSION AND IMPLICATIONS FOR PRACTICE

The human relations tradition of organizational research has long emphasized that supportive behaviors among employees can directly affect a variety of work-related outcomes. Taken together, the present results suggest that CIS may not always simply have positive (main) effects on employee reactions but that in certain situational or cultural environments CIS may interact with the experience of career stressors such as an intracompany job transfer in affecting outcome variables. The data reported here confirm the idea that in the United States and the United Kingdom, CIS will be especially beneficial for individuals experiencing a stressful career transition. Specifically, it was found that CIS among British/American R&D professionals had significantly stronger beneficial effects on job involvement, intention to leave, and career satisfaction for recently transferred employees than for a comparison group of not transferred respondents. In the British/American sample the present findings provide tentative support for the buffering effects of CIS in the case of a job transfer. This finding is consistent with recent theories regarding job transfers in particular (Brett, 1984; Fisher et al., 1982; London & Mone, 1987; Nicolson, in press; Pinder & Walter, 1984) and the nature of (re)socialization processes following career transitions of various sorts in general (Nelson, 1987; Pinder & Schroeder, 1987).

Based on the rationale that promotional and lateral transfers are career stressors that differ in their inherent opportunities, constraints, and demands, this study also hypothesized that the positive buffering effects of CIS would be more consistently found when laterally transferred employees (as opposed to promotional transferees) were compared to a no-transfer group. In the British/American sample, the overall pattern of results tends to support this prediction. This result as well the work of a number of other authors (e.g., Brett, 1984; Burke, 1974; Latack, 1984; Pinder & Schroeder, 1987) suggests that there are important differences in the processes associated with lateral as opposed to promotional transfers. As outlined earlier, lateral transfers appear to provide less positive opportunity stress than do promotional transfers. The present research corroborates this assumption indirectly: in both samples, the lateral transfer group had significantly lower job involvement ($p < .028$ and $p < .002$ for British/American and German respondents, respectively), career satisfaction (British/American: $p < .004$; Germans: $p < .003$), and work satisfaction (British/American: $p < .022$; Germans: $p < .007$) than the promotional transfer group.

Practitioners often assume that lateral transfers are helpful to overcome the negative consequences of blocked promotional career opportunities. However, the data here suggest that a personnel policy fostering lateral transfers appears to achieve its desired outcomes much better or sometimes only if it can be ensured that lateral transferees experience high levels of CIS at their new workplace. A lateral transfer per se is not necessarily a source of positive stimulation. In contrast, because a promotional move is generally perceived as an eustressful career experience, work-related attitudes of recently promoted transferees tend to be less affected by the degree of CIS among colleagues.

It should be noted that CIS does not emerge as a panacea for all transfer-related strains. There is evidence to suggest that contradictory findings may be partially explained by differences in the type of work organization. Whereas most blue collar and many white collar workers used as subjects in prior research appeared to be assigned to highly individuated tasks, the present samples consisted of R&D professional employees who are frequently only nominally supervised and hence rely heavily on their professional colleagues for informational support and evaluative feedback (cf. Boden-steiner, Gerloff, & Quick, 1989; House, 1981, p. 83). It appears that in this type of work or occupational context the buffering effects of CIS are more likely to occur than in occupational contexts in which tasks are less interrelated and professionally demanding (e.g., plumbers, lower level bank employees). Further, cultural as well as occupational work differences must be considered. It is tempting to conclude that work values and social relationships typically prevailing in organizations rooted in the British/American culture (little emphasis on uncertainty avoidance, considerable emphasis on mutual influence among professionals; cf. Hofstede, 1980) are important cultural factors influencing the likelihood that CIS may act as a buffer against career stressors.

The results of this research are also interesting from the perspective of what they do not tell us. While the findings do indicate that CIS had differential impacts for transferred and non-transferred British/American professionals, but not for West German R&D workers, we do not know why different findings were obtained for British/American versus West German respondents. As mentioned above, cross-cultural correlation differences between CIS and work-related outcomes for British/American vs. West German lateral or promotional transferees could be explained on the basis of Hofstede's (1980) work. Accordingly, due to the strong preference of West Germans to avoid uncertain situations, they should rely more heavily than their British/American colleagues on hierarchical integration devices and less on more informal CIS among colleagues in managing adaptational demands of transfers. However, future research addressing cultural differences is needed.

The results of the present study must be regarded as tentative since a post-test only design with nonequivalent groups as employed here provides only limited support for hypotheses which ideally should have been tested in a longitudinal pretest-posttest study. In addition, this study differed from pertinent prior research in that it employed an objectively measurable job stressor instead of perceptual measures of sources of organizational stress (e.g., role conflict). This approach avoids some of the response-response bias that has plagued prior research but it neglects potential mediating psychological process variables.

A further limitation of this research is its focus on work-related support among R&D professionals in two different cultures. Since different sources of support (colleagues, supervisor, spouse, etc.) may have different impacts on work-related outcomes, additional research might examine the relative impact of colleague, supervisor, and spouse support on additional outcome variables (e.g., performance, physiological symptoms) in different occupations across a larger range of culturally different samples.

IMPLICATIONS FOR PREVENTIVE STRESS MANAGEMENT: ENGENDERING CIS

Despite its limitations, this study does have important practical implications since preventive action in real world settings cannot wait for foolproof evidence but must be based upon the best available information (cf. Quick et al., 1987, p. 7). Specifically, this research indicates that in British and American industrial R&D units policies and practices to improve informal helping relationships among technical professionals should first be directed at recently transferred employees, paying special attention to laterally transferred individuals.

While the importance of CIS for transferees in their new jobs seems intuitively appealing and straightforward, engendering supportive transactions in organizations in which work is characterized by high levels of interdependence, complexity, uncertainty, and competitiveness, as well as by high demands for professional excellence, is often a very difficult undertaking. Based on numerous in-depth interviews with R&D personnel, I have found the following seven major reasons for why transferees frequently do not receive an optimum level of CIS from colleagues:

1. A lack of awareness that the problem exists; that is, technical professionals do not appreciate how they contribute to their transferred colleagues' career stress and, accordingly, little time is devoted to orienting and helping recently transferred coworkers.
2. An attitude of non-involvement in the affairs of others dominates, especially in technology-driven organization subunits;

this attitude promotes a general inability both among transferees and not transferred individuals to form informal supportive
relationships with others at work. (cf. Burke, Weir, & Duncan, 1976; Quick, Nelson, & Quick, 1987)
3. A lack of open communications.
4. A fear of a loss of power among non-transferees.
5. A lack of involvement of professionals in the transfer decisions of higher level management that affect the composition
of their work group.
6. A failure to assign formal responsibilities for transferee integration, to monitor continuously levels of support provided by
colleagues of transferees, and to reward those professionals
who were extraordinarily supportive for transferees.
7. Reward systems exclusively emphasizing individual contributions and neglecting interindividual dependencies and team
functioning.

Organizational decision makers should pay attention to each of
these factors since they may serve as starting points for preventive
management actions helping technical professionals to deal with
transfer-induced career stress. Such actions, which always require
visible strong support from senior management, might include
(House, 1981; Keller, 1986; Pinder & Schroeder, 1987) the thorough orientation and public recognition of the status and prior contributions of a transferee (especially after a lateral move), formal
assignment of sponsorship/assistance responsibilities to a more senior colleague of the transferred individual, and shortening physical
distances between the transferee and other group members.

In addition, interpersonal skill training programs not only for supervisory but also for non-supervisory technical professionals can
help them understand the different roles non-transferred colleagues
can play in assisting transferees in their adaptation. First, they can
serve as a source of information regarding informal background
knowledge needed to master a new assignment. Second, they may
at times stand in the stead of the transferee at critical moments when
the transferred person becomes overloaded with the demands of her
new job. Finally, such training can teach R&D professionals how to
judge their colleagues' and their own needs for CIS.

Specific analytical methods that may be helpful in assessing one's own and one's colleagues' networks of professional relationships and their nature in terms of different degrees of supportiveness have already been proposed by Francek (1987, pp. 258-259) and Bodensteiner, Gerloff, and Quick (1989). What is needed is further research to investigate the efficacy of various organizational interventions directed toward providing the support necessary in the context of job transfer-induced career stress.

REFERENCES

Aram, J. D., Morgan, C. P., & Esbeck, E. S. (1971). Relation of collaborative interpersonal relationships to individual satisfaction and organizational performance. *Administrative Science Quarterly, 16,* 289-296.

Bateman, T. S., Karwan, K. R., & Kazee, T. A. (1983). Getting a fresh start: A natural quasi-experimental test of the performance effects of moving to a new job. *Journal of Applied Psychology, 68,* 517-524.

Beehr, T. A. (1985). The role of social support in coping with organizational stress. In T. A. Beehr & R. S. Bhagat (Eds.), *Human Stress and Cognition in Organizations: An integrated perspective.* New York: Wiley.

Bhagat, R. S. (1983). Effects of stressful life events on individual performance effectiveness and work adjustment processes within organizational settings: A research model. *Academy of Management Review, 8,* 660-671.

Bodensteiner, W. D., Gerloff, E. A., & Quick, J. C. (1989). Uncertainty and stress in an R&D project environment. *R & D Management,* in press.

Brett, J. M. (1980). The effect of job transfer on employees and their families. In C. L. Cooper & R. Payne (Eds.), *Current concerns in occupational stress.* Chichester: Wiley.

Brett, J. M. (1984). Job transitions and personal and role development. In K. M. Rowland & G. R. Ferris (Eds.), *Research in personnel and human resources management* (Vol. 2). Greenwich, CT: JAI Press.

Brief, A. P., Schuler, R. S., & Van Sell, M. (1981). *Managing job stress.* Boston, MA: Little, Brown & Company.

Burke, R. J. (1974). Personnel job transfers: Some data and recommendations. *Studies in Personnel Psychology, 6,* 35-46.

Burke, R. J., Weir, T. & Duncan, G. (1976). Informal helping relationships in work organizations. *Academy of Management Journal, 19,* 370-377.

Cobb, S. (1976). Social support as a moderator of life stress. *Psychosomatic Medicine, 38,* 300-314.

Cohen, J., & Cohen, P. (1983). *Applied multiple regression/correlation analysis for the behavioral sciences* (2nd ed.). Hillsdale, NJ: Erlbaum.

Cohen, S., & Wills, T. A. (1985). Stress, social support, and the buffering hypothesis. *Psychological Bulletin, 98,* 310-357.

Cooper, C. L., & Makin, P. (1985). The mobile managerial family. *Journal of Management Development, 4*(3), 56-66.

Cramer, E. M., & Appelbaum, M. I. (1980). Nonorthogonal analysis of variance: Once again. *Psychological Bulletin, 87,* 51-57.

Dailey, R. C. (1978). The role of team and task characteristics in R&D team collaborative problem solving and productivity. *Management Science, 24,* 1579-1588.

Doering, M., Rhodes, S. R., & Schuster, M. (1983). *The aging worker: Research and recommendations.* Beverly Hills, CA: Sage.

Dohrenwend, B. S., Krasnoff, L., Askenasy, A. R., & Dohrenwend, B. P. (1978). Exemplification of a method for scaling life events: The PERI life events scale. *Journal of Health and Social Behavior, 19,* 205-229.

Etzion, D. (1984). Moderating effect of social support on the stress-burnout relationship. *Journal of Applied Psychology, 69,* 615-622.

Ferris, G. R., & Rowland, K. M. (1987). Tenure as a moderator of the absence-intent to leave relationship. *Human Relations, 40,* 255-266.

Fisher, C. D., Wilkins, C., & Eulberg, J. (1982). *Transfer transitions.* Report No. TR-ONR-5, Office of Naval Research. College Station, TX: College of Business Administration, Texas A & M University.

Francek, J. L. (1987). Employee assistance programs: A strategy for managing stress. In J. C. Quick, R. S. Bhagat, J. E. Dalton, & J. D. Quick (Eds.), *Work Stress: Health care systems in the workplace.* New York: Praeger.

Gelb, B. D., & Hyman, M. R. (1987). Reducing reluctance to transfer. *Business Horizons, 30*(2), 39-43.

Gerpott, T. J. (1988). *Karriereentwicklung von industrieforschern.* Berlin: De Gruyter Publishers.

Greenhaus, J. H. (1987). *Career management.* Chicago: Dryden Press.

Harman, H. H. (1976). *Modern factor analysis* (3rd ed.). Chicago: University of Chicago Press.

Hofstede, G. (1980). *Culture's consequences: International differences in work-related values.* Beverly Hills, CA: Sage.

Holmes, T. H., & Rahe, R. H. (1967). The social readjustment rating scale. *Journal of Psychosomatic Research, 11,* 213-218.

House, J. S. (1981). *Work stress and social support.* Reading, MA: Addison-Wesley.

Katz, R. (1980). Time and work: Toward an integrative perspective. In B. M. Staw & L. L. Cummings (Eds.), *Research in organizational behavior* (Vol. 2). Greenwich, CT: JAI Press.

Kegan, D., & Rubenstein, A. H. (1973). Trust, effectiveness and organizational development: A field study in R&D. *Journal of Applied Behavioral Science, 9,* 498-513.

Keller, R. T. (1986). Predictors of the performance of project groups in R&D organizations. *Academy of Management Journal, 29,* 715-726.

Latack, J. C. (1984). Career transitions within organizations: An exploratory study of work, nonwork, and coping strategies. *Organizational Behavior and Human Performance, 34,* 296-322.

Latack, J. C., & Dozier, J. B. (1986). After the ax falls: Job loss as a career transition. *Academy of Management Review, 11,* 375-392.

Lodahl, T. M., & Kejner, M. (1965). The definition and measurement of job involvement. *Journal of Applied Psychology, 49,* 24-33.

London, M., & Mone, E. M. (1987). *Career management and survival in the workplace: Helping employees make tough career decisions, stay motivated, and reduce career stress.* San Francisco: Jossey-Bass.

Louis, M. R., Posner, B. Z., & Powell, G. N. (1983). The availability and helpfulness of socialization practices. *Personnel Psychology, 36,* 857-866.

Moss, L. (1981). *Management stress.* Reading, MA: Addison-Wesley.

Nelson, D. L. (1987). Organizational socialization: A stress perspective. *Journal of Occupational Behavior, 8,* 311-324.

Nicholson, N. (in press). The transition cycle: A conceptual framework for the analysis of change and human resource management. In K. M. Rowland & G. R. Ferris (Eds.), *Research in personnel and human resources management* (Vol. 5). Greenwich, CT: JAI Press.

Payne, R. L. (1980). Organizational stress and social support. In C. L. Cooper & R. Payne (Eds.), *Current concerns in occupational stress.* Chichester: Wiley.

Pinder, C. C., & Schroeder, K. G. (1987). Time to proficiency following job transfers. *Academy of Management Journal, 30,* 336-353.

Pinder, C. C., & Walter, G. A. (1984). Personnel transfers and employee development. In K. M. Rowland & G. R. Ferris (Eds.), *Research in personnel and human resources management* (Vol. 2). Greenwich, CT: JAI Press.

Pines, A. (1983). On burnout and the buffering effects of social support. In B. A. Farber (Ed.), *Stress and burnout in the human service professions.* New York: Pergamon Press.

Quick, J. C., & Quick, J. D. (1984). *Organizational stress and preventive management.* New York: McGraw-Hill.

Quick, J. C., Quick, J. D., Bhagat, R. S., & Dalton, J. E. (1987). Introduction to "Work stress: Research and practice." In J. C. Quick, R. S. Bhagat, J. E. Dalton, & J. D. Quick (Eds.), *Work stress: Health care systems in the workplace.* New York: Praeger.

Quick, J. D., Nelson, D. L., & Quick, J. C. (1987). Successful executives: How independent? *Academy of Management Executive, 1,* 139-145.

Rook, K. S., & Dooley, E. (1985). Applying social support research: Theoretical problems and future directions. *Journal of Social Issues, 41,* 5-28.

Russell, D. W., Altmaier, E., & Van Velzen, D. (1987). Job-related stress, social support, and burnout among classroom teachers. *Journal of Applied Psychology, 72,* 269-274.

Schuler, R. S. (1984). Organizational and occupational stress and coping: A model and overview. In R. S. Schuler & S. A. Youngblood (Eds.), *Readings in personnel and human resource management* (2nd ed.). St. Paul, MN: West Publishing.

Sykes, I. J., & Eden, D. (1985). Transitional stress, social support, and psychological strain. *Journal of Occupational Behavior, 6,* 293-298.

Turner, R. J. (1983). Direct, indirect, and moderating effects of social support on psychological distress and associated conditions. In H. B. Kaplan (Ed.), *Psychosocial stress: Trends in theory and research*. New York: Academic Press.

Werbel, J. D. (1983). Job change: A study of an acute job stressor. *Journal of Vocational Behavior, 23,* 242-250.

Merger and Acquisition Stress: Fear and Uncertainty at Mid-Career

Michael T. Matteson
John M. Ivancevich
University of Houston

SUMMARY. In recent years merger and acquisition activity has increased significantly in the United States. Such activity can be stressful for all employees, particularly those at mid-career. This article examines the stress potential of mergers and acquisitions, with a particular focus on the mid-career employee. It provides a framework for examining merger and acquisition stress and discusses four approaches for stress prevention and management: realistic merger and acquisition previews, individual counseling, merger and acquisition stress management training, and outplacement services.

The level of merger and acquisition (M&A) activity among American businesses during the last decade has increased dramatically, to levels unprecedented in our history. Mergers and acquisitions have become a big business themselves, spawning new careers for those who play roles in some aspect of a merger process. There is even specialization, with some experts concentrating on horizontal mergers, others on vertical mergers, still others on concentric mergers, and others still on conglomerate mergers. Investment firms now have M&A research departments, and federal laws and Securities and Exchange Commission requirements have been modified in response to the increase in the number of such transactions (Porter, 1980).

Reprints may be obtained from Michael T. Matteson, Department of Management and Organizational Behavior, University of Houston, 4800 Calhoun Road, Houston, TX 77004.

139

Further indication of the level and importance of M&A activity is the fact that corporate takeovers, and the activities and behaviors associated with them, have given birth to a new business lexicon. Terms such as bear hugs, golden parachutes, greenmail, Pac-man defenses, poison pills, shark repellent, ten-day windows, and white knights have either entered our vocabulary or taken on new meanings germane to merger and acquisition activity (Byars, 1987).

While the term "mergers and acquisitions" is a commonly used one, it should be noted that there are differences between mergers on the one hand, and acquisitions on the other. Mergers typically involve a higher degree of cooperation and interaction between the two parties; acquisitions generally occur where one firm "takes over" another. Further, mergers tend to involve firms of approximately equal size, while in acquisitions one firm is typically larger and more powerful than the other.

How extensive is M&A activity? During the last decade over 23,000 mergers and acquisitions have been consummated. Eighty-two of those acquired were *Fortune* 500 companies. The 10 largest mergers in 1984 directly affected the lives of more than 250,000 employees (Magnet, 1984). In 1986 alone, M&A activity involved over 4,200 transactions with combined assets of approximately $200 billion, and affected millions of employees. There is no question that corporate America is being bought, sold, spun off, split up, and otherwise restructured at a rapid pace (Nahavandi & Malekzudeh, 1988; Pritchett, 1987).

The human dimension of M&A activity is no less real than the business, investment, and financial ones. Consider the following description of personal tragedy and frustration:

"Don't go down the cellar," Chris's suicide note warned his family. That is where the 38-year-old economist hanged himself, four days after he lost his $63,000-a-year job, when his company was acquired by another firm. (Magnet, 1984)

After four months of rumor, gloom and gossip, Joan, a financial control staff specialist, comments on the recent takeover of her company: "One day we are in business and the next day we disappear from the face of the earth. I'll have to start all over again learning the job, the policies, the people. Is it really worth it?'' (Schweiger & Ivancevich, 1985)

These incidents indicate the growing and critical effect that mergers can have on individuals and families. Concern with being merged or acquired by another company seems to be on the minds of many Americans employees today. Will I keep my job? Will I be transferred? Will I be demoted? Will I lose my accumulated benefits? Will employer expectations change? These are just a few of the questions being asked by those associated with merged or acquired firms.

Corporate M&As are potentially powerful events that can create severe trauma and stress which can result in negative outcomes not only for companies, but more importantly, for the individuals involved. M&A stress is a very real and potentially a very debilitating experience for many workers in the labor force today. In this article we will provide a framework for examining the M&A stress process, consider the important role of individual appraisal in that process, and offer some suggestions for merger stress prevention and management. In so doing we will focus primarily, although not exclusively, on the mid-career employee.

Since in most mergers or acquisitions the reorganization that follows is usually less than the formation of an entirely new company, our focus on prevention will be primarily from the perspective of the acquiring company or entity. The specific prevention strategies are offered as a program for acquiring organizations to implement; as a practical matter, the power and authority to implement such programs will typically rest with the acquiring firm.

STRESS AND THE MID-CAREER EMPLOYEE

A typical individual's occupational life will span a period of forty years or more. During this period people will pass through a number of career stages. The concept of career stage, which grew out of the work of Erikson (1950), refers to a more or less orderly sequence of distinctly different sets of experiences and activities that are associated with virtually all careers. A number of career stage taxonomies have been developed to describe different career phases (see, for example, Greenhaus, 1987; Hall & Nougaim, 1968; London, 1985; Miller & Form, 1951; Schein, 1978; Super, 1980). In keeping with the organization of this volume we will categorize such stages as beginning, mid-career, and end-career.

Needs and expectations change as individuals move into and through each of these stages. Consequently, potential stressors assume greater or lesser importance at different stages. Thus, for example, work overload is less likely to be a significant stressor for someone at the beginning career stage and more significant at the end stage. Similarly, lack of role clarity is a more potent potential stressor at the beginning stage than at career end (for two excellent discussions of need and expectation changes at different career stages see Feldman, 1988, and Greenhaus, 1987).

The mid-career stage is a very critical one; it may represent a period of continued growth and achievement, of simple maintenance where one "hangs on" to what has already been accomplished, of decline, or of some combination of these. Mid-career is also a potentially difficult stage, occurring as it does during midlife where individuals are forced to realize that they have stopped growing up and have begun growing old (Jaques, 1965). Many individuals will experience the infamous "midlife crisis" which may be triggered by fears of lost youth and missed opportunities. Consequently, the mid-career period is one in which individuals are particularly susceptible to fears and uncertainty as they come face to face with unrealized dreams, the physical changes of aging, and their own mortality. Since fear and uncertainty is a common byproduct of M&A activity, it is not difficult to understand why those at mid-career are especially vulnerable to merger and acquisition stress.

The stress associated with being a member of an organization that is being merged or acquired is in part a function of particular stressors growing out of, or intensified by, the nature of the process. For example, if a firm is being acquired is it a friendly acquisition or a hostile one? What is the desired degree of integration? That is, will one organization be absorbed by the other, will they remain operationally separate, or will the degree of integration be somewhere in between?

No one, regardless of career stage, is immune to M&A stress. Those at the beginning or end stage of their careers may find being a member of a merged or acquired organization is most distressing. Nonetheless, beginning stage individuals are not as likely as those at mid-career to have achieved the degree of socialization resulting in the internalization of organization goals, norms, and culture that may be significantly altered as a result of being merged or acquired. Likewise, those at the end-career stage are less likely to be as heavily invested in their career as those a mid-career. A process of disengagement (London & Stumpf, 1982) may already be underway as end-career individuals focus on balancing central non-career life interests and contemplate preparing for retirement.

It is those at mid-career, who may be psychologically most committed to the organization and their specific careers, at a time when they may be already having to deal with a midlife transition, who may find a merger or acquisition experience the most potentially disruptive, threatening, and stressful. At that period in their lives where order and stability may be the most important, they may instead find disorder and change as a result of being a member of a merged or acquired firm.

THE MERGER AND ACQUISITION STRESS PROCESS

The effect of a merger or acquisition on employees generally, and mid-career employees specifically, is a function of a number of factors. Basically mergers and acquisitions create, or intensify already existing stressors. Whether these stressors result in stress and its associated negative outcomes depends on the nature of both the individuals and the organizations involved, including the organizations' plan (if any) for systematic intervention to assist employees in preventing and/or managing M&A stress.

A general model of the merger stress process is depicted in Figure 1. This model suggests that various merger stressors, like job loss, and changes in job characteristics such as power and status can lead to stress. This stress, in turn, may result in dysfunctional out-

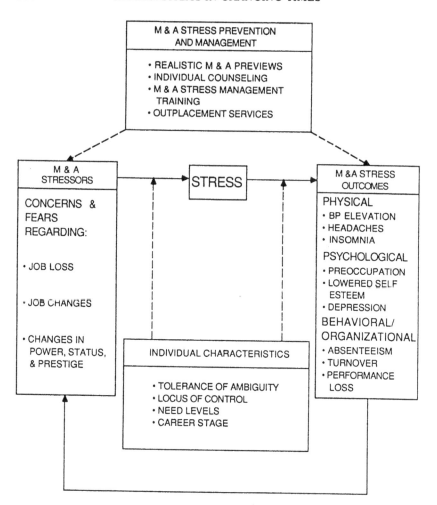

FIGURE 1. MERGER & ACQUISITION STRESS PROCESS

comes which we have categorized as physical, psychological, and behavioral/organizational. The model also suggests that a number of individual characteristics such as tolerance of ambiguity, self-esteem, and locus of control play a role in moderating the relationship between stressors, stress, and outcomes. We will briefly examine the major components of the M&A process.

M&A Stressors

It is reasonable to assume that because of changes, uncertainty, ambiguity, and fears, some employees will experience significant stress when organizations merge. Often well before a merger or acquisition is publicly announced, rumors and office gossip regarding the possibility create uncertainty and insecurity. The concerns and fears surrounding possible job change or possible job loss act as potent stressors. These concerns grow out of employee perceptions of what might happen and how their careers will be affected, and lead in turn to anticipatory stress. Essential to understanding the intensity of M&A stressors is the realization that people respond to their perceptions of the changes rather than to the actual or objective changes themselves. In the initial stages of a merger or acquisition these perceptions are frequently the least accurate with respect to the actual effects of the process.

These anticipated consequences of the merger, regardless of how accurate the perceptions may be, will tend to increase anxiety levels and exacerbate the stress. It is essential during this process that inaccurate perceptions of the changes that will occur and the stress that they create be dealt with in a timely manner by the acquiring or surviving organization. In a very real sense, the major M&A stressor is change. Change for most employees means a disruption in the life and work patterns to which they have become accustomed and comfortable with over time, a state of affairs particularly threatening to the mid-career employee.

A specific example is the fear of job loss. A reduction in force is not at all uncommon for merged or acquired companies. After Texaco acquired Getty Oil Company, the employee roster shrunk by over 6,000. In April of 1984 Chevron acquired Gulf, and a year later almost 20,000 jobs had been lost (Schweiger & Ivancevich, 1985). Anxiety associated with such a stressor often involves spouses and other family members in the stress experience, since it directly affects them as well. While actual M&A changes may be positive rather than negative, it is often the case that the initial shock and disbelief, with its accompanying uncertainty and threat of change, will create negative cognitions and stress. If this stress is allowed to intensify it is quite possible that the positive potential of the process may be damaged or unrealized for both the organization and the individuals who are involved.

M&A Stress Outcomes

M&A stress, like any kind of work related stress, can have a number of negative consequences for both the individual and the organization. Medical and behavioral stress researchers have clearly demonstrated that dramatic changes can have a pronounced physiological impact on those experiencing them. Physiological outcomes may include elevated blood pressure, increases in serum cholesterol, and immune system suppression, among others, which in turn may lead to insomnia, digestive problems, headaches, and various other negative health outcomes (Matteson & Ivancevich, 1987).

From a psychological perspective, one typical M&A stress outcome is preoccupation. In many cases, employees find it quite difficult to concentrate on their work during a merger or acquisition period, especially if they do not think that they will be retained in their job. This preoccupation frequently manifests itself in daydreaming and aimless wandering about the organization. To aid in coping with uncertainty, employees may seek each other out during work to check the validity of rumors or to get the latest available information.

Other psychological outcomes may include lower job, career, and life satisfaction and lower self-esteem. Common behavioral outcomes include increased absenteeism, turnover, quantitative and qualitative performance decrements, and even destructive behaviors. Under some conditions a merger or acquisition, because of its powerful psychological impact, can result in resentment and hostility toward the acquiring firm and its representatives. Anger directed toward others may show up in terms of covert activities such as sabotage. If the labor market is such that jobs are plentiful, key employees may elect to leave and seek employment elsewhere; key individuals nearing retirement may also elect to end their careers early to escape an uncertain and changing situation. Outcomes of M&A stress such as these are at best nonproductive for both individuals and organizations, and at worst are painful, counterproductive, and destructive.

Individual Characteristics

How employees respond to a merger or acquisition is not only a function of the merger or acquisition itself. Some will deal with the changes and ensuing uncertainties and insecurities better than others. Various individual characteristics play a major role in moderating the relationships between stressors, stress, and outcomes. In some cases the effect is to intensify stress; in others to reduce it (Schweiger & Ivancevich, 1985). Need levels such as a high need for achievement, for example, can serve to intensify experienced merger stress if conditions and uncertainties of the merger process operate to block goal accomplishment. The upward striving mid-career employee may be particularly vulnerable in this situation.

Numerous other examples are possible (for an excellent treatment of the role of individual differences in work stress see Payne, 1988). Individuals with low self-esteem are more likely to be threatened by the degree of change that is part of being involved in a merger or acquisition. Employees with an internal locus of control may feel particularly threatened as increasingly their lives are affected by environmental events beyond their control. A low tolerance for ambiguity has obvious negative implications in the unsettled environment of mergers and acquisitions. Many other factors such as previous experience with mergers, degree of available social support, alternative job opportunities, and the presence of other stress factors in one's life may also play an important role. As was previously suggested, those at mid-career may be already experiencing stress associated with a midlife transition, making them uniquely vulnerable to M&A stress. The nuances of many aspects of the relationships between individual characteristics and merger and acquisition stress remain a fertile ground for future research.

THE IMPORTANT ROLE OF APPRAISAL

Not all employees in merged or acquired organizations will consider the experience to be a stressful one. What is viewed as threatening by some will be seen as an opportunity by others. Like any potentially stress inducing event, whether a merger or acquisition will be a source of dysfunctional stress will depend on how each person appraises and evaluates the significance of the event. This concept of appraisal and evaluation has been a prominent theme in the biological tradition of stress (Lazarus, 1966) and is useful in considering M&A stress.

Lazarus and Folkman (1984), in considering primary appraisal (which focuses on the main evaluative issue of, "Am I in trouble or better off because of the situation?"), postulate that the process of appraisal results in three categories of events: irrelevant, benign-positive, and stressful. This is a particularly useful typology for understanding M&A stress. If a merger or acquisition is perceived as having no implications for the well-being of the appraising individual, it is considered to be *irrelevant*. That is, nothing is to be gained or lost by the employee as a result of the M&A process; consequently it becomes, for that employee, a "non-event."

A *benign-positive* appraisal occurs if an event is construed as positive. With respect to M&As, a benign-positive appraisal might occur when the event is viewed as an opportunity to maintain or enhance one's position, stature, power, or self-esteem. Essentially, it is characterized by pleasurable and comfortable feelings. A benign-positive appraisal of one merger was verbalized by a mid-career employee who stated, "I know my job and I know I'm needed. It really doesn't matter to me who's steering the ship. What's important is that the ship can't get back to port without me and my knowledge of the job."

It is the third category, that of the *stressful* appraisal, which has the potential for high individual and organizational costs, particularly for mid-career employees. The stressful appraisal can be subdivided into its own three categories: harm/loss, threat, and challenge. A harm/loss appraisal indicates that there has been some damage to the appraising individual, such as a sense of powerlessness or the actual loss of a job, accompanied by loss of self-esteem. One obviously distressed employee working for a recently acquired company expressed his feelings this way: "After seventeen years of working hard, trying to work toward the top, it's clear I no longer have the chance to make it. This [merger] changes my whole life."

While harm/loss indicates that damage has already been sustained, threat suggests a view by the appraising individual that the *potential* for damage is very real. "I don't know if I am going to have a job and be able to feed my family or what is going to happen to my career if this merger goes through" is the kind of statement that exemplifies the threat appraisal, where there are perceptions of harm or loss that have not yet occurred but are anticipated.

The third stress appraisal, challenge, differs from threat in that the appraisal focuses on the potential for gain or growth and is characterized by pleasurable emotions such as eagerness, excitement, and exhilaration. Challenged mid-career personnel have obvious advantages over their threatened counterparts with respect to their physical and psychological health, as well as in terms of organizationally important factors such as morale, commitment, and productivity.

Numerous factors contribute to understanding why the same merger rumors, facts, and activities would be appraised as a threat by some and an opportunity by others. As we have already seen, career stage is an important variable. Additionally, a variety of individual characteristics may influence the appraisal process. As one example of the latter, consider the concept of *hardiness* (Kobasa, 1988; Kobasa, Hilker, & Maddi, 1980). Hardy individuals are those who retain mental and physical balance during periods of exposure to potentially dysfunctional stressors. They are characterized by a sense of *commitment* to various aspects of their lives; they believe that they are in *control* of their lives; and they actively embrace novelty and *challenge*, as opposed to familiarity and security. It is not difficult to understand how a hardy mid-career person's appraisal of a merger would differ from that of a "non-hardy" one.

Work, and the careers associated with it, is an integral part of most people's lives and it assists them in attaining those things they value. Mergers and acquisitions are powerful events that have the potential to change these relationships. Job loss, demotion, change in salary and compensation packages, changes in work colleagues, managers, and subordinates, and alterations in company culture are only a few of the possible changes a merger or acquisition can initiate. With these changes M&As can threaten people's ability to attain and protect those things they value in life. M&A stress can also spill over into life outside of work and effect friendships and families. Clearly, however, not all reorganizations threaten the outcomes and value that work provides; many may significantly enhance value attainment.

To the extent that the events created by a merger or acquisition are expected to, or actually do, challenge or change the relationship between work and value attainment, a response will result. The appraisal process is critical in shaping the nature of that response. If the changes are perceived to threaten or diminish the ability of an individual to continue to attain those things that are valued, stress levels will increase. If merger events are appraised as enhancing value attainment (that is, benign/positive), there will be little or no dysfunctional stress. Where there is no perceived effect on value attainment (that is, irrelevant) there will be no response.

Viewed from a stress prevention perspective then, creating a situation where the merger process is likely to be appraised as either irrelevant or benign/positive is desirable. While there is no way to insure such an appraisal outcome for all individuals involved, there are steps which can be taken to minimize the likelihood of a stressful evaluation. These steps, and others, are an important part in M&A stress prevention and management.

M&A STRESS PREVENTION AND MANAGEMENT

Mergers, because they involve change, are by their very nature stressful; this will be true even if the changes are positive and beneficial (Marks & Mirvis, 1985). Effective merger stress prevention and management strategies, however, can be valuable in reducing the threat associated with change and in assisting employees to cope more effectively with the stress already experienced.

The upper part of Figure 1 shows the relationship of prevention and management actions to the M&A stress process. As can be seen from the figure, some actions are designed to minimize the stress producing potential of M&A stressors, while others are designed to help employees deal with M&A experienced stress and minimize dysfunctional outcomes. We will examine four possible strategies: realistic M&A previews, individual counseling, M&A stress management training, and outplacement services. The main elements of each of these strategies are summarized in Table 1.

Table 1
Summary of M&A Stress Prevention and Management Strategies

Strategy	Elements
Realistic M&A Previews	Communication of M&A information regarding -organization goals -company philosophy -changes in work schedules -changes in compensation -training & development plans
Individual Counseling	Personal adjustment counseling Educational counseling Mid-career counseling
M&A Stress Management Training	Voluntary in nature Knowledge acquisition oriented Coping skill development
Outplacement Services	Pretermination consultation Crisis intervention Resume preparation Job postings Self-help meetings

Realistic M&A Previews

Many of the most potent M&A stressors are related to concerns and fears which grow, at least in part, out of the uncertainty surrounding mergers and acquisitions. "How will I be affected by this change" is a question asked universally by employees of merged or acquired organizations. Simply having information to answer this question, even if the information is not positive, can reduce uncertainty, and consequently, anticipatory stress. Perhaps the single most important step that can be taken to prevent M&A stress is ensuring an information flow designed to clarify what implications the merger process has for employees. One way of accomplishing this is through the use of realistic M&A previews.

Realistic job previews, an accepted organizational strategy, involve providing prospective employees with enough information about the job itself and the larger job environment to provide a picture of what to expect; consequently, they can cope more realistically with job demands (Feldman, 1988; Premack & Wanous, 1985). Similarly, realistic M&A previews (RM&AP) can be developed for a merged or acquired firm's employees. As is the case with realistic job previews, RM&APs can be provided through a film, videocassette, booklet and/or in a large group setting. Some research suggests that a variety of different media may be most beneficial (Popovich & Wanous, 1982).

The intent of a RM&AP is to improve the mid-career employee's understanding of the M&A events and activities and their implications. Employees should be presented with information on what they can realistically expect in terms of organizational goals; management style; changes in work schedules, benefits, and compensation; implications regarding job security, career paths and opportunities and training and development plans; and, any significant alterations in company philosophy and organizational culture and expectations.

Planning for RM&APs may best be accomplished by a "transition team" comprised of managers and employees from both the acquiring and the acquired organization. The utilization in such teams of key individuals from both organizations can foster a broader information base and a greater degree of commitment from those effected (Jemison & Sitkin, 1986). While the thoughtful use of RM&APs will not mean that there will be no unwanted outcomes of the merger or acquisition process, it will have the effect not only of reducing fears and uncertainty, but also of providing a visible sign that the management of the resulting organization is sensitive to these kinds of employee concerns.

Individual Counseling

Realistic M&A previews will most likely not be sufficient in all cases to deal with fears and concerns. Consequently, it can be useful if voluntary individual counseling is available. Three, not entirely independent types of counseling may be of help: personal adjustment counseling, educational counseling, and mid-career counseling. In each type, one-to-one interaction between a counselor and an employee is desirable. The objective of such counseling is to aid the employee in coping with problems associated with M&A stress. Personal adjustment counseling emphasizes individual emotional responses to the M&A process. Here, the counselor is concerned with helping the individual identify stress responses and dysfunctional outcomes. The counselor also attempts to identify one or a series of coping methods that can reduce the psychological and/or physiological distress that is being experienced.

Educational counseling is concerned with providing mid-career employees with further information about the merger or acquisition or to reinforce information already disseminated. The RM&AP may not have been sufficient to alleviate some employees' uncertainties, and they may request additional detail. Ideally, this type of counseling should also be on a one-to-one basis.

Mid-career counseling in M&As involves issues dealing with job choices and opportunities. Making adjustments to an acquiring firm's management system and culture can be an important part of this counseling. The identification of career paths and objectives in the new organizational arrangement can be critical information for employees. Such counseling can be of value by aiding employees in working through questions and uncertainties regarding career goals, pathways, and opportunities. For those at mid-career this may be the last major opportunity to change career paths, and such employees can genuinely use outside guidance in thinking realistically about their options (Feldman, 1988).

Counselors in each of these three types of counseling need to be skillful in listening and communicating as well as understanding. Additionally, they must have sufficient knowledge about the acquiring firm and its orientation to understand the emotions that are projected in the counseling sessions and to provide reality-based feedback and support. Unskilled counselors who are not knowledgeable about the acquiring firm's orientation can intensify, rather than diminish, the problem.

M&A Stress Management Training

As an alternative (or, perhaps in addition) to individual counseling, some mid-career employees may benefit from a M&A stress management training course. Any such program should be voluntary and offered in a manner that does not discourage participation for fear of being viewed as a troubled employee.

While the specific content of such programs may vary and such a discussion goes beyond our scope here, a few comments are in order. The purpose of M&A stress management training programs, as is true for most stress management training, is to help the employee deal more effectively with M&A stress. Such programs can have one, or a combination, of two objectives.

Knowledge acquisition programs are designed primarily to provide information to mid-career employees that will help them understand the stress process and its potential outcomes. The underlying assumption is that by educating individuals with respect to what stress is and how it affects them, they are in a better position to deal with potential stressors and stress itself in ways that are positive rather than negative.

Skill development programs are designed to impart specific skills: cognitive skills, interpersonal skills, problem-solving skills — all directed toward improving individuals' abilities in coping with stress. Such skills may be classified as either instrumental (problem-focused) or palliative (emotion-focused) (Lazarus & Launier, 1978). In either case, the emphasis is on teaching specific techniques which have been found to be useful for dealing with stress. Skill development programs generally are more extensive, require more time, and have a higher initial cost than knowledge acquisition programs, which may amount to not much more than a "stress lecture." They are also generally thought to be of greater benefit to the employees electing to participate in them.

Outplacement

Frequently the fears and concerns mid-career employees may have about job loss are reality based; that is, some loss of employment is a fact of life in more mergers and acquisitions than not. Research suggests that not only are mid-career employees the most traumatized by job loss, they are also the least able to cope with it (Jackson & Warr, 1984; Leana & Ivancevich, 1987). For example, Hepworth (1980) found that mid-career individuals had the most negative attitudes toward job loss and experienced the greatest amount of stress. Since job loss tends to be a traumatic experience that has been associated with a number of negative physical and mental outcomes (see, for example, Kasl & Cobb, 1982), a critical intervention relates to assisting individuals cope with this stressful event. One mechanism of value in this regard is outplacement.

Morin and Yorks (1982) define outplacement as a systematic process by which terminated employees are trained and counseled in the techniques of self-appraisal and securing new employment appropriate to their needs and talents. It does not necessarily include placement of the employee in a new job. Pretermination consultation is a part of outplacement and is designed to help the organization's management think through their options, objectively choose an approach that is consistent with company policy, and review the package of support services for those being terminated. This is a critical phase of outplacement that, if handled well, can significantly reduce the stress experienced by those losing their jobs (DeFrank & Pliner, 1987).

An important part of outplacement services is outplacement counseling which is essentially a crisis intervention process. The role of the counselor is to facilitate the venting of negative feelings, leading, it is hoped, to the development of positive attitudes about the outplacement process and aimed at rebuilding (or increasing) the mid-career individual's self-esteem and sense of personal worth. Additionally, a variety of outplacement services such as resume preparation, job postings, resource materials, and informal supportive self-help meetings may be part of the outplacement package. All such activities are designed to reduce M&A stress by facilitating positive cognitive and affective changes, as well as faster reemployment (DeFrank & Pliner, 1987).

CONCLUSION

Mergers and acquisitions are stressful events to which hundreds of thousands of employees have been subjected in recent years; there are no indications that the level of such activity is going to significantly decrease in the near term. While it is naive to think that M&A stress can be eliminated, it is also true that a great deal of it can be prevented and better managed with the expenditure of relatively little effort. The payoffs in terms of human happiness and health (not to mention organizational health) can far exceed the investment of time, money, and energy.

We have identified four specific strategies which can be helpful in reducing M&A stress and its negative outcomes for mid-career employees; many other specific approaches are also available. At a more general level, however, there are two keys to successful M&A stress prevention and management: *awareness* and *action*. It is imperative that there is awareness of the fact that mergers are stressful events and that M&A stress has potentially dysfunctional outcomes for both individuals and organizations. It is also important to know how merger and acquisition activity can contribute to these unintended and undesirable consequences. Based on this awareness, action should be taken to decrease the uncertainty that can be such a potent stressor and to reduce the likelihood of destructive physiological, psychological, and behavioral/organizational outcomes.

There is no single recipe for effectively preventing M&A stress. Nonetheless, organizations with well-prepared plans, based on consideration of the human beings involved, can play a major role in helping mid-career employees adjust and cope successfully with what otherwise could be a major trauma. Such employees, individually and collectively, deserve no less.

REFERENCES

Byars, L. (1987). *Strategic management*. New York: Harper & Row.

DeFrank, R. S., & Pliner, J. E. (1987). Job security, job loss, and outplacement: Implications for stress and stress management. In J. C. Quick et al., (Eds.), *Work stress*. New York: Praeger.

Erikson, E. (1950). *Childhood society*. New York: W. W. Norton.

Feldman, D. C. (1988). *Managing careers in organizations*. Glenview, IL: Scott, Foresman.

Greenhaus, J. H. (1987). *Career Management*. Chicago: Dryden Press.

Hall, D. T., & Nougaim, K. (1968). An examination of Maslow's need hierarchy in an organizational setting. *Organizational Behavior and Human Performance, 3*, 12-35.

Hepworth, S. J. (1980). Moderating factors of the psychological impact of unemployment. *Journal of Occupational Psychology, 53*, 139-46.

Jackson, P. R., & Warr, P. B. (1984). Unemployment and psychological ill-health: The moderating role of duration and age. *Psychological Medicine*, *14*, 605-614.

Jemison, D. B., & Sitkin, S. B. (1986). Corporate acquisitions: A process perspective. *Academy of Management Review*, *11*, 145-163.

Kasl, S. V., & Cobb, S. (1982). Variability of stress effects among men experiencing job loss. In L. Goldberg & S. Breznitz (Eds.), *Handbook of stress: Theoretical and clinical aspects*. New York: Free Press.

Kobasa, S. C. (1988). Conceptualization and measurement of personality in job stress research. In J. Hurrell, L. Murphy, S. Sauter, & C. Cooper (Eds.), *Occupational stress*. New York: Taylor & Francis.

Kobasa, S. C., Hilker, R. R., & Maddi, S. R. (1980). Remaining healthy in the encounter with stress. In *Stress, work, health*. Chicago: American Medical Association.

Lazarus, R. S. (1966). *Psychological stress and the coping process*. New York: McGraw-Hill.

Lazarus, R. S., & Cohen, J. B. (1984). *Stress, appraisal, and coping*. New York: Springer.

Lazarus, R. S., & Launier, R. (1978). Stress-related transactions between person and environment. In R. Pervin & L. Lewis (Eds.), *Perspectives in interactional psychology*. New York: Plenum.

Leana, C. R., & Ivancevich, J. M. (1987). Addressing the problem of involuntary job loss: Institutional interventions and an agenda for research. *Academy of Management Review*, *12*, 301-12.

London, M. (1985). *Developing Managers*. San Francisco: Jossey-Bass.

London, M., & Stumpf, S. A. (1982). *Managing careers*. Reading, MA: Addison-Wesley.

Magnet, M. (July, 9, 1984). Help! My company has just been taken over. *Fortune*, 44.

Marks, L. M., & Mirvis, P. (1985). Merger syndrome: Stress and uncertainty. *Mergers & Acquisitions*, *20*, 50-61.

Matteson, M. T., & Ivancevich, J. M. (1987). *Controlling work stress*. San Francisco: Jossey-Bass.

Miller, D., & Form, W. (1951). *Industrial Sociology*. New York: Harper & Row.

Morin, W. J., & Yorks, L. (1982). *Outplacement techniques: A positive approach to terminating employees*. New York: AMACOM.

Nahavandi, A., & Malekzadet, A. R. (1988). Acculturation in mergers and acquisitions. *Academy of Management Review*, *13*, 79-90.

Payne, R. (1988). Individual differences in the study of occupational stress. In C. L. Cooper & R. Payne (Eds.), *Causes, coping, and consequences of stress at work*, New York: John Wiley.

Popovich, P., & Wanous, P. (1976). The realistic job preview as a persuasive communication. *Academy of Management Review*, *1*, 570-578.

Porter, M. E. (1980). *Corporate Strategy*. New York: Free Press.

Premack, S. L., & Wanous, P. (1985). A meta-analysis of realistic job preview experiments. *Journal of Applied Psychology*, *70*, 706-19.

Pritchett, P. (1987). *Making mergers work*. Homewood, IL: Dow Jones-Irwin.
Schein, E. H. (1978). *Career dynamics: Matching individual and organizational needs*. Reading, MA: Addison-Wesley.
Schweiger, D. L., & Ivancevich, J. M. (November, 1985). Human resources: The forgotten factor in mergers and acquisitions. *Personnel Administrator*, 47-61.
Super, D. E. (1980). A life-span, life-space approach to career development. *Journal of Vocational Behavior*, *16*, 282-298.

Staying with or Leaving the Organization

Judith Pliner

Drake, Beam, and Morin, Inc.

SUMMARY. Corporate restructuring activities in American corporations during the 1980s have created a variety of dilemmas for individuals in the mid-career years. This article proposes a two dimensional framework for understanding the experience of those facing these mid-career restructuring dilemmas. One dimension is whether the individual leaves the organization or remains in the organization. The other dimension is whether the decision is voluntary or involuntary. Interviews indicate that those most successful in managing the transitions of this career period are flexible in response to changing circumstances, have a high level of awareness, are characterized by information seeking behavior, and have the capacity to venture beyond previous boundaries and known ground.

In their chapter in this volume, Matteson and Ivancevich addressed the tasks and issues facing the individual at mid-career. This stage may offer continuing opportunities for advancement and achievement, or merely the chance to "hold on" to what has already been attained. It is typically a time when the individual begins to reflect on career/life achievements (hopefully with some measure of satisfaction) while recognizing that options have narrowed and upward mobility is likely to be restricted. Often it is the time to grapple simultaneously with unrealized aspirations, lack of career fulfillment, and increasing financial demands as children enter college and retirement is anticipated.

During the last decade major business events and trends have produced several complicating mid-career issues. A pervasive anxi-

Reprints may be obtained from Judith Pliner, Drake, Beam, and Morin, Inc., 1099 18th Street, Suite 200, Denver, CO 80202.

159

ety in corporate America about job security has arisen in response to merger and acquisition activity and the severe cutbacks in major industry sectors (Schane, personal communication, November 9, 1988). The result of slashing middle management ranks by over 1/3 or by one million jobs is a lack of advancement opportunities for younger managers, as well as a threat of job loss and career plateauing, burnout, and disillusionment. What this means to the individual at mid-career in 1989 is that there is a strong likelihood of being faced either with an involuntary termination or the decision to exit from a company with or without a financial inducement. If one stays with an organization by choice or by "missing the ax" in 1989, there is a good chance of no upward or lateral movement for 2-5 years.

To learn about the experiences of people who stayed and those who left organizations both in times of reorganization/downsizing and during times of relative stability, the author interviewed nine individuals who faced significant changes at the mid-point of their careers. What was sought in the interviews was an understanding of the key factors in the decision to stay with or leave an organization (if there was a choice to be made). How did they cope with the stress associated with their particular situations? What factors enabled them to make successful adjustment (either to a new job, a changed organization, or a static organization)?

For the purposes of this study those interviewed were divided into the following four categories (see Figure 1):

1. Those who were terminated involuntarily as a result of a downsizing, reorganization, or other reasons (cell 1);
2. Those who left an organization as the result of a personal decision that may have included a financial inducement to leave (cell 2);
3. Those who were retained by a changing, downsizing organization but would have preferred a financial inducement to leave (cell 3);
4. Those who remained with a changing organization by surviving a downsizing and who preferred to stay (cell 4).

WHO CHOOSES

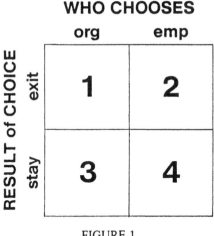

FIGURE 1

CELL 1 – "YOU'RE FIRED"

Of these four groups, people who leave jobs involuntarily have most often been the subjects in business and psychological research. The health effects of job loss, including physiological and psychological changes, have been extensively researched and reviewed (DeFrank & Ivancevich, 1986; Kasl, Grove, & Cobb, 1975). The focus in the first half of this chapter is the perceptions of individuals undergoing voluntary or involuntary job changes – how they view their careers, how they reacted to changes, and how they coped with the challenges that confronted them.

Sarah

Sarah worked for twenty years with a major state bank and then joined a smaller, financial services organization. After seven years there she held the position of Senior Vice President/Chief Operating Officer and was a member of its Board of Directors.

When she joined the company she was instrumental in its development from a small, unsophisticated, barely profitable organization into a professional, profitable one – a nice career progression for a woman with a high school education, who started as a keypunch operator. She was not suffering from mid-career issues of stagnation and lack of career satisfaction. In fact, she described the current status of her career as "very exciting"; she "took great enjoyment in developing senior managers." So what happened?

Her former company, which is privately owned by a small group of investors, underwent an ownership change in December of 1987, and the President bought a major share in the company. The next summer he released six senior managers, including Sarah, as part of a major reorganization. The shock of being terminated was so great that she was unable to begin the outplacement process for a week, even though she met a representative of the consulting firm handling her outplacement the day she was released. It took her weeks to unravel her identity from that of the company and the process of disengaging took even longer.

Sarah dealt productively with the stress she experienced by doing a lot of talking about what happened and why it happened. Not being the type of person to move quickly past hurtful situations, she dug in and went through the painful process of self-examination. Through this process she was reminded of positive things she already knew about herself—her strength and ability to be productive while under stress, how highly she was regarded professionally, and her ability to maintain a positive attitude. She also gained some insight about her inclination to do a better job managing down than managing up; she became more aware of the dynamics that were present among the management group during the six months preceding her termination; and she learned about her own repetitive behavior patterns that were not always adaptive in the workplace.

Sarah had two other major tools she used in combatting stress. One was the continuous use of "to do" lists to structure her time and help her feel productive everyday. The other was an extremely close and supportive family and close professional friendships.

Bill

Unlike Sarah, Bill started his career with the right credentials. Following completion of an M.B.A. degree, he began a credit training program with a major New York bank. Progressing over a 10 year period into a senior position in the Petroleum Department, he guided the application of the bank's services to several major oil companies and suppliers to the energy industry. His work was on the leading edge of worldwide petroleum financing. For several years Bill served in this capacity, and in assessing his next career step at the bank, decided that it was not one he wanted to take.

He opted instead to accept a CFO position with a major independent oil company in the western part of the United States. The offer arose out of the consultative relationship he had already established with this company while at the bank. The financial rewards and opportunities were great; and for a two-year period things went well. Then came 1985 and a severe downturn in the industry. In addition, there was dissension among the senior management group, which escalated into a hostile three against one power struggle. After eighteen months of feeling powerless and frustrated, Bill decided it was time to negotiate his exit.

Did Bill leave voluntarily? While he did engineer the specifics of his departure, in his mind he really had no choice. He was determined, however, in leaving to learn from the experience by reflecting in depth about himself and his career. As part of his exit agreement, he insisted upon outplacement assistance and the services of an industrial psychologist, someone in his words who would "be tough on him."

The year following Bill's departure from his company was difficult. The difficulties stemmed primarily from the stock market crash of 1987 which devastated the financial community and left thousands of talented people jobless. He also was in a poor cash situation. Fortunately, the intense financial pressure was alleviated temporarily by the opportunity to consult again with his former company. The chance to repair the working relationships was beneficial — a time for healing after the previous, painful eighteen months. As a consultant Bill worked well in the company; as an employee he was less effective.

For his family the situation has had a positive side as well. His two children grew up with all the comforts afforded them by their father's career efforts. Their response to his being unemployed was to assume more financial responsibility for their college expenses. Of perhaps greater importance, they did not seem to take things for granted as they used to, according to Bill, and they probably learned an important lesson about business realities.

Sam

Sam left public school teaching early in his career and began an executive training program with a major retailer 14 years ago. He was promoted quickly into a buying position and then to assistant merchandise manager. Five years later he accepted a job in store management with another major retail organization on the east coast. He soon realized that he preferred the buying end of the business and sought an internal opportunity to work as a division merchandise manager which he was given several months later. A company reorganization resulted in a transfer to a western city in 1986, a lateral move.

Sam describes his first boss in the new city as very difficult to work with. "I was his whipping boy," he said. Then, after a merger with another department store chain, the company replaced his former manager with a general merchandise manager from the acquired company. The relationship started out well enough, according to Sam, but deteriorated quickly. The new manager was critical of his management style and became very involved in the details of Sam's operations. It was a tough year for retailers in this city whose economy was tied to oil and gas. Shortly after the first negative performance review of his career, Sam was terminated.

Sam's exit from his company was not unlike the experience of thousands of middle managers in the 1980s. It followed a history of success, then organizational change which resulted in an incompatible manager/subordinate match in the context of a toughening business environment.

What makes Sam's situation more insidious than Sarah's or Bill's is his response or lack of response to it. For example, in the interview Sam stated that he was dissatisfied with the general direction of and specific events that occurred in his career for a five year period. His rationale for not taking action is that the retail industry was in such turmoil during that time that trying to make a change seemed like a less desirable course of action than staying where he was. Even in the western city where his career was quickly falling apart, Sam did not even consider looking for another job once the first boss was fired.

Sam is also handicapped by a failure to recognize the role he played in his downfall. He blames the company for what happened, and believes the company has not been fair with him. Five months after the termination Sam is still visibly angry.

Sam, Sarah, and Bill are all still seeking full-time professional positions. Both Sarah and Bill are involved in temporary consulting assignments which provide some financial relief. All three have exhausted their severance benefits. All three face the possibility of having to relocate and sell houses in a "soft" real estate market. All three have families and financial obligations. For each of them the future is difficult to predict.

If there is one differentiating factor among them, Sarah's and Bill's demonstrated ability to gain something positive from their experiences is noteworthy. All three executives could claim they were treated unfairly; each could claim to have been ensnared by circumstances. Two of them, however, have gained some insight about themselves in the process; and therefore, the likelihood of getting entangled in similar situations at some future time seems reduced.

CELL 2 – "VOLUNTARY EXITS"

Of the 8.5 million people who were out of work in 1986, 10.4% left their jobs voluntarily (Leana & Ivancevich, 1987). The primary reasons appear to be either a financial inducement which permitted early retirement for the older workers or opportunities for younger workers to start afresh, or an intense discomfort related to disillusionment, fatigue, burnout, and overall lack of career satisfaction. Nick, Jerry, and Mike are interesting examples.

Nick

Nick made a voluntary exit from his company, a small marketing information services company in late 1987. He did this without benefit of severance pay or even unemployment benefits since he resigned from his position. The resignation was the culminating event in a series of career decisions which alternately reflected his need for work enjoyment and the desire for advancement.

In 1984 he resigned from a Fortune 100 company as the Director of Marketing to join the smaller company. He did so in order to "get away from climbing the ladder," join a small, humanistic company, and "focus on the job not egos and politics."

While the job was a step down in title, and involved direct selling, he enjoyed his first year and had quite a bit of success. Then, by his own admission, he started getting "greedy and ambitious," and wanted to be part of the exclusive "men's club," i.e., senior management. As it became clear to him that he was not viewed as senior management and never would get admitted to the "club," Nick became depressed and began to see the company which he formerly experienced as a "small, intimate boutique" turning into a "small, crowded playing field."

At about the same time that Nick was beginning to feel trapped, an outside consultant was retained to write a strategic plan for the company. One of several steps outlined in the strategic plan was the creation of the Director of Marketing position. While Nick was interviewing internally for the position, he was simultaneously telling his wife that taking it would be a no-win situation because of the high expectations the owners would have for immediate concrete results. Over a two-year period in the new position Nick felt increasingly estranged from his management, felt his career was veering farther off track, and saw himself and his staff become less productive. Things approached a crisis and Nick resigned.

Nick is an example of a bright and talented young man with very high expectations of himself and his career. He described leaving the job as a stress reducer, in spite of the financial hardships and uncertainty he and his family endured during the seven months it took for him to secure another position. He gained solace through rigorous introspection and philosophical examination of his priorities and values, which left him with a sense of satisfaction about himself and his relationships with his family and God. After a tumultuous seven months of job seeking he began a new position in a Fortune 500 company with philosophic acceptance. "It's time to get back on the log and start floating downstream."

Jerry

Jerry did not appear to experience the angst that Nick did about his life and career, but nevertheless is an individual with definite expectations of his career. He joined the Bell System immediately after completing his undergraduate work in engineering. Placed on a management track for high potential employees, Jerry held a series of progressively responsible positions across several functional areas for the next 13 years. During the early 1980s he observed that upward opportunities were declining as competition in the industry emerged for the first time.

During this period Jerry made and implemented several strategic career decisions. It was a three-point plan: (1) get out of the regulated side of the telecommunications business and seek out an opportunity in one of the new competitive businesses within the Bell System; (2) get an M.B.A. degree to get positioned in and exposed to the external marketplace; and (3) begin developing plans for starting a new business on his own.

In 1984, following the divestiture of the company, Jerry got the chance he was looking for and became the Vice President-Marketing for a wholly-owned Bell subsidiary that was an unregulated business. He was required to give up a generous Bell System pension and benefits.

The years that followed were challenging and stimulating, albeit difficult. Two years later the parent company decided to consolidate several incubated subsidiaries which had been marginally successful. The belief was that collectively they would be more viable. Two years and another reorganization later Jerry was faced with a choice: return to one of the larger company entities or leave altogether.

At this point Jerry had four years' experience in a very competitive business environment. He had completed his M.B.A. and had analyzed his plan for starting his own business as a class assignment. The other members of his Executive M.B.A. class represented the range of businesses in that city, and the professors were an integral link to senior management in many companies.

Jerry made the choice to leave. His only real concern was that his wife, a homemaker who was very security-oriented, and their three children would suffer. While he did leave with severance pay and outplacement assistance, Jerry was mentally prepared for the job search process (he had abandoned the idea of starting a business) to take a year.

It was no surprise that Jerry approached the task of finding a job as systematically and rationally as he had approached the rest of his career. He found several things of particular help to him. Psychological testing confirmed much of what he had always believed about his interests, personality, and strengths. He appreciated the methodology and structure provided by an outplacement program. He credits his M.B.A. classes in marketing and finance with enabling him to assess companies he was considering working for and project a broader business understanding during interviews.

Jerry located an executive position in an excellent company four months after voluntarily leaving his employer of 18 years. He is currently active in establishing himself in his new position and getting on with his career.

Mike

In contrast to Jerry's straightforward progression, Mike described himself in the interview as having a "checkered" career. After completing a Ph.D. in English Literature at a time when there was little opportunity for doctoral level graduates in the humanities, he accepted a position as technical writer for the United States Agricultural Service. Three years later he was recruited into a major oil company in the employee relations area. He spent a total of eight years working for this company in a variety of human resources functions and for five of those years was in a managerial role.

Mike's decision to leave the company was not an impulsive one. During his tenure there he accepted several promotions and one transfer, and declined others. He survived a major reorganization and downsizing in 1986, but before then had been told he would probably not rise into the senior management ranks. He was extremely well paid and well regarded.

Mike's career might have continued in this vein for another 20 years. However, he felt under-utilized, and given the state of the oil industry, felt this situation would continue at least for another five years. When he first began to recognize the warning signs of having reached a plateau, Mike began getting his financial life in order to leave. When he finally told the company of his plans, he was positioned to sustain himself for two years with no outside income. At this juncture, the company countered with an offer of another job in a desirable location for more money. In assessing this opportunity, Mike judged it to have the same job content, and therefore, still represent under-utilization of his skills. Like Jerry, without benefit of severance pay, he resigned.

While not having his career road map as clearly marked to all the destinations as Jerry, Mike knew himself well enough to know that his career was derailing. One of the first things he did was to engage the services of an industrial psychologist and get some outside assessment of his strengths, interests, and personality. What he learned from the psychologist was a verification of what he had always believed to be true of himself. With his conceptual ability, creativity, and love for writing identified as three major career variables, Mike was able to see how the various threads of his career were actually woven together. This gave him the confidence to proceed with planning his next step—a consultancy in a partnership with a more marketing-oriented professional.

Mike stated that resigning his position reduced his level of stress. His wife, who had a fifteen-year career in banking, has been extremely supportive. He finds that he is working far harder for himself now than he did for his former company and deriving much more satisfaction. He feels successful and intends to take the time periodically for self-assessment and reflection.

Nick, Jerry, and Mike are markedly different from one another in personality and professional experience and credentials. Yet, they have three striking similarities. While some people stay in jobs when they are miserable and know that the jobs are wrong for them, other executives will risk making changes. This was the case for Nick, Jerry, and Mike.

The first similarity among the three men is in their personal circumstances. They are all around the age of forty; and all of them have wives who are homemakers and two or more children. Therefore, one can assume that a spouse's financial contribution was not a key ingredient in the decisions to resign. All three men earned at least $75,000 a year. Jerry was the only one to leave with severance benefits.

The second similarity is in their evaluations of intraorganizational career opportunities. All three found the career options that were open to them at their respective organizations were unacceptable. They recognized the subtle or not so subtle messages being sent about what opportunities would be open to them in the future. They acknowledged their lack of satisfaction and discomfort to themselves.

The third similarity is found in their senses of themselves. Healthy self-concepts and self-confidence made this awareness possible as did the support of their wives. All are men who are inclined toward introspection and struggle continually to gain clarity about themselves, their values, and their priorities, and what would lead to career satisfaction. They were willing to abandon the "known" and venture into the "uncertain."

In summary, all three men assumed financial risks, in spite of their personal financial responsibilities, with an eye toward long-term benefits and gains. The enabling factors for them were their healthy self-concepts and confidence in themselves, their personal psychological support systems, and their knowledge and understanding of their organizational and career circumstances.

CELL 3 – "I NEED A CHANGE"

For the plateaued, burned-out, dissatisfied, would-be job or career changer, the absence of an opportunity to bail out of a company with assistance is a disappointment. Not all employees are as risk-oriented or determined as Nick, Jerry, and Mike. Chuck is a good example of an employee who feels frustrated and believes that at his company the "those who leave get a better deal than those who stay."

Chuck

"If I had a six-month package, I'd walk," Chuck told me during our interview. The recent reorganization at his company left him demoted out of a branch manager job, which he had begun only a year ago after transferring from a city 2000 miles away. Chuck has worked for this electronics company for four years, the first three years of which he was a highly successful salesman. With an undergraduate degree in engineering, an M.B.A., and an excellent track record in high-technology sales, Chuck is the quintessential young man on the move.

The difficulties the company is having have slowed his rapid ascent, however, and caused hardship for him and his family. Much of the hardship has stemmed from several, recent corporate relocations. When he accepted the branch manager job, he and his wife had just unpacked the last of their boxes in a new custom-built home. His wife and children remained behind to finish out the school year while Chuck went on to the new job in the new city. Six months later they were a family again, and Chuck contracted to build another custom home. Two months later he learned that the reorganization would take place. He would have a job, albeit a demotion, but he would not be offered a severance package and the encouragement to take his career elsewhere. His last official act as branch manager was to terminate a dozen of his subordinates.

Chuck stated that he experienced a lot of stress associated with his concern for his people and his loyalty to them. He was disturbed by the minimal severance assistance provided. "I spent a lot of time working toward this management position. Maybe it's not all it's cracked up to be." He stated that he has less concern for himself and his own career. "I got derailed, but its temporary. I made transitions before; I can do it again."

His wife, however, has been angry and emotional for months. She would like for him to quit and move the family back to the former city.

While Chuck would not admit to having much concern for himself or his career at this point, he was willing to tell me that he has learned through this experience that he is not invincible. To counteract the stress he has been feeling, he exercises, immerses himself in a hobby, and spends a lot of time on the phone with his peers around the country. During these calls, "we're not talking about business." Obviously, what they are doing is commiserating with one another and providing psychological support to one another.

Chuck is aware that his career has veered off track and would have preferred his company enable him to leave. If after assessing the restructured organization Chuck cannot predict career growth for himself, staying will most likely spell further derailment. My prediction, however, is that once he re-stabilizes he will begin looking for opportunities outside the company.

CELL 4 – "SURVIVORS"

Increasing attention is being paid to the "survivors" of corporate reorganizations as management acknowledges the trauma experienced by those who do not lose their jobs. Some of the more typical reactions of this group are a continuing high level of anxiety, a sense of loss and guilt, anger toward management and others, depression, and loss of commitment. Practically speaking, "survivors" often find themselves doing more work with fewer resources. They wonder why they continue to work hard. They have concerns about losing their jobs in the future and being disadvantaged because they would be entering the job market later than their predecessors. They question whether their companies will provide equal severance benefits to those previously given if they are released. In this author's experience this is not an unwarranted concern, having been a consultant to companies which gave less generous benefits to later groups of terminees. This typically is the result of budget restrictions, not a lack of concern for employees.

It is not complete consolation, obviously, merely to have a job when all the dust settles after a reorganization. Nancy and Judy both survived major downsizing as a result of reorganizations. In their interviews they evidenced perceptiveness about their responses and those of fellow workers to organizational upheaval.

Nancy

Nancy has a master's degree in social work, but left the field to pursue a higher-paying career. Her interpersonal skills quickly led her to a job in human resources where she has worked for the last ten years. For the last five of these she has worked for a major state bank. During the preceding year the bank was forced to reduce its work force by 50% due to sharply declining profits. All levels, from clerk to senior management were affected.

Initially the reaction of the employees was shock about the true financial condition of the bank. One year and no raises later, those who have opportunities are leaving; those who cannot leave are bitter and resentful. Management, in an attempt to be more communicative, has apologized in employee meetings for withholding such important information in the past. However, the apologies and frequent communications about current performance seem to be falling on deaf ears and in Nancy's own words: "Management is viewed as able to do nothing right."

As a human resources professional Nancy is sensitive to the reactions of employees to company developments and is in touch with a large number of them. She has observed the demoralization, alienation, and hostility of the remaining work force. However, as far as the effect on Nancy herself, she states that it has been tempered by past experience and her present domestic situation. She claims that having lost one job through a layoff enabled her to "step back and look at the (the present) situation analytically." "We had no choice" even though "it could have been handled better."

The previous layoff from an oil shale company was more traumatic for Nancy—in her own words it was devastating. She witnessed highly specialized, technical employees become "unemployable" overnight. She also witnessed the striking disintegration of employees' behavior on and off the job after the layoff announcement was made.

Two events in particular are part of her painful memories. One year after the layoff her boss committed suicide. At about that same time she boarded a city bus and saw that the driver was a former high level manager.

Nancy was fortunate to find her next job (the one she holds currently) very quickly. Within a year of beginning the new job she had a baby and was able to change her work schedule from full-time to part-time. Having a husband with a professional job made this possible. Nancy finds her schedule ideally suited to her own and the family's needs. Even though a new structure in the Human Resources area left her with a narrower function, resulting in a less satisfying role to play, Nancy does not complain. In her own words, "working three days a week is worth so much to me that I could put up with anything."

Judy

Like Nancy, Judy has had a unique vantage point from which to experience a corporate reorganization. As corporate counsel for a Fortune 500 company, she gained tremendous legal experience during a debt restructuring which followed a period of very high profits.

Judy began her career as a paralegal and worked for a number of years for the city's most prestigious firm. She attended law school in the evenings and following graduation was hired by her firm — an uncommon occurrence. Then for two years she worked the typical long hours of the associate in a prestigious firm, but had little close client contact. It added up to a lack of job satisfaction so she turned to corporate practice as a reasonable, alternative career track. She was quickly recruited by one of her client companies.

Seven years ago when Judy joined the company it was enjoying a period of profitability and great national prestige. She thrived on her involvement in the business and the close working relationships with senior management. Within two years of her arrival, however, the company began making mistakes — capital improvements during a steeply inflationary cycle. Several years later the company had huge debts.

In 1986 the company prepared for bankruptcy, providing Judy with challenging and exciting work. She personally felt in no jeopardy due to the key role she was playing in keeping the business going. Then the cost-cutting and reduction-in-force began. The company continued in its well-entrenched paternalistic style and awarded generous severance packages to those who lost jobs. Judy was aware of the need to rid the company of excess fat, "but it was awful to watch the trauma." As time went on, the company's financial situation became even more desperate. Ironically, the more severe the crisis, the more interesting and professionally challenging her job became. Judy was in a very strange position through this period. She had intimate knowledge of the company's worsening condition, but continued to have no fear for her own job security.

The cuts continued until 1986. By this time people with essential skills had also been released. Then, after a foreign company bought a controlling interest, all of senior management was fired. Gone were the paternalism and generous severance packages. The new management group regarded employees from the old organization as part of the problem. A "we/they" culture developed.

Judy began questioning her decision five years previously to join the company. Her friends at the law firm were doing well and moving into partnerships. She was way behind them financially and believed that her professional stature was not being enhanced by her current employment. Then, as the local economy worsened, Judy finally began to get nervous about job security. After two anxious years of holding on, Judy eventually started to relax and quit looking over her shoulder. Nonetheless, she was resentful of the new management's attitude toward the old employees. She also reflected with sadness about the physical and mental breakdowns, sudden deaths, and alcohol abuse among the group of plant managers who had been asked to do the impossible, then terminated.

At the time of our interview, Judy summarized the company's financial condition by saying that the debt had been restructured but the company still was not profitable. "Now they would love to get rid of the lawyers" were her concluding words during our interview.

As a postscript, the company did eliminate Judy's position after our discussion. The "ax" finally fell, giving her the opportunity to seek another corporate position.

Nancy and Judy both "survived" corporate reorganizations in that they both retained their jobs after a downsizing. To say that either of them received any assistance from their respective organizations would be inaccurate, however. There was a notable absence of transition management in both instances. The process of transition management involves the creation of temporary policies and procedures, the promotion of cohesion within the organization and within work units, the continuing acknowledgement of old issues and losses that resulted from the changes, reminding people of the reasons for the change and focusing them toward a positive future, creating new communication channels and using them, protecting employees from any unnecessary changes, and monitoring the change process (Bridges, 1988). By addressing, rather than ignoring the issues people have amidst the chaos of organizational change, management should be better positioned to achieve its number one goal – productivity. Ignoring the issues can easily lead to a protracted period of confusion, demoralization, and anxiety and a lack of focus and productivity.

CONCLUSIONS

Much of the stress people experience is related to their work – either the lack of it, the fear of losing it, the demands of the work itself, or the peculiarities of the work environment. Because this is not likely to change in the foreseeable future, an important component of stress management is career management.

Career management may be defined as the assumption of responsibility by an individual for selecting a career direction, monitoring progress toward defined goals, and identifying and acquiring skills needed in the future to insure marketability. It encompasses the notion of individual initiative and proactive behavior, rather than the expectation that an organization will provide a defined career path.

What twentieth-century Americans have come to expect as a birthright, i.e., a job, is, in fact, a "social artifact" (Bridges, 1988). Jobs as we know them are the result of the industrial revolution. Prior to that people earned a living by raising crops and livestock, or independently producing goods that could be traded. Those who performed tasks for others were typically paid for tasks, not guaranteed full employment.

Bridges points out that the present is not the first time in history when large numbers of workers were displaced. At the end of the crusades unattached soldiers who were trying to find an outlet for their skills and experiences were known as "free lancers."

This idea of contracting to perform specific tasks is highly relevant in today's marketplace. Contractual employment is far more prevalent today than it was in the past. By adopting the mental set that certain skills are required to execute specific tasks and that someone else is willing to pay to have these tasks performed, one maintains a "free lance" attitude. This attitude is a core component of an overall career strategy and is a primary prevention technique in managing career stress.

Unfortunately, many of us have been lulled into complacency after years of working for an organization. We begin to feel that the organization owes us our salaries, our titles, our benefits, and a secure future. We are genuinely hurt, surprised, and terrified when told by the organization that our services are no longer required. Sarah, Bill, and Sam faced the stress of major career crisis. All of them had received signals that their employment was in jeopardy. It was too late for primary prevention.

Once the trauma of separation from employment has occurred, as it did to several of the executives discussed earlier in this chapter, managing the stress is a major challenge. Losing control of one's career through an involuntary separation is particularly devastating. However, most of the six individuals in the case studies who changed jobs developed effective means of coping. Some of the tools they used were introspection, discussion with and formal assessment by professionals to gain insight about themselves, structured approaches in making career changes and looking for a job, reliance on family members and close friends for psychological support, and activities such as exercise or immersion in a hobby.

Of the executives interviewed, the most successful in managing their careers have certain shared characteristics and behaviors. They all demonstrated flexibility in response to changing circumstances; they all had a high level of awareness of themselves and the marketplace; they constantly sought out information about themselves and trends in business and employment; and finally, they were not afraid to venture beyond their existing boundaries.

REFERENCES

Bridges, W. (1988). *Surviving corporate transition*. New York: Doubleday.

DeFrank, R. S., & Ivancevich, J. M. (1985). *Job loss effects: An individual level model and review*. Unpublished manuscript.

Kasl, S. V., Grove, S., & Cobb, S. (1975). The experience of losing a job: Reported changes in health, symptoms and illness behavior. *Psychosomatic Medicine, 37*, 106-122.

Leana, C. R., & Ivancevich, J. M. (1985). *Job loss effects: An individual level model and review*. Unpublished manuscript.

The Middle Years:
Career Stage Differences

Joseph J. Hurrell, Jr.

National Institute for Occupational Safety and Health

Margaret Anne McLaney

National Council Research Association

Lawrence R. Murphy

National Institute for Occupational Safety and Health

SUMMARY. This paper examines career stages from an occupational stress perspective. Specifically, relationships among job demands, career stages, and health-related strains are analyzed in a sample of over 6,000 United States Postal Workers. Results from these analyses suggest that for individuals in the middle stage of their careers, job stressors lose some of their potency in affecting physical health status while stressful events outside of the job domain become increasingly deleterious. Moreover, the beneficial effects of social support on mental health were found to vary by career stage, being most pronounced among middle career workers. Findings from the study emphasize the necessity for stress researchers to consider career stress effects.

Over the past decade, there has been a growing interest among industrial and organizational researchers in individual career stages and their relationships to work behaviors and attitudes (Gould, 1979; Gould & Hawkins, 1978; Rabinowitz & Hall, 1981; Slocum

Reprints may be obtained from Joseph J. Hurrell, Jr., Motivation and Stress Research Section, Division of Biomedical and Behavioral Science, NIOSH, 4676 Columbia Parkway, Cincinnati, OH 45226.

179

& Cron, 1985; Stumpf & Rabinowitz, 1981). While empirical investigations in this area are currently lacking in specificity and hampered by methodological problems, there is reason to believe that distinct career stages exist and that values, needs, and expectations of employees change as they go through them (Hall & Mansfield, 1975; Rhodes, 1983). Moreover, there is increasing evidence that relationships between perceived job conditions and such organizationally valued outcomes as job satisfaction (Gould, 1979) and job involvement (Rabinowitz & Hall, 1981) vary with career stage.

Despite the implications of these findings for occupational stress research, no attempts (with the exception of those in this volume) have been made to systematically examine relationships between job demands and health-related (strain) outcomes within career stages. Rather, stress researchers have generally either ignored age (and by consequence career stage) in their study designs or treated age as a confounding factor and controlled for its effects in examining relationships between job demands and health. This paper represents an attempt to consider career stages from an occupational stress perspective in which health-related outcomes are of primary concern.

Career Stages

Career stages have been viewed as a sequence of positions occupied by a person during his or her lifetime (Super, 1957), as a decision tree portraying decision points at various times (Flannigan & Cooley, 1966) and, perhaps most commonly, as a series of stages in which various career concerns (Super, 1957), values, and needs (Hall & Nougaim, 1968; Miller & Form, 1951) are associated with each stage. Unfortunately, there is little agreement in the field concerning the specific measurement of career stage. In general, career stage researchers, beginning with Super (1957), have tended to divide a person's working life (generally ages 20-65) into three phases. While the specific titles and age-related descriptions of these phases vary, they are most often described using the terms "early career," "mid-career," and "late career."

In this paper, the effects of job stress on health-related outcomes are modeled separately for individuals in early, mid, and late stages of their careers. The resulting models are then contrasted. Special emphasis is placed on examining the mid-career stage. During this stage, people have usually chosen an occupation and have made serious attempts to reach personal goals (Super, 1980). Yet, mid-career is a time for reexamination of personal values and needs during which conflicts regarding the meaning of life, work, and family occur and require resolution (Hall, 1976).

METHOD

Subjects and Procedures

Data used in the present analysis were collected as part of a comprehensive investigation of job stress among a group of workers subject to machine-paced work conditions. Questionnaires designed to examine perceived stressors and to characterize health status were mailed to 6591 postal workers engaged in machine-paced Multiple Position Letter Sorting Machine operations (termed MPLSM operators) and 5722 other postal workers (drawn from five different non-machine-paced jobs) at 48 US Postal Service facilities. The 48 survey sites (16 per cent of the 300 MPLSM facilities in the continental United States) were chosen using multi-stage stratified random sampling (see Hurrell, 1985). At each survey site, 50 percent of the MPLSM operators and a nearly equal number of non-paced workers were randomly chosen from employment rosters. Each selected participant was sent a questionnaire for anonymous completion, along with a pre-addressed, postage-paid, return envelope. A follow-up mailing was made to selected participants approximately six weeks after the initial mailing. All participants were mailed one dollar as a token payment.

These procedures resulted in completed returns from 3263 MPLSM operators and 3160 non-paced postal workers, representing response rates of 50 and 55 percent respectively. As the survey was anonymous, follow-up mailings to individual non-respondents to assess the potential for bias in the data could not be conducted. Several factors, however, suggest that the data are free of large scale systematic bias. First, the response rates for paced and non-paced workers were similar, suggesting an absence of major bias related to the type of work performed; secondly, large differences in response rates between the various survey sites were not found, indicating the absence of systematic regional bias.

MEASURES

The effects of four types of variables (demographic characteristics, stressful life events, work stressors, and social support) on four different health-related outcomes were examined in respondents from three career stages.

Career Stage

The sample was divided into three age groups corresponding to the Early (ages 21-34), Mid (ages 35-50), and Late (ages 51 and above) career stages. These career stages have been previously used by Hall and his colleagues in examining changing career experiences in professional engineers and scientists (Hall & Mansfield, 1975) and in blue collar transportation workers (Rabinowitz & Hall, 1981).

Demographic Characteristics

Age, gender, level of education, marital status, job tenure, and job type were included in the analyses. Two levels of marital status were used—married and not married, the latter including both single and divorced respondents. Job type encompassed two categories—machine-paced and non-machine-paced workers. The number of years in the current job at the Postal Service was used to determine job tenure.

Stressful Life Events

The Social Readjustment Rating Scale (SRRS: Holmes & Rahe, 1967) was used to assess sources of stress not associated with job task requirements. The 43 items of this checklist are intended to represent fairly common situations arising from family, personal, and financial events that require or signify change in ongoing adjustment.

Work Stressors

Multi-item rating scales assessing five different job stressors — cognitive demands, organizational satisfaction, work pressure, pay equity, and skill underutilization — were used in the current investigation. These scales were factor analytically derived from items from Quinn and Shepard (1974), Caplan, Cobb, French, Harrison, and Pinneau (1975), and House and Wells (1978). Scale scores for each of the stressors were computed by summing the responses to the items on each scale, with a high score indicating more of the construct being measured. Scale descriptions and internal consistency reliability coefficients (alpha: Nunnally, 1967) are provided below.

Cognitive demands. This five-item scale (alpha = .71) assessed job-related concentration requirements, memory, and attentional demands of the job. Ratings were made on a four-point scale from (1) "strongly agree" to (4) "strongly disagree."

Organizational satisfaction. Satisfaction with supervisory relationships, work evaluation methods, performance feedback, and promotions was measured using an eight-item index (alpha = .83). Ratings were made on the four-point, "agree – disagree," scale described above.

Work pressure. This ten-item scale (alpha = .79) measures feelings of excessive workload, time urgency, ability to meet job demands, and control of job activity. Ratings were made on a four-point "agree – disagree" scale.

Pay equity. Four items (alpha = .78) were used to gauge feelings concerning adequacy and fairness of pay in comparison to the work performed. Ratings were made on a five-point scale ranging from (1) "very much less than I ought to get" to (5) "more than I ought to get."

Skill underutilization. Perceptions of challenge, and use of skills and training, were assessed using seven items (alpha = .84). Respondents were asked to rate how often their jobs involved these elements on a six-point scale ranging from (1) "never" to (6) "very often."

Social Support

Three, four-item scales from Caplan et al. (1975) were included to evaluate potential differences in social support from supervisors, co-workers, and family/friends. Alpha coefficients for these scales were .87, .76, and .85 respectively.

Outcome Measures

Four outcome measures were used, two of which tapped affective reactions (job satisfaction and mood state) and two of which assessed physical status (perceived ill health and somatic complaints). These measures are described below.

Job satisfaction. A four-item scale developed by Caplan et al. (1975) was used to measure content-free job satisfaction (i.e., satisfaction irrespective of job content). The alpha coefficient for this scale was .85.

Mood disturbance. Psychological strain was assessed using the Profile of Mood States (McNair, Lorr, & Droppleman, 1971). This instrument measures six mood or affective states and yields a Total Mood Disturbance (TMD) score.

Perceived ill health. Perception of general health was measured by a single item scale that rated overall health from poor to excellent, with a high score indicating poorer health. This item has been widely used in other survey research and has been shown to be highly correlated with morbidity and mortality (see Goldstein, Siegel, & Boyer, 1984).

Somatic complaints. Frequency of occurrence of fifty-two somatic symptoms relating to respiratory, nervous system, gastrointestinal, musculoskeletal, circulatory, and visual functions was assessed by an index constructed for this study. Respondents were asked to indicate how frequently they experienced each symptom on a four-point scale ranging from (1) "never" to (4) "constantly.'' An overall index was computed by summing responses to each item.

ANALYSES

Hierarchical multiple regression analyses were conducted separately at each career stage to determine the proportion of variance in each of the four outcome variables attributable to demographic characteristics, stressful life events, work stressors, and social support. Predictors were entered into the regression equation for each dependent variable as sets (Cohen & Cohen, 1975). The set of demographic characteristics (six variables) was entered into the regression equation first and the resulting R^2 was computed. The stressful life events total (LET: one variable) was added in the second step to determine the increment in R^2. Work stressors (five variables) were entered in the third step and the set of social support variables (three variables) in the fourth step, with the increment in R^2 computed at each step. Thus, at the end of the fourth step the proportion of variance accounted for in each of the dependent variables was based on all fifteen predictors. The step immediately prior to that at which the increment in R^2 became non-significant ($p > .05$) was chosen as the most appropriate model for each dependent variable. The final models include all the variables entered into the regression equations up to and including that step. However, to facilitate interpretation, only those variables with significant ($p < .05$) beta weights will be discussed in the text and presented in the figures (betas significant at $p < .01$ are acknowledged in the text). The demographic characteristics and life events score were entered in the first two steps to control for their effects. The social support variables were entered last since social support has been found to have moderating effects on mental and physical health (cf. Ganster & Victor, 1988).

A test for multicollinearity among the 15 independent variables was included in the regression analyses for each career stage (Belsley, Kuh, & Welch, 1980). The results of these tests indicated that there were no collinearity problems among the independent vari-·ables for any of the three career stages.

RESULTS

Career Stage Differences

Means and standard deviations of all variables used in the analyses are presented in Table 1 for each of the three career stages. Percentages for categorical variables are also included.

As can be seen from Table 1, at least 60 percent of the workers in each stage were men and at least 57 percent of the workers in each stage were married. A greater number of machine-paced workers than non-machine-paced workers were in the Early Career group while this relationship was reversed for the Mid- and Late Career groups. Individuals in the Early Career group had significantly more education, higher stressful life events scores, higher under-utilization scores, and higher mood disturbance scores than those individuals who were in the Mid-Career and Late Career groups. Early Career workers also had higher scores for social support from spouse and family than the Mid-Career group, but did not differ from individuals in the Late Career group.

Individuals in the Late Career group were in their current jobs longer, had significantly higher cognitive demand scores, more social support from supervisors and co-workers, and had higher organizational satisfaction and overall job satisfaction scores than the other two groups. Late Career workers rated their pay as more equitable than individuals in the Mid-Career group, but they did not differ from the Early Career group. Late Career workers also had higher self-reported poor health scores; however, they reported fewer somatic complaints than the other two groups. Work pressure was the only variable for which individuals in the Mid-Career group had higher scores than their Early and Late Career co-workers. Lastly, with the exception of work pressure, the relationships between career stages and the stressor and outcome variables appear to be linear, indicating that multiple regression analyses are an appropriate analysis strategy.

Correlations among demographic characteristics, life events, work stressor, social support, and outcome variables for each of the three career groups are shown in Table 2, while Table 3 presents correlations among the outcome variables for each age group. As can be seen from Table 2, correlations among the stressor variables, with the exception of organizational satisfaction, were relatively small, as were correlations among the social support variables. The outcome variables, as shown in Table 3, were moderately intercorrelated; however, the interrelationships were relatively stable across the three career stages.

Regression Analyses

The results of the regression analyses at each step for the four outcome variables are presented in Table 4.

Job satisfaction. As shown in Table 4, the final prediction equations for job satisfaction for each of the three career stage groups contained demographic variables, LET score, and stressor variables. Figure 1 displays standardized beta coefficients for the significant ($p < .05$) predictors from the final equations.

As shown in Figure 1, three demographic variables predicted job satisfaction for the Early Career group. Here, older workers ($p < .01$), less educated workers ($p < .05$), and MPLSM operators ($p < .01$) tended to be more satisfied with their jobs. Women ($p < .05$) were more satisfied with their jobs in the Late Career stage. As indicated above, LET was significantly ($p < .01$) associated with job satisfaction for the Early and Mid-Career groups. For both groups, having lower LET scores was associated with greater satisfaction.

Underutilization, as shown in Figure 1, was the single best predictor ($p < .01$) of job satisfaction for all three groups, and most potent for those in Mid-Career. In all groups, less underutilization (i.e., better utilization) was associated with greater satisfaction. Organizational satisfaction was the second best predictor ($p < .01$) of satisfaction for all three groups. It was, however, slightly less predictive for those in the Mid-Career group.

Like underutilization and organizational satisfaction, work pressure was associated ($p < .01$) with job satisfaction for all three groups, with less pressure being associated with greater satisfaction. The effects of work pressure, however, tended to decrease as workers progress from the Early to Late Career stages. Lastly, pay

TABLE 1. Means and standard deviations for demographic characteristics[a], life events, work stressors, social support, and outcome variables.

	Early N=2782	Middle N=2086	Late N=1117	F	Group Comparisons[b]
	%	%	%		
men	60.5	66.3	75.3		
women	39.5	33.7	24.7		
MPLSM	74.1	46.8	20.5		
NMPLSM	25.9	53.2	79.5		
married	57.1	71.8	76.7		
not married	42.9	28.2	23.3		
	X(sd)	X(sd)	X(sd)		
age	28.72(3.32)	42.22(4.71)	56.51(4.12)	20492.81**	L > M > E
education	6.77(1.51)	6.34(1.52)	6.03(1.63)	106.99***	E > M > L
job tenure	4.01(2.83)	7.22(5.08)	11.75(7.92)	963.39***	L > M > E
life events	196.01(129.48)	146.86(111.45)	112.91(95.31)	196.53***	E > M > L
skill underutil.	30.58(7.96)	25.93(8.83)	23.52(8.70)	320.69***	E > M > L
work pressure	26.28(5.86)	27.84(6.20)	26.03(5.91)	118.16***	M > E > L
cog. demands	14.12(3.44)	15.43(3.34)	15.74(3.38)	131.42**	L > M > E

pay equity	13.71(3.27)	13.53(3.38)	13.82(3.29)	3.22*	L > M
organiz. satis.	15.85(5.29)	15.87(5.40)	16.63(5.92)	8.76**	L > E,M
superv. supp.	8.81(3.53)	9.35(3.68)	10.16(3.63)	54.47***	L > M > E
home supp.	13.42(2.96)	13.12(3.37)	13.15(3.37)	5.66**	E > M
coworker supp.	10.50(2.71)	10.83(2.70)	11.33(2.71)	36.07***	L > M > E
ill-health	1.74(.65)	1.86(.65)	2.03(.68)	76.43***	L > M > E
som. complaints	70.13(10.98)	69.33(11.34)	67.74(12.12)	17.73***	E,M > L
mood disturb.	26.60(33.97)	17.01(31.80)	10.27(29.31)	99.98***	E > M > L
job satis.	8.82(2.37)	9.74(2.30)	10.33(2.24)	191.48***	L > M > E

* $p < .05$; ** $p < .01$

ᵃ Men = 0, women = 1; NMPLSM = 0, MPLSM = 1; not married = 0, married = 1.

ᵇ E = early, M = middle, L = late.

TABLE 2. Correlations among demographic characteristics, life events, work stressors, social support, and outcome variables for all age groups.

	1	2	3	4	5	6	7	8	9	10	11	12	13	14	15	16	17
1. Gender		-.15*	-.13*	-.07*	.14*	.11*	.14*	.02	.16*	.01	-.08*	0	-.11*	.12*	.22*	.11*	-.07*
2. Age			-.18*	.52*	-.30*	-.33*	-.20*	-.21	-.01	.05*	.15*	-.04*	.11*	.16*	-.09	-.22*	.26*
3. Education				-.17*	.09*	.13*	.03	-.11*	-.14*	-.04*	-.03*	.02	-.01	.11	-.02	.04*	-.14*
4. Job Tenure					-.19	.12*	-.13*	.08*	.04*	-.03	.04*	-.03*	.05*	.14*	.06*	-.12*	.10*
5. Life Events						.08*	.09*	.05*	-.07*	.08*	-.11*	-.04*	-.05*	.06*	.26*	.29*	-.14*
6. Skill Underutilization							.43*	-.31*	-.00	-.48*	-.40*	-.06*	-.20*	.03	.22*	.30*	-.69*
7. Work Pressure								.26*	-.05*	-.24*	-.28*	.00	-.18*	.07*	.27*	.25*	-.41*
8. Cognitive Demands									-.05*	.17*	.11	.05*	.00	.06*	.02	-.12*	.20*
9. Pay Equity										.16*	.08	.01	.05*	.04*	-.03	.05*	.11*
10. Organizational Satisfaction											.65*	.05*	.15*	.05*	-.14*	-.18*	.48*
11. Supervisory Support												.11*	.25*	.05*	-.15*	-.19*	.39*
12. Home Support													.24	-.08*	-.05*	-.17*	.04*
13. Co-worker Support														-.07*	-.10*	-.15*	.16*
14. Perceived Ill Health															.34*	.22*	-.09*
15. Somatic Complaints																.45*	-.25*
16. Mood Disturbances																	-.35*
17. Job Satisfaction																	---

*p<.01

TABLE 3. Correlations among outcome variables for each age group*

	1	2	3
EARLY			
(21-34)			
1. Job Satis.			
2. Mood Disturb.	-.29		
3. Ill Health	-.13	.26	
4. Somatic Compl.	-.27	.43	.38
MIDDLE			
(35-50)			
1. Job Satis.			
2. Mood Disturb.	-.33		
3. Ill Health	-.13	.27	
4. Somatic Compl.	-.25	.46	.37
LATE			
(>50)			
1. Job Satis.			
2. Mood Disturb.	-.37		
3. Ill Health	-.14	.26	
4. Somatic Compl.	-.14	.45	.29

*All correlation coefficients are significant at $p < .01$.

equity was a predictor ($p < .01$) of satisfaction for all three groups, and was slightly more predictive for those in the Late Career stage. In summary, underutilization and life events were better predictors and organizational satisfaction a poorer predictor of job satisfaction for the Mid-Career group.

Mood disturbance. The final prediction equations for the Early and Mid-Career groups contained demographic variables, LET score, stressor variables, and social support variables, while the equation for the Late Career group contained only the first three sets of variables (see Table 4).

As shown in Figure 2, a number of demographic variables predicted mood disturbance for both the Early and Late Career stage

TABLE 4. Hierarchical multiple regression analyses for all outcome variables.

		Early		Middle		Late	
		R^2	$\angle R^2$	R^2	ΔR^2	R^2	ΔR^2
Job Satisfaction							
Step #1	Demographics	.05		.06		.02	
#2	Life Events	.05	0	.07	.01*	.02	0
#3	Stressors	.49	.44**	.51	.44**	.47	.45**
#4	Social Support	.49	0	.51	0	.47	0
Mood Disturbance							
Step #1	Demographics	.02		.02		.02	
#2	Life Events	.08	.06**	.08	.06**	.05	.03*
#3	Stressors	.17	.09**	.16	.08**	.13	.08**
#4	Social Support	.20	.03*	.20	.04**	.14	.01
Perceived Ill-Health							
Step #1	Demographics	.04		.04		.004	
#2	Life Events	.06	.02**	.06	.02**	.01	.006**
#3	Stressors	.07	.01**	.06	0	.04	.03**
#4	Social Support	.07	0	.06	0	.04	0
Somatic Complaints							
Step #1	Demographics	.07		.07		.03	
#2	Life Events	.13	.06**	.14	.07**	.05	.02*
#3	Stressors	.20	.07**	.20	.06**	.08	.03*
#4	Social Support	.20	0	.20	0	.08	0

* $p < .05$
** $p < .01$

groups. No demographic variables were predictive for the Mid-Career group. For the Early group, being female in an MPLSM job and having relatively more tenure in the job were associated with less mood disturbance. For the Late group, being older, married, and in an MPLSM job were associated with less mood disturbance.

The stressful life events measure was a significant ($p < .01$) predictor of mood disturbance for all three groups and was the single best predictor of mood disturbance for both the Early and Mid-Career groups. Its ability to predict, however, decreases with ad-

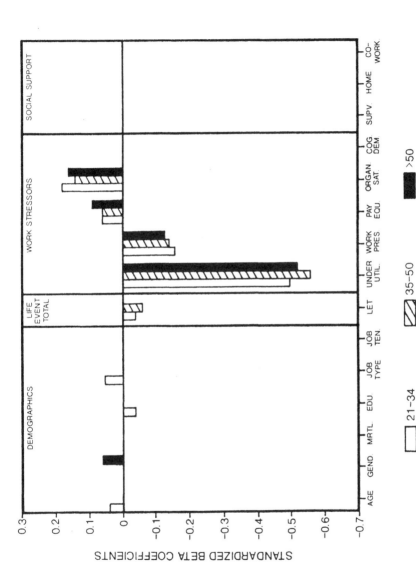

FIGURE 1. Significant ($p < .05$) standardized beta coefficients from final regression models predicting job satisfaction for each career stage group.

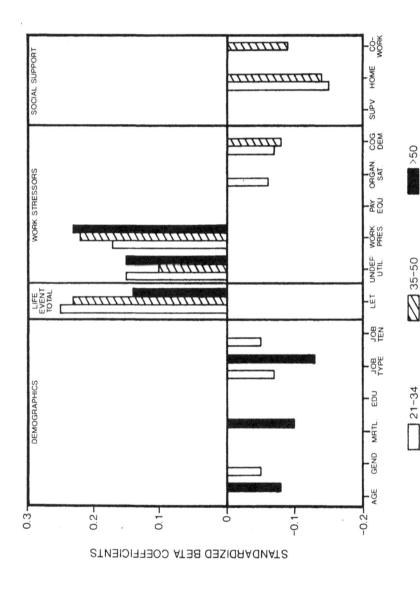

FIGURE 2. Significant ($p < .05$) standardized beta coefficients from final regression models predicting mood disturbance for each career stage group.

vancement through career stages. Of the work stressor variables, work pressure was the most potent predictor of mood disturbance for all three groups. As shown in Figure 2, the effects of work pressure appear to increase as workers move from the Early to Late stages of their careers. Indeed, work pressure was the single best predictor of disturbance for those in the Late Career stage. Like work pressure, underutilization was a significant ($p < .01$) predictor for all three groups and was equally potent for those in the Early and Late groups, but less potent for those in the Mid-Career group. Cognitive demands was a predictor for the Early and Mid-Career groups, with greater perceived demands being associated with less mood disturbance. Lastly, greater organizational satisfaction was associated with less mood disturbance in the Early Career group.

As indicated above, social support variables were predictors of mood disturbance for those in the Early and Mid-Career groups. As shown in Figure 2, social support from home (family and friends) and from co-workers were significant ($p < .01$) predictors for the Mid-Career group, while home support was a predictor for those in the Early stage. In all cases, having increased support was associated with decreased mood disturbance.

In summary, underutilization and demographic variables were poorer predictors and social support from co-workers a better predictor of mood disturbance for Mid-career workers.

Perceived ill health. The final models predicting perceived ill health for the Early and Late Career groups contained the demographic variables, the LET index, and stressor variables, while the final model for the Mid-Career group contained only the demographic variables and LET index (see Table 4).

Age was positively ($p < .01$) related to perceived ill health for the Mid-Career group and was the best predictor in the set of demographic variables for this group (see Figure 3). Gender ($p < .01$), education ($p < .01$), and job tenure ($p < .05$) were significant predictors for both the Mid-Career and the Early Career groups. Poorer health was reported by women in both career stages, less educated Mid-Career employees, and more educated Early Career employees. Poorer health was also reported by individuals in the Early and Late Career stages who have been on the job longer. Job type was related to poor health only for those in the Late Career stage, with MPLSM operators reporting better health than their

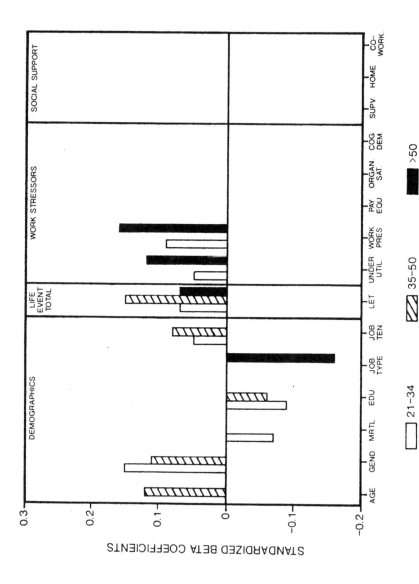

FIGURE 3. Significant ($p < .05$) standardized beta coefficients from final regression models predicting perceived ill health for each career stage group.

non-MPLSM co-workers. As only 21 percent of the workers in the Late stage were MPLSM co-workers, this relationship may reflect a survival/natural selection effect, with workers who continue in MPLSM jobs representing those who have learned to adapt to the demands. Lastly, marital status was a significant predictor only for those in the Early Career stage, with single employees reporting better health.

LET (as shown in Figure 3) was a significant ($p < .05$) predictor in models for each age group; however, it was substantially more predictive of perceived ill health for the Mid-Career group. Indeed, of all variables in the equation, LET is the single best predictor for the Mid-Career group.

Figure 3 indicates that work pressure followed by underutilization of skills were the job stressors most predictive of poor health for the Early and Late Career Groups. As indicted above, no job stressors were found to be predictive for the Mid-Career Group.

In summary, demographics and life events were better predictors while work stressors did not predict perceived ill health among Mid-Career workers.

Somatic complaints. The final prediction equations for the three Career groups contained the demographic variables, the LET score, and the job stressor variables (see Table 4).

As can be seen in Figure 4, gender was a significant predictor of somatic complaints for all three career groups. Here, women reported more frequent complaints than their male co-workers, with gender being less predictive going from Early to Late Career. Age was a significant ($p < .01$) predictor of somatic complaints for both the Early and Mid-Career groups, with increasing age being associated with increasing complaints in each career group. As was the case with perceived ill health above, less educated workers in the Mid-Career stage reported more somatic complaints. Job type was a significant predictor for both the Mid- and Late Career groups. Here, Mid-Career MPLSM operators reported more complaints than their non-MPLSM co-workers, while Late Career MPLSM operators reported fewer complaints than their non-MPLSM counterparts.

Life events were highly associated with somatic complaints for all three groups. As seen in Figure 4, LET was the single best pre-

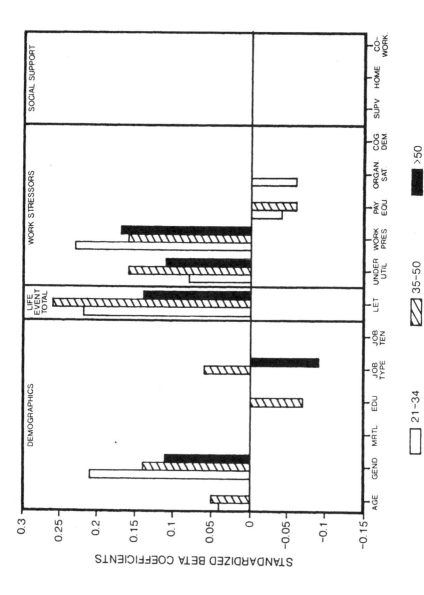

FIGURE 4. Significant ($p < .05$) standardized beta coefficients from final regression models predicting somatic complaints for each career stage group.

198

dictor of somatic complaints across all predictor categories for the Mid-Career group, and was a relatively better predictor for the Mid-Career group than for the Early or Later Career groups.

Both skill underutilization and work pressure were significant ($p < .01$) predictors of somatic complaints for all three groups, with underutilization being a relatively better predictor for the Mid-Career group than for the other two groups (see Figure 4). Work pressure was the best predictor of somatic complaints for the Early and Late Career group. Pay equity predicted ($p < .05$) somatic complaints for both the Early and Mid-Career groups, with perceptions of inequitable pay being associated with more complaints. Pay equity was a relatively better predictor for the Mid-Career group. Lastly, organizational satisfaction was a significant predictor for the Early group, with less satisfaction being associated with more complaints.

In summary, demographic, life events, and underutilization were better predictors and work pressure a relatively poorer predictor of somatic complaints for Mid-Career workers.

DISCUSSION

Previous vocational research has found that job characteristics are more strongly related to job satisfaction and job involvement in the early and late career stages, while individual difference variables operate more during the middle career years (e.g., Hall, 1976; Katz, 1976; Levinson, Darrow, Klein, Levinson, & McKee, 1978). More so than in early or late stages, workers in the middle career years tend to reexamine personal values, attempting to increase personal self-direction (Levinson et al., 1978). Super (1980) characterizes the middle years as a "stabilization period" when workers need less guidance from their supervisors and are more concerned with maintaining a certain lifestyle than building new skills and developing competencies at work. Increasingly, satisfaction and fulfillment are garnered from areas outside of work, due to (1) the routinization or lack of challenge of work that accompanies the proficiency workers gain during the early career stage, and (2) the need to resolve conflicts regarding the meaning of life, work, and family.

Although vocational studies have not examined physical and

mental health status as a function of career stage, the present results provide support for the above propositions. For those in the Mid-Career stage, job stressors seem to loose some of their potency in affecting physical health status. Indeed, none of the job stressor variables were found to be related to the perceived ill health measure in the Mid-Career group, while both work pressure and under-utilization were significant predictors for the Early and Late Career groups. Similarly, work pressure was found to be a better predictor of somatic complaints for both the Early and Late Career groups than the Mid-Career group. This result is not due to Mid-Career workers merely reporting less work pressure than the other groups. Indeed, workers in the Mid-Career group actually reported more work pressure than their Early and Late Career coworkers.

Underutilization of abilities does, however, affect Mid-Career workers and was more strongly related to both job satisfaction and somatic complaints among this group than among either the Early or Late Career groups. Findings with respect to job type are also interpretable in this context. That is, MPLSM work is machine-paced and was found to be correlated with perceptions of underutilization. For those in the Mid-Career group, MPLSM work was associated with increased somatic complaints, while for workers in the Early Career group, MPLSM work was associated with fewer somatic complaints.

Life events clearly have a greater impact on Mid-Career workers than their Early and Late Career counterparts. For the Mid-Career group, life events was a significant predictor of all four dependent measures and, of all the independent variables included in the analyses, was the best single predictor of all but the job satisfaction variable. With one exception, the Life Events score was a better predictor of each of the four dependent variables in the Mid-Career group than other career groups. (The life events score was a better predictor of mood disturbance for those in the Early Career stage.) Of particular relevance (as seen in Table 1) is the fact that Life Events scores decreased significantly ($p < .01$) from Early to Mid- to the Late Career stages. Indeed, nearly all 43 events composing the weighted index decreased monotonically from the Early to the Late Career stages. These findings clearly suggest that the events themselves are interpreted quite differently by Mid-Career individuals, such that they have a more potent effect on mental and physical health.

Recent literature has suggested that social support is related to mental and physical health status (e.g., LaRocco, House, & French, 1980). Most of the evidence indicates that health status is better among persons with higher levels of support than those with low support (e.g., Ganster & Victor, 1988). The present study found evidence of social support effects, but only on the mood disturbance measure and only for the Early and Mid-Career groups. Social support from one's spouse, family and friends (home support), and coworkers (coworker support) was associated with lower mood disturbance scores for the Mid-Career group. In the Early Career group, only support from spouse, family, and friends was associated with lower mood disturbance. Social support from one's supervisor was not significant for any career group, and no effect of social support was found for self-rated health, somatic complaints, or job satisfaction.

These results suggest that social support is more influential with respect to mental health than physical health, and that this influence varies with career stage and source of support. Previous social support research has not stratified data on the basis of age before assessing the influence of social support on health. The present results argue for such stratification.

Similarly, gender was found to be decreasingly important over career stage in predicting self-rated poor health and frequency of somatic complaints. That is, in the Early Career stage, women reported substantially poorer health and more somatic complaints than their male coworkers. In the Mid-Career stage, these differences were less pronounced, and in the Late Career stage even less pronounced. These results suggest that research focusing on gender differences in work stress/health relationships should control for stage of career development or should confine analyses to differences within specific stages.

Research investigating the link between psychosocial factors at work and worker mental and physical health (i.e., job stress research) has generally treated age as a nuisance variable that is either ignored or controlled statistically. The present results clearly suggest that this approach should be abandoned in that the relationship among psychosocial work factors and health status changes according to stage of career development. In particular, Mid-Career workers, in comparison to their younger and older coworkers, were found to be less affected by job-related sources of stress and more affected by sources of stress external to the work environment. Moreover, the salubrious effects of social support were found to vary with career stage. Thus, it appears that the inclusion of career stage as an independent variable in organizational stress research may enhance understanding of the complex relationships among job factors, individual differences, and worker health.

Finally, it bears mentioning that since this study was based on cross-sectional data, cohort explanations of the results are possible. Such explanations argue that particular socialization experiences occurring during the formative years of a cohort create distinctive shared values which remain stable over time. Longitudinal studies are needed to determine cohort vs. career stage effects. In the absence of longitudinal studies, however, the current results emphasize the necessity for stress researchers to consider career stage effects.

REFERENCES

Belsley, D. A., Kuh, E., & Welsch, R. E. (1980). *Regression diagnostics*. New York: John Wiley & Sons.

Caplan, R. D., Cobb, S., French, J. R. P., Harrison, R. V., & Pinneau, S. R. (1975). *Job demands and worker health*. DHHS (NIOSH) Publication No. 75-160. Washington, DC: U.S. Government Printing Office.

Cohen, J., & Cohen, P. (1975). *Applied multiple regression/correlation analysis for the behavioral sciences*. New Jersey: Lawrence Erlbaum & Associates.

Flanagan, J. C., & Cooley, W. W. (1966). *Project talent: One year follow-up studies*. Pittsburgh: School of Education, University of Pittsburgh.

Ganster, D. C., & Victor, B. (1988). The impact of social support on mental and physical health. *British Journal of Medical Psychology, 61*, 2-19.

Goldstein, M. S., Siegel, J. M., & Boyer, R. (1984). Predicting changes in perceived health status. *American Journal of Public Health, 74*, 611-613.

Gould, S. (1979). Age, job complexity, satisfaction, and performance. *Journal of Vocational Behavior, 14*, 209-223.

Gould, S., & Hawkins, B. L. (1978). Organizational career stage as a moderator of the satisfaction-performance relationship. *Academy of Management Journal, 21*, 434-450.

Hall, D. T. (1976). *Careers in organizations*. Santa Monica, CA: Goodyear.

Hall, D. T., & Mansfield, R. (1975). Relationships of age and seniority with career variables of engineers and scientists. *Journal of Applied Psychology*, *60*, 201-210.

Hall, D. T., & Naugaim, K. (1968). An examination of Maslow's need hierarchy in an organizational setting. *Organizational Behavior and Human Performance*, *3*, 12-35.

Holmes, T. H., & Rahe, R. H. (1967). The social readjustment rating scale. *Journal of Psychosomatic Research*, *11*, 213-218.

House, J. S., & Wells, J. A. (1978). Occupational stress, social support and health. In A. Mclean (Ed.), *Reducing occupational stress*. DHEW (NIOSH) Publication No. 78-140. Washington, DC: U.S. Government Printing Office.

Hurrell, J. J., Jr. (1985). Machine-paced work and the Type A behavior pattern. *Journal of Occupational Psychology*, *58*, 15-25.

Levinson, D. J. Darrow, C. N. Levinson, M. B., & McKee, B. (1978). *The seasons of a man's life*. New York: Knopf.

McNair, D. M., Lorr, M., & Droppleman, L.F. (1971). *Profile of Mood States (POMS)*. San Diego, CA: Educational Testing Service.

Nunnally, J. C. (1967). *Psychometric theory*. New York: McGraw Hill.

Quinn, R. P., & Shepard, L. J. (1974). *The 1972-1973 quality of employment survey*. Ann Arbor, MI: Survey Research Center.

Rabinowitz, S., & Hall, D. T. (1981). Changing correlates of job involvement in three career stages. *Journal of Vocational Behavior*, *18*, 138-144.

Rhodes, S. (1983). Age-related differences in work attitudes and behavior: A review and conceptual analysis. *Psychological Bulletin*, *93*, 328-367.

Slocum, J. W., & Cron, W. L. (1985). Job attitudes and performance during three career stages. *Journal of Vocational Behavior*, *26*, 126-145.

Stumpf, S. A., & Rabinowitz, S. (1981). Career stages as a moderator of performance relationships with facets of job satisfaction and role perceptions. *Journal of Vocational Behavior*, *18*, 202-218.

Super, D. E. (1980). A life-span, life-space approach to career development. *Journal of Vocational Behavior*, *16*, 282-298.

Super, D. E. (1957). *The psychology of careers*. New York: Harper & Row.

Mid-Career Transition

Jack Davis

St. Mary's University

Eduardo S. Rodela, Jr.

Department of Veterans Affairs

SUMMARY. The era of change is now the rule rather than the exception. Organizations are adapting to environmental demands such as an expanding international market, individual work techniques in manufacturing are being replaced by work group techniques because of increasing competition, and the individual himself/herself is experiencing changes in values through the maturation process as well. At mid-career these transitions pose difficult questions for the individual; he/she is concerned with maintaining work competency and managing change related stress. A strategy involving the continuous scanning of organizational, work and individual issues may assist the mid-careerist in answering these questions. Learning, understanding, predicting and acting, and controlling are the elements required in the process of problem-solving and decision-making for the individual as he manages his/her mid-career transition through this myriad of organizational, work, and individual change.

A conspicuous part of a major Southwest city's skyline is a 24 story office building, the headquarters of a Fortune 500 energy company. Inside are about a thousand employees, many of whom face crucial concerns about their careers right now, in a few months

---

This work was completed while Jack Davis was Manager of Employee Training & Development at Valero Energy Corporation.

Reprints may be obtained from Jack Davis, St. Mary's University, Alkek Building, School of Business Administration, 1 Camino, Santa Maria, San Antonio, TX 78228-8607.

or in a few years. At any one moment, in a number of offices or work areas, there are a large number of people, particularly those in their middle years of age and work, mentally wrestling with serious issues about their jobs and future. For example:

> Room 1530 — Harry N., 47, upper middle manager heading an important technical group; some college with extensive military training; 10 years with the company, the last 5 as group head. His thoughts at this moment as he views the city's panorama from his 15th floor window: "I have started the needed reorganization of the group. The group has to be more responsive to our customers. I know the boss approved the plan, but does it show him I'm executive material, that I'm strategically minded? Am I going to be a part of the top management team taking the company into the 21st century?"

> Room 605 — Ted F., 42, lower level manager, mechanical engineer; responsible for 30 field operational people; a hard working Vietnam veteran who loves the technical side of the job. As he sits behind his desk and a pile of paper, he is saying to himself, "What the hell am I doing pushing all this paper? I've never liked doing this pencil work and never will. I told the company I didn't want to be a manager. Why didn't I stay a senior engineer where I would be doing the things I really like to do?"

> Work area 31 — Martha E., 34, an accountant, 8 years with the company having had job assignments in finance, accounting and data processing areas. Her self-talk as she prepares a report on a new data processing procedures, "Does the company really appreciate what I have been doing in my job? I have worked my buns off for years, and what has it got me? My boss won't talk to me about what may be in store for me in the next couple of years. I'd like to be given a shot at supervising, but I doubt that will ever happen. I may have to leave the company to get ahead."

This kind of self-talk is very likely going on in almost every organization across the country. People, particularly those in the middle of their careers, are wondering and worrying about their professional futures. Many workers in the 30 to 50 year age bracket feel mired in a confusing mid-career malaise that creates inaction, indecision or uncertainty. What actually may be involved here is a multi-level series of forces which must be identified and understood by all those caught up in the pursuit of a career. It is the contention of the authors that the careerists, especially at or near the halfway mark of life, will face several serious transitions or changes and must react or adapt well to them in order to achieve a positive career continuance and avoid negative, destructive stresses. There are three principal transitional forces categories: (1) Changes in the organization, (2) changes in the ways jobs are structured and designed, and (3) changes in the individual's psycho-physiological make-up. Failure to grasp the full meaning of each of these three complex, interacting transitional dynamics may cause severe stress and counter productive consequences for the careerists. What follows is a description of (1) these three major mid-career transitional forces and (2) an approach to help a mid-careerist deal with the resultant demands for change.

MAJOR CAREER TRANSITIONAL FORCES

Transition for the Organization

The careerist is defined as a working person who is quite serious about examining the current job, doing well in it, and doing those things necessary to advance in the future. The careerist in mid-life today, however, very likely has a narrow self-view of the vocational world. Few probably have the inclination or take the time to see the powerful forces operating on the organization to change it. The authors believe such a restricted perspective must be enlarged to recognize the organization's past, its current transitioning and to some degree its future in order to effectively answer questions about one's career. It is as though the careerist must see with the eyes of the Chief Executive Officer (CEO) of the organization.

How does the CEO look at the organization today? What are the pressing concerns in the present environment for the CEO and the organization? In a word, it is "change." Peters (1986) goes to the extreme of calling it "chaos." Drucker (cited in Trotter, 1986) claims that the head of an organization can no longer set five year strategic plans, but must reexamine the fundamental direction of the organization constantly because of the rapidity and degree of change. The factors at work to create such an unstable environment for the organization are numerous. Both the CEO and careerist have to understand the impact of such factors as restructuring, internationalization, deregulation/regulation, competition, and productivity improvement.

Restructuring may be somewhat an outdated word in the vocabulary of the CEO replaced by another term such as merging or demerging, streamlining, downsizing, or even disaggregation. In any case, Peters, Waterman, and Phillips (1980) suggested several years ago that fresh approaches are needed to efficiently and effectively utilize organizational resources. Mintzberg (1981) pointed out at about the same time that "organizations need above all to innovate in complex ways" and presented "ad hocracy" as a key structural configuration deserving fuller consideration. Layers of management in the traditional hierarchies are being removed. Asset divestment is now commonplace as a result of the actions of corporate raiders like Pickins and Icahn. The question to centralize or decentralize is ever present. When the careerist fails to be cognizant of these issues, there is the ignoring of an important framework for one's job and career.

The factors of internationalization and competition have the adverse effect of attempting to eliminate totally the aforementioned organization framework for job and career. The CEO and careerist have to look at survival as a paramount concern given that world class competitors are expanding U.S. market share and are exporting jobs overseas. Current balance of payments deficits are staggering. BMW, Sony, Volvo, Seiko, Royal Dutch Shell, and OPEC are just some of the well known foreign organizations which have sparked changes in the way the United States and the world do business. If an American organization is not completely appreciating these overseas challenges, then that organization and the jobs that go with it run the real risk of disappearing.

Similarly, regulation/deregulation and productivity improvement are playing sizeable roles in altering the shape and actions of U.S.

organizations today. CEO's and job holders in the medical health care, communications, airlines, banking and natural gas industries, to name a few, know well the meaning and extent of governmental oversight or involvement. As government control has been emphasized or deemphasized, organizations have been turned topsy-turvy. To make things worse for American organizations, the highly publicized declining rate of productivity improvement has cast a heavy cloud on the ability of managers and workers to achieve both quantity and quality. C. Jackson Grayson (1981) of the American Productivity Center of Houston, Texas has closely monitored this faltering record and has publicized organizational programs to correct the dismal trend. John Bookout (cited in Mack, 1986), CEO of the unusually successful Shell Oil Company, has said that his guiding philosophy during the energy industry's turbulent decade of the 1980s can be summarized in three words, "efficiency, efficiency, efficiency."

The above list of forces attacking the organization is not exhaustive. It is provided to illustrate that there are outside forces which require organizational transitions and changes. The experienced and alert mid-life careerist can and should understand the need for organizational streamlining, intensified international manufacturing and marketing efforts, and the drive for productivity efficiencies. The careerist has to view the world broadly, as the CEO does, looking at what has been happening, what is, and what will be happening to the organization. The mid-life careerist, for selfish reasons, must actively begin to seek answers to such questions as:

1. Do I know what is strategically taking place with my organization; if not, how do I find out?

2. Am I anticipating the priority functional needs, such as marketing or manufacturing, of my organization; do I have the interests and skills to aid the organization in these areas?

3. Where can I contribute the most in my job to the survival and success of my organization in these rapidly changing times; what am I doing to build my skills and abilities in high contribution areas?

Transitions in Job Structure and Design

Just as there is vast change today in organization structure so there is to be much change to come in job structure. The former necessitates the latter. The organization can be pictured as a complex network of jobs linked horizontally and vertically in the traditional triangular shape. If a layer of management jobs is removed, does this mean less work at lower standards of quality is to be done? The reverse is what job holders face.

Many people may be confused with the flattening of an organization. A layer of management is cut out from an organization and spans of control are increased. People may see fewer opportunities for advancing; however, much more opportunity exists for advancing one's job rather than one's job title. As an unneeded layer is eliminated, it may be true that there will be fewer manager titles to be passed around, but it will certainly not mean reduced responsibilities, less teamwork and problem-solving, or lowered technical competence or production. On the contrary, demands for greater initiative, participation and involvement, innovation, autonomy, and skill development and utilization will increase. The thrust for advancement in the future will be away from a "glorified" single leader or manager type of job to the professional, technically competent team player type of worker.

It is apparent that the careerist must look differently at job advancement and job structure. A good starting point is the way jobs have been defined in the past. To define jobs traditionally has meant to have them written by a job analyst for pay purposes, both to determine pay equity and merit increases. To put it simply, job descriptions have been pay driven, not performance driven. Yesterday's job descriptions and definitions were static; now there is a great need to move to a kinetic format of thinking and acting upon jobs and the accompanying duties and responsibilities. The defining and structuring of jobs has to take on a changing and flowing quality to keep up with the change forces operating on the organization.

Hayes (1985) has written extensively about the importance of having the highest technological competence at the lowest organizational level, no small feat of job structuring. Drucker (1986) has also explored at length the significant ramifications of redesigning jobs. He states that the organization and its personnel department "will have to redirect itself away from concern with the cost of employees to concern with their yield." A big factor to cause this redirection is changing technology. Drucker (1986) goes on to elaborate . . .

> The shift to knowledge work and knowledge workers also creates a need to rethink and to restructure career ladders, compensation and recognition. The traditional career ladder in most business has only managerial rungs. But for most knowledge workers a promotion into a management job is the wrong reward. The good ones usually would much prefer to keep on doing professional or technical work – they are good at it and enjoy it. And not very many of them are particularly good at management. This is not a new problem. Thirty years ago General Electric Co. established "parallel ladders" of advancement and rewards for "individual professional contributors." In most other large business all we have done, however, is to establish a good many positions with managerial titles – e.g., director or vice president – but without managerial function, thus creating a lot of non-jobs, a lot of confusion and title inflation. The shift to knowledge work as the new center of gravity of the work force will altogether force us to rethink the traditional organizational structure. The existing structure derived from the 19th century military – sees the manager as the "boss" with everybody else as the "subordinate." In the knowledge based organization knowledge workers are the "bosses" and the "manager" is in a supporting role as their planner and coordinator. But this means that jobs, their responsibilities, their relationships, their rewards, have to be thought through and have to be redesigned. (p. 14)

It is prophetic for those working in the personnel function that this message from Drucker (1986) should come from a Wall Street Journal article titled "Good Bye to the Old Personnel Department." The CEO and the boss of the careerist must take on the major responsibility in causing everyone in an organization to visualize how jobs can and must grow with organization change.

Mid-life careerist can aid in the process of job restructuring by drawing on their many years of job experience and by responding professionally to several questions concerning the way a job should best be structured in a non-homeostatic organization environment:

1. Have I been looking at my job in a static way; what must I do to build a kinetic quality into my job?
2. How can I get my boss's help in enriching my job?
3. Are there human resource specialists who can aid me in re-structuring my job; where else can I get assistance in this effort?

Transitioning Dynamics Within the Careerist

The third major force, one that is very personal and internal to the careerist, that must be dealt with by the careerist especially at the mid-point of life, is personal change. Levinson (1986) has reported that the early 30s is a period of "settling down," followed by a series of stages between 35 and 45 of "becoming one's own person," "mid-life transitioning," and "restabilization." In this ten year span of 35 to 45 the individual nurtures a principal "dream," fosters a "mentorship," and grapples with four large polarities of life: (1) youth versus age, (2) destruction versus creativity, (3) masculinity versus femininity, and (4) attachment versus separateness. Dalton (cited in Davis and Gould, 1981) has described four sequential stages in one's professional career. The primary roles or activities in these four stages are (1) the apprentice who learns and helps, (2) the colleague who is independently contributing, (3) the mentor who is training and integrating and (4) the sponsor who is shaping the direction of the organization.

Schein (1987) believes it is useful "to examine the internal career from a dynamic evolutionary perspective." He notes that at stage six of his nine stage career model there is a mid-career crisis and reassessment, stating that:

There is mounting evidence that most people go through some kind of difficult self-reassessment when they are well into their career, asking themselves questions about their initial choice ("Have I entered the right career?"), their level of attainment ("Have I accomplished all I hoped to?" "What have I accomplished and was it worth the sacrifices?"), and their future ("Should I continue or make a change?" "What do I want to do with the rest of my life, and how does my work fit into it?"). (p. 156)

Schein (1987) believes that during stage six every person develops a distinct career defined self-concept which enables the individual to answer several crucial career questions. According to Schein, a very important part of that self-concept is the career anchor or "that element in our self-concept we will not give up, even if forced to make a difficult choice."

It is clear that the careerist faces much self change at mid-life. This inner evolutionary process holds the potential for future improvement or frustration or lack of fulfillment. Davis and Gould (1981), Levinson (1986), Dalton (cited in Davis and Gould, 1981), Schein (1987) and others indicate that career dissonance occurs to one degree or another in the mind and body of every adult because of subtle but irrefutable individual change.

WAYS OF DEALING EFFECTIVELY
WITH MID-CAREER TRANSITIONAL FORCES

What is the careerist to do when caught up in the complexity of all this multi-level change? It would appear that an essential prescription is the using of all of one's faculties not only to learn and know what is going on in the world of work but also to develop the knowledge and skill to understand, predict, and control as much as possible the three major mid-career transitional forces. The alternative is the adverse stress that can harm job performance and job advancement.

Sutton and Kahn (1987) have developed a theory which states that prediction, understanding, and control are the main reducers of harmful stress. From their theory may be derived a practical straightforward action taking model for reducing job and career stress. This model enjoins the mid-life careerist to (1) *learn* actively about one's self, job, and organization, (2) *understand* fully the meaning of this vital information, (3) *predict and act* skillfully using the knowledge, and (4) *control* the job and career over time in spite of continuous change. If the mid-life adult is able to keep each phase fully operating over the long term, the opportunity exists to achieve better decision-making and problem-solving results regarding job and career.

Learning

It is almost too basic and obvious to state that to be minimally stressed the careerist has to develop and keep an "open-mindness," to develop and maintain an intelligence gathering capability that is ever searching and incorporating any and all relevant data that impacts the organization, the job and the personality of one's self. However, a heightened sensitivity by the careerist to all these patently needs to exist.

Learning cannot be taken for granted in our increasingly complicated world. The intelligent and educated adult can and does hide from or refuse to accept for many different reasons critical information that threatens the security or ego of the individual. Similar to Roger's (1961) "ambivalent desire to learn," Maslow (1962) has described the human learning dilemma as a great "need to know" but an equally great "fear of knowing." The mid-life adult has to confront and remove any reluctance to learning, particularly about himself or herself.

With any single event or trend taking place, the careerist needs to identify and note it in order to start any interpretation or evaluation as to whether it is a positive opportunity or negative constraint. To alert one's faculties to what is going on in the environment and within oneself is the initial move that must be taken to establish a stable stance for understanding, predicting, and acting.

Technology is an example where learning is continually needed by the careerist. The careerist needs to constantly read journals or talk with cohorts to collect information about what is happening in the careerist's technical field. One technology may be expanding and needed by the organization (a positive opportunity); the current technology being used by the careerist may be dying and as a result is a potential negative career restraint. In the latter situation, failure to identify this adverse circumstance prevents adequate understanding, predicting, and action-taking which, in turn, most likely will lead to mounting stress for the mid-life adult.

Understanding

Closely associated with the learning phase in career and stress management is the phase of understanding. Some may argue they are the same, not deserving any differentiation. The significant distinguishing aspect of the two are shown in four questions that a mid-life careerist needs to ask regularly in the two stages.

1. Is my mind open and alert to what is going on around me? (Learning)
2. Am I working to get good relevant information? (Learning)
3. Am I seeing the information for what it really is? (Understanding)
4. What does this data mean to me in terms of how it impacts me, my job, and my organization? (Understanding)

The fourth question makes it clear that the careerist must make a strong effort to use reasoning and judgment to establish cause and effect relationships. Question three also demonstrates a definite higher order of mental processing. In some ways this question isolates a large complication in the way a person views things. The careerist's analyzing or interpreting ability concerning newly acquired information operates in conjunction with a wide array of unique individual factors: the careerist's values, experiences, education, cultural background and perceptions. These color the way new information is seen, acting as a filter in the careerist's evaluation or assessment approach. Knowledge that these factors exist and the refinement of their use can enable the careerist to deal with personal, job, and career matters better. An increased awareness of the overall process of understanding and the special insightful tools involved can bring a much better view of career forces and how they can best be managed through a competent prediction, action-taking and controlling series of steps.

An example of the importance of the understanding stage is one's primary motivation or need. Is the person's primary motivation or need at mid-life one of security, challenge, autonomy, money or a combination of these? If there is deeper comprehension of the fundamental drives that are predominantly active for an individual, then learning and understanding can lead to more effective predicting, acting, and controlling.

Predicting and Acting

As with the last section on understanding, using a series of questions may aid in explaining what is meant by the third phase of predicting and acting. The questions are:

1. How do I deal with change as it relates to my job and organization?
2. If I deal with change on a reactive basis, why is that the case?
3. Could it be that I am not sure that I am getting good and complete information about my job and organization and that I am not able to draw accurate conclusions?
4. Could the cause be that I am unable to forecast with any high degree of probability what may happen; therefore my usual behavior is to take no action or to take action only when I am forced to do so?
5. Is my usual prediction concerning my job and organization: Things are going to stay the same?

Predicting and acting enlivens the cause/effect reasoning or judgment just discussed in the understanding phase. Predicting is the basis on which action is taken. It is only when the individual has done well in learning (gathering information), understanding (seeing important relationships clearly) and predicting (concluding about consequences) that a person can pursue an action with the confidence of some probability of success. Predicting and action taking are inextricably tied together.

A more common term for predicting and acting is coping. It may be helpful to discuss predicting and acting from the positive and negative aspects of this more familiar word. In coping well, an individual may be using the self-talk of "I understand the causes of the change and stress and here's what I am going to do about that change and stress." On the other hand, a person who does not cope well may be saying something to the effect, "I am seeing signs of stress; I am not sure of the causes of stress and I wonder if it will worsen and show itself in even more harmful ways." The individual may be getting caught in a negative web that can capture only negative prophesies or negative outcomes because of the inability to learn, understand and predict in a skilled problem-solving way.

Controlling

Controlling is the culminating phase of the four part model being proposed. It is the phase that provides a *continuous, coordinating* of the other three phases. This condition of recycling is necessary because the world of work is ever changing. Controlling is the thermostat standing permanent guard over what is taking place in the turbulent vocational environment. It is the process instrument gauging the quality of knowledge and skill used in learning, understanding, predicting and acting as these phases attack problem after problem over a lengthy period of time.

This fourth encompassing stage of controlling is the developing and using of a scorecard to self-report how much knowledge and skill have been employed by the mid-life adult in playing the career game. If the score or result is not what the individual wants, then the careerist has to make those changes needed to get a better or "winning" score in the latter half of the game. There is no more significant scorecard that can be kept because it represents the health and satisfaction one has in his or her job, career, and life.

CONTRIBUTING TO MORE EFFECTIVE MID-CAREER TRANSITIONING

The mid-life careerist in today's world faces enormous change on many different fronts. The question is not "Will the changes occur," but "what do I, the mid-life adult, do about the changes?" To meet the problems and challenges of the transitioning inner and outer spheres of adult life, knowledge and skill are needed in four fundamental human behaviors: (1) learning, (2) understanding, (3) predicting and acting, and (4) controlling. Some people are more naturally talented in functioning well in these areas. Some must work hard at educating themselves and improving their abilities in these categories. Examples do exist that it is possible to enhance one's knowledge and skill in these basic but significant activities. The results are the positive handling of change in one's job and career and the safeguarding of one's psychological and physical health.

REFERENCES

Davis, S., & Gould, R. (1981, July-August). Three vice-presidents in mid-life. *Harvard Business Review, 59* (4), 118-130.
Drucker, P. (1986, May). Good bye to the old personnel department. *Wall Street Journal*, p. 9.
Grayson, C. J. (1981, June). Three Scenarios for the U.S. in the 1980's. *Productivity Letter*, Houston, TX: American Productivity Center.
Hayes, R. (1985, November-December). Strategic planning—forward in reverse. *Harvard Business Review, 85* (6), 111-119.
Levinson, D. J. (1978). *The seasons of a man's life*. New York: Ballantine.
Mack, T. (1986, October). It's time to take risks. *Forbes, 138* (7), pp. 125-133.
Maslow, A. (1962). *Toward a psychology of being*. Princeton: Van Nostrand.
Mintzberg, H. (1981). Organizational design: Fashion or fit. *Harvard Business Review, 59* (1), 103-116.
Peters, T. (1986). *Thriving on chaos*. New York: Alfred A. Knopf.
Peters, T., Waterman, R. H., & Phillips, J. R. (1980, June). Structure is not organization. *Business Horizon, 23*, 14-26.
Rogers, C. (1961). *On becoming a person*. Boston: Houghton Mifflin.
Sutton, R., & Kahn, R. (1987). Prediction, understanding, and control as antidotes to organizational stress. In J. Lorsch (Ed.), *Organizational behavior* (pp. 272-285). Englewood Cliffs, NJ: Prentice-Hall.
Schein, E. (1987). Individuals and careers. In J. Lorsch (Ed.), *Organizational Behavior* (pp. 155-171). Englewood Cliffs, NJ: Prentice-Hall.
Trotter, H. D. (1986, Summer). Straight talk from Peter Drucker. *Best Business Quarterly, 8* (2), pp. 12-14.

IV. THE END GAME

Why Retire Early?

Ann E. McGoldrick

Manchester Polytechnic

Cary L. Cooper

Manchester School of Management

SUMMARY. Early retirement trends in the United States, United Kingdom and other industrialized societies are examined in relation to changing manpower requirements and economic forces. The results of a United Kingdom study of early retired men are presented, demonstrating the strategies adopted in retiring early. Factor analysis was used to examine the detailed considerations of respondents. A suitable financial basis was generally seen as the necessary prerequisite. In addition, a double-edged strategy emerged: a strategy for coping with changes and pressures in the work environment, and a more positive developmental strategy. Implications considered include the responsibility of organizations, the costs of early retirement, and alternative approaches for the future.

In addressing the question of why employees wish to retire early, or at least are increasingly tending to so do, we must briefly exam-

This study was funded by a grant from the United Kingdom Economic and Social Research Council. Reprints may be obtained from Ann E. McGoldrick, Department of Management, Manchester Polytechnic, Aytoun Street, Manchester, England, M1 3GH.

219

ine retirement trends in the United States, United Kingdom, and other industrialized societies. An accelerated trend towards earlier retirement was first demonstrated in the United States in the 1950s and 1960s. Since then, corresponding patterns have been detected far more widely, in response to similar economic forces and changes in population structures. Likewise, technological advancement and associated developments in labor force and skill requirements have had significant effects on the current labor need profile. Accurate manpower planning and management of human resources have become critical to company survival and growth, as well as for national economic prospects. These changes have also brought significant growth in potential stresses for individual employees in terms of increasing demands and pressures in their jobs, threats of job loss and growing insecurity in the work environment, the changing management-personnel interface, and the interaction of work and home domains. The purpose here is to examine one major response to such changes and the potential for individual and organizational action to counteract the negative effects.

In the United States, in the later 1950s and throughout the 1960s, provision at the state level and changes in private occupational pension scheme terms facilitated the growth in early retirement. At the national level, Social Security rules were relaxed, eligibility ages reduced and coverage extended (Brousseau, 1981; Work in America Institute, 1980). At the same time dramatic expansion in private pension schemes meant that many more employees had access to such benefits. The existing unemployment rate, combined with growing concern about the effects of technological change and automation on future labor force requirements were, in fact, forcing not only Government and industry, but also trade unions to try to find acceptable ways of adjusting labor force supply. Early retirement was a major response and pension scheme terms were developing, which actively encouraged it. Unions were not only willing to co-operate, but applied active pressure (Slavick, 1966). As early as the mid-1960s, this growth in early retirement was clearly demonstrated in national statistics (Shoemaker, 1965), while the increasing liberalization of company private benefits was monitored. Schemes generally became more appealing: eligibility ages were reduced, early retirement became a right in many schemes, benefits at less than actuarial reduction were more widely available, and various supplemental payments were being offered (Burrows, 1971; Jackson, 1972; Walker, 1975). The combination of this with state provision resulted in a significant decline in the labor force participation of older employees throughout these years (US Bureau of Census, 1975; US Department of Labor, 1978).

In the United Kingdom similar developments have followed. There were equivalent needs for manpower reduction and changing emphases in the workforce profile. This was acknowledged at the national level in the Job Release Scheme of 1977, which was directly seen as a means to create vacancies and offset high unemployment rates (Department of Employment, 1978). Weaknesses in the terms of the scheme, however, limited its attractiveness to individuals and organizations, resulting in a more modest response than was initially forecast (Makeham & Morgan, 1980; McGoldrick & Cooper, 1989). Similar schemes have been adopted in other advanced industrial societies such as the Netherlands, Sweden, Australia, France, West Germany, and Finland (Casey & Bruche, 1983; Fisher, 1975; Gaullier, 1985; Howe, 1980; Tracey, 1979).

Private pension provision in the United Kingdom, although not as widespread as in the United States, was nonetheless covering growing proportions of the employed population (Government Actuary Department, 1986). Increasingly, early retirement was being utilized to accomplish manpower objectives. It could assist not only in overall numbers' reduction, but in respect of other personnel problems: workforce bulges, developing promotion prospects, response to new technology, dealing with redundant skills and poor performers, establishing a younger and healthier workforce, increasing general security and a reward for older, long-service employees. Response was two-fold. With trade union support and encouragement, companies began to increase the generosity of provision for early retirement in existing pension plans, removing or reducing eligibility barriers and diminishing negative financial implications (McGoldrick, 1984). At the same time, special schemes were also introduced to deal with specific manpower needs. These could involve enhanced benefits and ex-gratia payments. While initially many of these schemes were operated on a compulsory basis, union influence and concern regarding company-employee relations have dictated a shift towards voluntary options (McGoldrick & Cooper, 1978).

The effect has been that increasing numbers of United Kingdom employees have become eligible for early retirement arrangements on a standard basis (Government Actuary Department, 1986; National Association of Pension Funds, 1986), while many others have responded to these special company based initiatives (McGoldrick & Cooper, 1989). This has contributed to a comparable decline in the labor force participation of older workers to that which occurred earlier in the United States, particularly for men (Central Statistics Office, 1987; Department of Employment, 1987). While current economic pressures, organizational needs and developing technologies suggest that early retirement will be with us into the future, we need to assess also its desirability for and impact on the individual. Retirement has been seen in terms of a psychosocial crisis, bringing with it loss of identity, status and even deleterious health consequences. This view focuses on the impact of the withdrawal of what is assumed to be the central role of work in one's life.

Increasingly, this is being considered a narrow and simplistic approach, which does not take into account variations in its relevance or desirability for the individual. Empirical evidence (McGoldrick & Cooper, 1989) does not show a direct link between retirement and early mortality, nor can it be directly associated with health decline and may, in fact, result in improved health status. Likewise, studies (Kasl, 1980) have demonstrated that mental health problems do not occur for the majority, who are generally satisfied with post-retirement outcomes. Lower morale has been associated with the effects of advanced age, poor health and lower income, rather than retirement per se (Kasl, 1980; McGoldrick, 1989; McGoldrick & Cooper, 1985). The major study of earlier retirement in the United States, in fact, found a high level of satisfaction amongst automobile employees who had qualified for a liberalized pension plan (Barfield & Morgan, 1969). Three-quarters reported satisfaction, while the majority (89%) confirmed that their decision to retire early had been right. McGoldrick (1983), in a United Kingdom study, demonstrated similar outcomes. A large sample of early retirees from a variety of industries and employment levels showed high overall satisfaction with their experience and lifestyles (80%). Three-quarters would have retired early again, 60% reported improvement in their current life in comparison to working years, with a further 30% indicating that these were equivalent.

The Retirement Decision

An important issue investigated in the United Kingdom study was the employees' view of earlier retirement and their reasons for opting for it. Early studies had emphasized the part played in the retirement decision by poor health. Since financially viable schemes were rarely available employees were encouraged to work on as long as it was feasible (Corson & McConnell, 1956; Steiner & Dorfman, 1957; Shanas et al., 1968). The emphasis switched in later studies towards financial motivations, as a result of newly developed options (Boskin, 1977; Katona et al., 1969; Parnes & Nestle, 1981; Patton, 1977; Pollman, 1971; Prothero & Beach, 1984; Reno, 1971). While generally pension eligibility and post-retirement income were the variables investigated, Barfield and Morgan (1969) investigated economic factors in more detail, including the supportive effects of economic assets, savings, having fewer dependents, and a positive financial outlook.

Only a few studies have totally eliminated health factors (Schmitt et al., 1979; Schmitt & McCune, 1981). Evidence exists that self-appraised health and the belief that health may improve or be better maintained through retiring may be influential (Jacobson, 1972a). Connected to this are the stresses and problems individuals may encounter in later years within the work environment. Limited evidence suggests that preference for early retirement may be associated with blue-collar work, higher rates of physical strain, and lower skill levels. Likewise, there is some indication that job attitudes and attributes may have an effect. Lower age preference has to a limited degree been associated with lower job satisfaction, less emphasis on the value of work, lack of autonomy, job related tension, poor working conditions, and the effects of job changes, particularly in respect to automation and new technology (Eden & Jacobson, 1976; Jacobson, 1972b; Jacobson & Eran, 1980; Schmitt et al., 1979; Streib & Schneider, 1971).

More generally, surveys of work attitudes have shown that the centrality of the work role has declined for many employees. Family and leisure roles have achieved greater significance, while more positive attitudes towards the retirement experience have been established (McGoldrick, 1989; McGoldrick & Cooper, 1985). Information on positive perception of retirement lifestyles or the potential of further employment is almost nonexistent, however, except with regard to a general desire for more free time (Kimmel, Price, & Walker, 1978; Price, Walker, & Kimmel, 1979) and some suggestion of the desire for more interesting, challenging activities (Schmitt et al., 1979).

A major deficit in research has been the lack of attention to the width of factors involved in the decision to retire, with many studies examining only small numbers of global variables (Orbach, 1969; Pollman, 1971). Sample sizes have frequently been small and limited to specific occupational groups (Owen & Belzung, 1967; Peretti & Wilson, 1975; Schmitt & McCure, 1981). Even national surveys of early retirees have been limited to small sample sizes (Parnes & Nestle, 1975).

Some studies have employed projective analyses with working populations (Hall & Johnson, 1980; Usher, 1981), but comparability between them has been limited because of differing age ranges. Differing preference choices have also been used, such as willingness to retire and desire to retire before 65, resulting in a lack of standardization. The overriding weakness, however, has been the lack of precision regarding retirement timing and decision criteria, on account of the likely effects of subsequent circumstances and events. Retrospective studies (Barfield & Morgan, 1969; Streib & Schneider, 1971; Schmitt et al., 1979) have the disadvantage of possible contamination from later experience, although they do offer an accurate measurement of retirement timing.

METHOD

Sample

A questionnaire, based on intensive home interviews of 120 early retired men and, where appropriate, their partners, was distributed to 1,800 men who had retired early from 16 United Kingdom organizations. These organizations represented a wide range of industry, differing organizational sizes, and the public and private sectors. This was considered to be more representative than a single company study in terms of organizational variables and permitted

the inclusion of individuals retiring under varying terms and circumstances. Full disability retirement had to be excluded, however,
as a distinct problem requiring separate study.

Response Profile

An overall response rate of 67% (N = 1,207) was attained, with
good representation across major sample characteristics. According
to company definitions the vast majority of retirements (74%) were
voluntary, although questionnaire responses varied from this according to personal circumstances and pressures experienced.
Thirty-four percent of the respondents indicated at least some degree of compulsion, even though they might have willingly accepted the outcome. Only 10% indicated that they had no choice at
all, however, and even then many had perceived positive aspects of
leaving earlier.

The respondents had retired between the ages of 44.5 and 64.8
years, with a mean of 58.8 years and the majority of retirements
taking place after age 56. Sixty-seven percent had retired within 8
years of the state norm of 65 and 85% had retired within 8 years of
their company norm.

All respondents received some form of special early retirement
financial package, although arrangements varied considerably. Just
over half (55%) received a full or upwardly adjusted pension, with
the remainder obtaining only credits earned. Two-thirds also received severance payments or chose to commute their pensions
(63.6%) for a lump sum, with only 6.6% retiring with neither.

At the time of the survey, the men were between 49 and 77 years
of age, with 70% under the state retirement norm of 65 years. The
vast majority were married or with a permanent partner (88.4%)
and had children (75.6%). Eighty-seven percent no longer had financial dependents other than their spouse.

Analysis of the Retirement Decision

Since previous work had tended to solicit response only to global
decision factors, the questionnaire contained an extensive list of
detailed criteria and considerations. These covered a range of factors relating to finances, health, work, leisure, personal circum-

stances, pressures, and attitudinal influences. Factor analysis was undertaken on the basis of 60 selected decision criteria, with varimax rotations employing an orthogonal procedure to eliminate collinearity between factors. The 13 factor solution was found to reduce repetition without meaningful loss of emerging constructs, while explaining 68% of the variance.

RESULTS

Strategies Adopted

Questionnaire results clearly pointed to the breadth of the decision process for many respondents, with a wealth of factors playing their part in the decision to retire or accommodation to compulsory retirement. A suitable financial basis was seen by the majority as a necessary prerequisite. Special financial inducements were of significance to many (75%) and a major decision criteria for over half (60%). At the same time, the appropriateness of their own finances and savings was of relevance to the majority (58%) and of major importance to over a third (38%), particularly those leaving under standard scheme terms. More detailed considerations included the provision of immediate benefits (77%), severance payments (62%), unemployment benefits (34%), savings and investments (34%), mortgage completion (37%), and the independence of children (34%).

Two major strategies emerged, which were not necessarily mutually exclusive: a strategy for coping and a more positive growth and development strategy (McGoldrick, 1983). Although the majority (81%) were generally satisfied with their working careers, a notable deterioration was found in later years (60%). This related to personal changes and the effects of aging, as well as changes in the industrial situation, technological advance, and growing insecurity in the workplace. Thirty-eight percent believed they were coping less well at work, often experiencing spill-over into their domestic life. A major area of concern related to satisfaction with the actual job and pressures such as technological changes, relocation and job changes, travel to and at work, poor work conditions, insecurity, overload, and boredom. Likewise, there was dissatisfaction in terms of the human interface of the work environment.

A major influence on the decision to retire early was a generally positive outlook on retirement, although pressures from management, unions, and fellow workers were also of importance. Likewise, wives and families played a role in the decision process, while the concern about the possibility of others being made redundant (13%) and youth unemployment (17%) also had an effect. Preservation of good health (36%) and active retirement prospects (46%) were similarly important, although about a third reported general health decline and tiredness, aging effects, reduced work performance, and disrupted domestic lives. Physical health problems and poor health were, in fact, reported by a quarter (24%), while smaller numbers had concerns regarding their partner's health status.

A more positive development strategy was relevant for the majority, including many of the compulsorily retired. Anticipated lifestyles after retiring varied considerably, ranging from the more traditional pursuits of home and family, grandchildren, and rest and relaxation to far more active plans. Significant minorities had anticipated involvement in holidays, clubs and societies, further education, and voluntary work. Further work was the objective of 21% of the respondents.

Factors in the Early Retirement Decision

Table 1 presents the results of the factor analysis on the detailed considerations. Four factors related to retirement opportunities, six were work related, two were discrete financial factors, and one related to the dimension of health.

Several factors were significantly related to social class, as is demonstrated in Table 2. The *Active Opportunities* factor was positively associated with higher social classes as was *Free Time and Leisure*, where the Eta-squared value of .012 reflects the departure from the linear approximation, with very similar scores for the skilled manual and non-manual categories. *Work Changes and Pressures* was also positively associated with higher social classes. Higher classes demonstrated stronger positive relationships with fi-

TABLE 1. Factor Analysis of Considerations Before Early Retirement (% of variance explained by each factor)

Factors (as extracted)	Variables Loading Significantly (at or above .30)	Factor Loadings
1. Free Time and Leisure (31.4%)	Wanted more free time	.77725
	Worked long enough/deserved	.64870
	Time for hobbies/recreation	.64362
	Always thought ER good thing	.60908
	Time with family and friends	.61996
	Rest and relaxation	.57556
	Healthier/more active retirement	.42798
	More time with family	.41026
2. Health Concerns (14.2%)	Job affecting health	.69459
	Tiredness	.64774
	Poor health	.63710
	Prevent future health problems	.59526
	Hard to keep up at work	.54210
	Feeling effects of getting older	.46067
	Pressures and stresses of job	.45426
	Overworked	.44975
	Rest and relaxation	.35409
3. Others at Work (10.1%)	Fellow workers generally	.65104
	People directly worked with younger	.62371
	Workers' attitudes	.51318
	Pressures from other workers	.50026
	People responsible for	.47510
	Unpleasant company atmosphere	.35230
	Unpleasant aspects of job	.32173
4. Work Changes and Pressures (7.2%)	Changes in the job	.60122
	Changes in the Company	.54715
	Less satisfaction with job/work	.44715
	Immediate boss(es)	.40649
	Management pressure	.40576
	Technological changes	.39866
	Overworked	.31873
	Pressures and stresses of job	.31130
	Need to change job	.30720
	Need to move location	.30126

228

5. **Wife and Family**
   (5.5%)

Help wife/household jobs	.59378
More time with family	.56864
Wife's health	.47156
Family circumstances	.45629
Time with family and friends	.42134
Wife/family wanted the ER	.38877

6. **Own Finances Right**
   (5.2%)

House mortgage paid	.60959
Own savings/investments	.51229
Children independent	.50382
Own finances and savings	.46435
Good pension	.30197

7. **Other Work Intended**
   (4.5%)

Chance of new job/career	.68436
Chance of reduced hours/part-time	.44698
Chance of own business	.41559

8. **Insecurity**
   (4.3%)

Insecurity of job/company	.61532
Company running down	.58999

9. **Unions**
   (4.0%)

Pressures from unions	.78272
Influence of unions	.59778

10. **Active Opportunities**
    (3.6%)

Wanted to do voluntary work	.52947
Time for societies and clubs	.52154
Opportunity for further education	.40943

11. **Financial Inducements**
    (3.4%)

Severance payment	.60027
Unemployment benefit	.46485
Immediate pension rights	.31782
Financial inducements good	.30954

12. **Social Conscience**
    (3.1%)

To prevent others being redundant	.56652
Younger people out of work	.50315
Friends/colleagues leaving	.32508

13. **Boredom**
    (2.9%)

Bored/not enough to do	.55643
Less satisfaction from job/work	.32807

TABLE 2. Factor Scores by Social Class

Factor	Social Class					F-Ratio	Eta-sq	r^2
	Professional	Intermediate	Skilled non-manual	Skilled manual	Part-non-skilled	(p =)		
Free time and leisure	.139	.037	-.022	-.016	-.225	(.009)	.012	.009
Health concerns	-.218	-.060	.013	.051	.257	(.000)	.022	.020
Others at work	-.194	-.172	.042	.157	.231	(.000)	.037	.035
Work changes and pressures	.118	.246	.063	-.295	-.338	(.000)	.078	.061
Wife and family	-.052	-.033	-.041	.036	.134	(n s)	.005	.004
Own finances right	.204	.291	-.062	-.164	-.446	(.000)	.103	.091
Other work intended	.347	.134	-.131	-.127	-.180	(.000)	.052	.040
Insecurity	.004	-.119	-.035	.052	.204	(.001)	.019	.012
Unions	-.174	.043	-.047	.125	-.001	(.020)	.011	.003
Active opportunities	.169	.052	-.023	-.074	-.114	(.006)	.014	.013
Financial inducements	.028	.061	.107	-.027	-.250	(.000)	.027	.015
Social conscience	-.076	-.122	-.003	.130	.162	(.000)	.022	.016
Boredom	.043	-.063	.034	-.016	.057	(n s)	.004	.001

nancial variables such as *Own Finances Right* and *Financial Inducements*. The former relationship probably results from the tendency among the professional group to have plans for returning to some form of work.

Four factors showed a positive association with lower classes. The Eta-square and the r^2 values indicate that the strong association of *Health Concerns* is close to linear in its form. A reasonable approximation to linear form is also demonstrated in respect of *Others at Work*, while *Social Conscience* demonstrated a definite inverse relationship to social class. *Insecurity* displayed a significant positive association with blue collar employees, a group of men who frequently felt that their jobs could easily be dispensed with or changed. The intermediate and skilled non-manual groups received negative scores on this factor while the professional category scored a relatively neutral value.

Unions showed an unusual relationship with social class with factor scores peaking among the skilled manual and intermediate groups but demonstrating a negative relationship with the other three classes. It can be conjectured that an association with supervisory/lower management problems and difficulties faced by foremen/chargehands were influential in these associations. Interview data supported this view.

A series of t-tests of the data from respondents who defined themselves as voluntarily retired versus those who reported they retired by compulsion showed that only two negative work factors, *Work Changes and Pressures* (p < .006) and *Insecurity* (p < .001), were significantly associated with compulsory retirement. The financial criterion *Own Finances Right* (p < .003) and *Other Work Intended* (p < .07), with its implication of further earnings, were associated with voluntary retirees. The compulsory group was slightly older on retiring and therefore less likely to seek or anticipate finding further work. Other positive lifestyle factors significantly associated with voluntary retirement were *Free Time and Leisure* (p < .001) and *Wife and Family* (p < .001). As might be expected, the *Social Conscience* factor was thus associated (p < 003). No significant differences were found between the groups on the other factors or the individual items contained within them.

DISCUSSION

The results of the study clearly demonstrate the multi-faceted nature of the retirement decision process, representing a double-edged strategy for many, both facilitating an earlier exit from their work situation and bringing the opportunity for a range of leisure and development options. The great changes occurring within industry in the last decades have made it a less equitable environment for many older employees, with growing stresses and pressures, which determine the necessity of an earlier move. While early retirement has proved a useful management tool in dealing with some of the current changes in manpower requirements, the individual too can benefit. Retirement may be the lesser stress, and it would seem that the view of retirement as a major life-crisis is proving untrue for many who perceive positive outcomes in terms of their post-retirement lifestyle and health.

The provision of adequate financial security is, however, of paramount importance as a foundation. This study demonstrates the wide range of financial factors which must be taken into account in deciding to retire early. Other analyses of satisfaction after retiring (McGoldrick & Cooper, 1989) clearly link this to achieving desired financial security at a level appropriate to lifestyle requirements.

The study also provides evidence of the particular difficulties of the blue-collar sector in the high technology environment prevailing within industry. Satisfaction with the working career was strongly associated with social class, with greatest dissatisfaction occurring among the partly/unskilled manual workers and the skilled non-manual groups. The former experienced a great deal of insecurity, including redeployment, job changes, and threats of redundancy. Further employment was known to be unlikely if they were made redundant. Lower status employees were also most affected by *Social Conscience* considerations, feeling pressured to make way for younger people and to accept an earlier retirement as a means to avoid redundancies for workmates.

Of importance is that this study was limited to men at the request of the sponsoring body. There is very little research into the retirement patterns and attitudes of women with virtually no studies concerning early retirement. In studies that have included women, numbers have frequently been small, making separate analysis impossible or at best tentative. It cannot be assumed that reactions and sets of decision criteria are comparable to those in the present study. The overall cost of early retirement must also receive consideration. The decline in labor force participation in the United States, together with increased life-expectancy and the changing population profile, is of concern. Expectancy of shorter working careers with lower fertility rates could make future labor shortages more likely. Ultimately workers could be deprived of benefits which they had worked to provide for others.

Forecasts for the United Kingdom are more positive with more balanced projections between the active and non-active sectors of the population at the beginning of the twenty first century. There still needs to be caution, however, if the early retirement trend continues to accelerate and pressures for reduced retirement ages succeed. In this case, increased costs of social support and maintenance would fall on the declining proportion of workers.

This study also raises concerns regarding ageism and the passing of the burden of unemployment to older age-groups. *Social Conscience* was certainly an important motivation found in this study for volunteering to retire, while many unions and individuals have supported policies of "making way." We cannot, however, ignore the evidence regarding the potential of earlier retirement for some, if it can be provided on a secure financial basis. Views on work and leisure are changing directly as a result of the evolving nature of industrial society and the rapidly shrinking size of the workforce. Leisure time is being redefined in terms, not of absence of work, but of a range of activities and commitments which can provide status, a positive self-image, and the opportunity for personal development.

The organization has a duty towards employees to attempt to prepare them financially and psychologically for the retirement transition. Compulsory retirees are frequently ill-prepared and can face many problems, as may those voluntary retirees who only leave on account of extreme pressure. Where feasible, individuals should be able to make the retirement decision to suit their specific circumstances. In the United States, legislation now exists to protect the older employee from being compelled to leave the workforce, although there is no equivalent in the United Kingdom. Flexibility to work beyond the age of retirement, when it is in the individual's interest to do so, is rarely discussed. Finally, it should be noted that about a fifth of those retiring early wanted alternative forms of work, while a third wanted to work again. We need to recognize the potential of training and development programs for second careers and mid-career change. We also need to be increasingly aware of older employees' capabilities as members of the workforce and to address their desire for shorter hours, part-time work, and easier or less stressful employment during their later working years.

REFERENCES

Barfield, R. E., & Morgan, J. N. (1969). *Early retirement: The decision and experience*. Ann Arbor: Institute of Social Research, University of Michigan.

Boskin, M. J. (1977). Social security and retirement decisions. *Economic Inquiry*, *15*, 1-25.

Brousseau, K. R. (1981). After age forty: Employment patterns and practices in the United States. In C. L.Cooper & D. P. Torrington (Eds.), *After forty*. Chichester: John Wiley.

Burrows, E. E. (1971). Liberalized early retirement: Where it is and what's ahead. *Compensation Review*, 4th October, 19-24.

Casey, B., & Bruche, G. (1983). *Work or retirement? Labour market and social policy for older workers in France, Great Britain, the Netherlands, Sweden and the USA*. Aldershot: Gower.

Central Statistics Office. (1987). *Social Trends* (No. 17). London: HMSO.

Corson, J. J., & McConnell, J. W. (1956). *Economic needs of older people*. New York: Twentieth Century Fund.

Department of Employment. (1978). Measures to alleviate unemployment in the medium term: Early retirement. *Department of Employment Gazette*, March, 283-285.

Department of Employment. (1987). Civilian labour force economic activity rates and projections. *Social Trends*, *17*, 4.

Eran, M., & Jacobson, D. (1976). Expectancy theory prediction of the preference to remain employed or to retire. *Journal of Gerontology*, *31*, 605-610.

Fisher, P. (1975). Labour force participation of the aged and the Social Security System in nine countries. *Industrial Gerontology*, *2*, 1-13.

Gaullier, X. (1985). *Technology, employment and aging: Early retirement policies in France*. Paper presented to the International Congress of Gerontology, New York.

Government Actuary Department. (1986). *Occupational pension schemes 1983: Seventh survey by the government actuary*. London: HMSO.

Hall, A., & Johnson, T. R. (1980). The determinants of planned retirement age. *Industrial and Labour Relations Review, 33*, 241-254.

Howe, A. (1980). Retirement and pensions: A survey of recent trends in Australia. *Work and Aging, 3*, 89-102.

Jackson, P. H. (1972). Early retirement: U.S. patterns and problems. *Benefits International*, June, 9-14.

Jacobson, D. (1972a). Willingness to retire in relation to job strain and type of work. *Industrial Gerontology, 13*, 65-74.

Jacobson, D. (1972b). Fatigue-producing factors in industrial work and pre-retirement attitudes. *Occupational Psychology, 46*, 193-200.

Jacobson, D., & Eran, M. (1980). Expectancy theory components and non-expectancy moderators as predictors of physicians' preference for retirement. *Journal of Occupational Psychology, 53*, 11-26.

Kasl, V. (1980). The impact of retirement. In C. L. Cooper & R. Payne (Eds.), *Retirement*. London: John Wiley.

Katona, G., Morgan, J. N., & Barfield, R. E. (1969). Retirement in prospect and retrospect. In H. E. Orbach (Ed.), *Trends in early retirement* (Occasional Papers in Gerontology No. 4). Ann Arbor, MI: University of Michigan.

Kimmel, D. C., Price, K. F., & Walker, J. W. (1978). Retirement choice and retirement satisfaction. *Journal of Gerontology, 33*, 575-585.

Makeham, P., & Morgan, S. (1980). *Evaluation of the job release scheme: Research paper 13*. London:Department of Employment.

McGoldrick, A. E. (1983). Company early retirement schemes and private pension scheme options: Scope for leisure and new lifestyles. *Leisure Studies, 2*, 187-202.

McGoldrick, A. E. (1984). *Equal treatment in occupational pension schemes*. Manchester: EOC.

McGoldrick, A. E. (1989). Stress, early retirement and health. In K. Markides & C. L. Cooper (Eds.), *Aging, stress, social support and health*. Chichester: Wiley.

McGoldrick, A. E., & Cooper, C. L. (1978). Early retirement for managers in the U.S. and the U. K. *Management International Review, 3*, 35-42.

McGoldrick, A. E., & Cooper, C. L. (1985). Stress at the decline of one's career: The act of retirement. In T. A. Beehr & R. S. Bhagat (Eds.), *Human stress and cognition in organizations: An integrated perspective*. New York: John Wiley.

McGoldrick, A. E., & Cooper, C. L. (1989). *Early retirement*. Aldershot: Gower.

Orbach, H. L. (1969). Social and institutional aspects of industrial workers' retirement patterns. In T. Donahue (Ed.), *Trends in early retirement*. Ann Arbor: University of Michigan.

Owen, J. P., & Belzung, D. (1967). Consequences of voluntary early retirement:

A study of a new labour force phenomenon. *British Journal of Industrial Relations*, *5*, 162-189.

Parnes, H. S., Fleischer, B. M., Miljus, R. C., & Spitz, R. S. (1975). *Pre-retirement years: Five years in the work lives of middle-aged men.* United States Department of Labor Manpower Administration.

Parnes, H. S., & Nestle, G. (1981). The retirement experience. In H. S. Parnes (Ed.), *Work and retirement: A longitudinal study of men.* Cambridge, MA: MIT Press.

Patton, C. V. (1977). Early retirement in academia: Making the decision. *The Gerontologist*, *17*, 347-354.

Peretti, P. O., & Wilson, C. (1975). Voluntary and involuntary retirement of aged males and their effect on emotional satisfaction, usefulness, self-image, emotional stability and interpersonal relationships. *International Journal of Aging and Human Development*, *6*, 131-138.

Pollman, A. W. (1971). Early retirement: A comparison of poor health to other retirement factors. *Journal of Gerontology*, *26*, 41-45.

Price, K. F., Walker, J. W., & Kimmel, D. C. (1979). Retirement timing and retirement satisfaction. *Aging and Work*, *2*, 235-245.

Prothero, J., & Beach, J. R. (1984). Retirement decisions: expectation, intention and action. *Journal of Applied Social Psychology*, *14*, 162-174.

Reno, V. (1971). Why men stop working before age 65. In V. Reno (Ed.), *Reaching retirement age: Findings from a survey of newly entitled workers, 1968-70.* US Department of Health, Education and Welfare. Social Security Administration, Office of Research and Statistics, Research Report No. 47.

Schmitt, N., Coyle, B. W., Rauschenberger, J., & White J. K. (1979). Comparison of early retirees and non-retirees. *Personal Psychology*, *32*, 327-340.

Schmitt, N., & McCune, J. T. (1981). The relationship between job attitudes and the decision to retire. *Academy of Management Journal*, *24*, 795-802.

Shanas, E., Townsend, P., Wedderburn, D., Friis, H., Milhoj, P., & Stenhouner, J. (1968). *Old people in three industrial societies.* London: Routledge & Kegal Paul.

Shoemaker, R. (1965). The quickening trend towards early retirement. *American Federationist*, March 13-17.

Slavick, F. (1966). *Compulsory and flexible retirement in the American economy.* New York: Cornell University Press.

Steiner, P. O., & Dorfman, R. (1957). *The economic status of the aged.* Berkeley: University of California Press.

Streib, G. F., & Schneider, C. J. (1971). *Retirement in American society: Impact and process.* Ithaca, NY: Cornell University Press.

Tracey, M. (1979). *Retirement age practices in ten industrial societies.* Geneva: International Social Security Association.

United States Bureau of Census. (1975). *Historical statistics of the United States* (Part I). Washington, DC: US Government Printing Office.

United States Department of Labor. (1978). *Employment and training report to the President.* Washington, DC: US Government Printing Office.
Usher, C. E. (1981). Alternative work options for older workers: Part 1: Employees' interest. *Aging and Work, 4,* 74-81.
Walker, J. W. (1975). The new appeal of early retirement. *Business Horizons,* June, 43-48.
Work in America Institute. (1980). *The future of older workers in America: New options for an extended working life.* New York: Work in America Institute.

Time to Move On?

James F. Quick

Rochester, New York

SUMMARY. Retirement, especially early retirement, is a stressful experience, though not necessarily a distressful one. This article addresses several issues related to making the process of retirement a beneficially stressful experience. It addresses the decision to retire, the planning process for retirement, and living in retirement. It addresses four factors which may be sources of stress — lifestyle and location, spousal concerns, finances, and health.

There always has been a certain mystique about early retirement. I recall seeing insurance advertisements of more than 50 years ago purporting to show that one could, with proper insurance, retire to go fishing at 55. With financial options improving in the years that have followed, I suspect that many people may be taking early retirement with little thought of the unpleasant — even painful — stress that might well follow if they do not plan with care.

Satisfying retirement and, in particular, early retirement requires careful attention to the retirement decision, to organizing retirement life, and to planning in advance for retirement. This chapter will consider each of these areas — deciding to retire, living in retirement, and planning for retirement — as well as the potential stress involved in the retirement process.

The time to move on, until about fifty years ago, was age 65 — if still alive and whether you liked the idea or not. Today you cannot be forced to retire before age 70. Within the last fifty years a proliferation of retirement ages — 55, 62, 65, now 70 — has been offered, in the Social Security Act as well as in company plans. Within the

---

Reprints may be obtained from James F. Quick, 1145 South Winton Road, Rochester, NY 14618.

239

last twenty years there has been a marked increase in the number of people taking early retirement. In some cases companies have used early retirement policies to lure people into early retirement as a means of reducing the payroll and achieving lower costs and higher profits. Now many have the opportunity to choose when to retire, while others are induced to retire early, like it or not.

The once standard age of 65 for retiring probably generated less stress because no subjective decisions had to be made about the time of retirement. You knew the date, you could plan your asset accumulations to match your needs at retirement, and statistics did not indicate more than eight or ten years of life would remain after retirement. It was a very acceptable arrangement for those who thoroughly enjoyed what they were doing and had no concern about the stability of their employment. For others not so happily situated or tempted by other possibilities, the opportunity to retire early with some financial support was welcomed. But regular retirement at 65 or 70, as well as early retirement, can generate severe stress. For the average American, fifteen to twenty years of life now remain at age 65, making retirement potentially a career in itself! One individual may move happily along to retirement at 65 or 70, but when faced with the last day of work, the future looms long and empty, familiar activities gone forever. As an associate said to me the day after he retired, "now there's nothing to do but sit around and die"—which he did, a year and a half later.

DECIDING TO RETIRE

Ideally, the time to "move on," in the sense of retiring from one's regular occupation, is when other activities have more appeal, and your careful analysis of all factors indicates that the change can be managed to your complete satisfaction—and your spouse's. The freedom to exercise one's choices would seem to be a desirable situation. Certainly it is better to choose whether or not to continue receiving a pay check based on one's own carefully developed plans, than to have one's employer make the decision for reasons over which you have no control. When the age of 65, and now the age of 70, had the support of custom and law, that made the date of retirement an impersonal matter. Stress could still be present in those who never gave much thought as to what they would do in retirement, but there was no assault on a person's pride or sense of worth. To those forced out well before normal retirement, even though the financial arrangements have been adequate, it comes as a surprise that the company will pay to get rid of them. The stress can be intense from what I've observed in some friends who have gone through that process. The news is broken suddenly—often on a Friday. One's pride is deeply injured. Those that have given thought to retirement over the years probably regain their composure more quickly; if they have found themselves in comfortable financial situations, they quickly proceed to review the plans for retirement that they had sketched out in the past.

My own approach to early retirement might not have been very unusual. About age 58 I suddenly realized that I had already lived beyond the ages at which my grandfather and my father died. If the pattern continued, I thought it quite possible I would have all too few years of retirement to enjoy. My wife and I wanted to take some long trips before age and inertia caught up with us. And work was not bringing the satisfaction which it once had brought.

But early retirement would be impossible if our financial situation could not support a comfortable standard of living. I had spent most of the first half of my business life with a small national company which had no established pension policy. When it was bought out, the sale of my stock doubled my net worth, but I was still worth considerably more dead than alive. The second half of my business life, therefore, demanded careful attention to increasing my resources, as well as the value of a modest inheritance my wife had received. Living on a modest scale and fortunate in investments, sons educated and our home paid for, it appeared I could take early retirement and we would not have to change our standard of living. From age 39 to 62 I kept a yearly record of growth in assets and that discipline contributed much to our comfortable situation.

There was a catch, however. When I joined my last employer I signed an agreement that, barring a serious health problem or death, I would not be able to leave the company before age 65 and still collect my deferred profit share. That engendered real stress. I considered testing the president's feelings. After the passage of years perhaps he might be lenient about my retiring at 62. Then again he might not be—and even make the last three years unpleasant. Of course, he might be glad to see me go! Tough on the ego. Yet I knew I could not afford to retire without having the income from my share of the deferred profits.

Several years went by. Suddenly the company was sold. The new owning company had very flexible retirement programs and leaving at age 62 would be no problem. There was, however, a certain excitement about the change in ownership. For a year and a half there was plenty to do in carrying through the changes desired by the new ownership. They worked in a new management team. While several areas of responsibility were proposed for me, none appealed more than early retirement. We still wanted to assure ourselves of as many healthy years of retirement as possible and I had determined that we now could afford it. So my sixty-second birthday was my last day at work.

LIVING IN RETIREMENT

My thoughts on retirement activities had included travel, volunteer work, and regular financial reading. A modest social calendar—including occasional lunches with former business associates, attendance at the Chamber of Commerce speaker series, and weekly lunch with fellow retirees—filled out the plan. My goal was to have a varied, but uncluttered, schedule of regular activities. Not having been a sports enthusiast during my younger years, travel and reading were for me what fishing and golfing were for some of my friends. Just as working life offers many different career opportunities, so too does retirement life offer limitless possibilities. It's not so much a matter of what activities one chooses to engage in, but simply that one choose to become involved in activities that are personally satisfying.

From my own experience as well as that of some of my friends, I think it is wise to plan some type of vacation shortly after retirement. This allows for a decompression period before embarking on a regular schedule of activities such as volunteer work, part-time employment, or hobbies.

For us travel plans developed quickly. Not long after I retired, my older son planned a wedding in Houston and my wife and I used that occasion to travel through the Great Smoky Mountains and to visit New Orleans on the way to the wedding. We returned by a northern route, stopping to see friends in Oklahoma, Nebraska, and Iowa on our way back to Rochester, New York. Several months later we sailed on a seven week voyage to Iceland, Scandinavia, and Russia. For most of my working life nonbusiness "travel" consisted of an annual two week vacation at a small lake in Canada. Since retirement, we have taken several one to two week trips each year to different parts of the country. Traveling with friends or visiting with family and friends, we have managed to stay within our retirement budget while enjoying more travel than we did before retirement.

Volunteer work provided the plank of my tripartite retirement platform. For volunteer work I had considered the Service Corps of Retired Executives (SCORE), my church, and the Red Cross. I joined SCORE before retiring and, according to plan, I became active in it about seven months after retirement. SCORE was established in the Nixon Administration as part of the Small Business Administration to provide would-be, fledgling, and floundering small businesses with free advice from experienced businessmen. It has been a very satisfying activity for many retired managers and executives. Over the last fifteen years my role in the local SCORE chapter has evolved from active membership, to chairmanship, and finally to a gradual taper to rather inactive membership in recent years. During my early years of retirement, every Thursday (except while traveling) was spent at the SCORE office doing initial or follow-up counseling. I found it interesting volunteer work, and from time to time was made to feel I had been very helpful in providing solutions to some serious problems.

During my second year of retirement my church asked me serve as an assistant to the treasurer, taking care of all incoming funds and producing individual quarterly reports for each pledging member. This "job" was ideal for me: it was work which needed doing, so I felt useful; it took only one or two short days each week; the church staff was small and quite pleasant; and I have always liked working with finances.

The third plank in my retirement platform, regular financial reading, had always been of interest to me. But it became mandatory several years before retirement when my father-in-law asked me to manage his financial affairs. I was both honored and concerned. Inflation was becoming a serious worry for everyone and had to be taken into consideration in every investment decision. My older son also asked me to manage his investments. I cannot see my way clear to give up this family "volunteer work." It will continue to make demands on my time that I find satisfying.

These activities have provided me with many satisfying volunteer hours over most of the last fifteen years. Now at the age of 77, I feel inclined to change my routines again. Travel continues, but at a reduced pace and frequency. My participation in SCORE has tapered and last spring I "retired" — with brass plaque and "retirement party" — after nearly fifteen years, from my volunteer retirement job at church. Financial reading is still as important as ever. I have felt none of the kind of stress or obsolescence associated with inactive retirement. My sense of satisfaction is in part good fortune, but planning for retirement was also an important factor.

PLANNING FOR RETIREMENT

The wise thing to do is plan no unplanned retirement. If you wish to thoroughly enjoy the freedom retirement brings, you must plan some activities that require attention on a regular basis. In some cases a part-time, paid job is indicated to fill in for a financial shortfall expected in retirement. A wide variety of volunteer jobs are available in every town of any size, and they require many different skills. Some like activities that have no relation to their work experience; others want to operate a small business of their own. The important thing is to plan ahead and be able to go into retirement with a chart to follow.

Every bit as important as how you plan to spend your time is how and what your spouse feels about your plan to retire. For a husband, there are some important caveats to consider. First of all, start talking about retirement just as soon as you begin to consider it yourself. There are two items, from my experience, that loom largest with a wife: "What's our standard of living going to be?" and "What are you going to do all day?" Husbands, it seems, do not make good house pets. If they can produce a plan that gets them out of the house — frequently — it should contribute to domestic tranquility. Spouses may have other concerns and anxieties, some very specific ("Shouldn't we move south when we retire?") and others rather diffuse (fear of the unknown). Effective retirement planning means effective communication between spouses. The inherently stressful process of retirement can be made even more stressful by absent or ineffective involvement of the spouse in the planning process.

Two earner families have been increasing over the last two decades. Retirement in such families presents added complications. Retirement of one spouse before the other may be the only way possible because of forced retirement. Will one spouse want the second to retire early so they can enjoy joint activities? Can they afford it? If the man retires and the wife does not, will he feel like a "kept man" and resent it? A mutual agreeable plan must be developed *before* retirement if life is to be agreeable after retirement.

Exactly what will the financial situation be in retirement? It should not be an unfamiliar subject. In fact, some companies advise their people to consult with the personnel department as much as five years before scheduled retirement to forecast what their income will be, health care coverage and any other benefits to expect when retired, and to determine if their needs will be met.

The earlier you plan the financial details of retirement the better. When you started on your first job it would not have been too soon to lay down some guidelines and start some programs. A regular pattern of saving, the start of a life insurance program, and the purchase of a home are all steps in building financial security. The difficulty is that so many of us do not think seriously about careful planning until mid-life. In spite of that, a great many people, with the combination of Social Security, company pension programs, and life and health insurance, find that at age sixty, when they look ahead to retirement at 70, they can expect a fair chance of retiring at 60-70% of their annual income from employment.

Within four or five years of retirement — whether you plan normal (age 70) or early retirement — you should make a complete check of your financial resources and your health. Work sheets for estimating your income and expenses in retirement can be found in many books on retirement, and in some bank and life insurance publications.

Ideally, to retire without having to change one's lifestyle is the way to go. Very often this is not possible because your income will not be 60-70% of your income during the last years of employment. Where do you cut? Is your present home too large to maintain on the expected retirement income? What about clubs, cars, or travel? Many choose to live in a different climate and in an area with lower living costs.

If your pension is from a source that adjusts it from time to time to reflect inflation, you are very fortunate. The lengthening of the life span assures us all that we will experience increases in cost of living. As far as you are able, you should have some investments in stocks appraised by experts as "income with some inflation protection." Social Security's adjustments to reflect inflation have been of critical help to most retirees during these last years of sharp inflation, and so have a number of common stocks. One brokerage house has for several years published a list of more than 250 stocks that have raised their dividends every year for the past ten years or more; most have outpaced inflation.

At all cost, try to avoid planning to spend a portion of capital each year to flesh out regular income. There are formulae that are designed to provide a "safe" percentage of capital that can be spent a year with assurance that funds will not be totally exhausted. This approach seems too risky, partly because we are living, on the average, ever longer, and partly because market fluctuations can distort results. It is not always possible to avoid spending capital, but it should be done only as the last possible solution.

Health insurance is very important. If your company provided health insurance, it may well be available to you in retirement. But it might not be sufficient coverage in retirement. Health becomes a costlier matter in retirement and you should search for the best available insurance in your area.

In preparing a financial plan for retirement, the first report to draw up is one listing all the sources from which to expect income, and all the assets of value that do not provide income at present. Next draw up another report listing by category all the expenditures for a year—food, taxes, doctors, dentists, insurance (life, home, health and car), clothing, and vacations.

In general, if you estimate that your retirement income will amount to about 70% of what your earnings in your last year before retirement, then you can expect to live about as you had been. If the available funds seem insufficient perhaps it would be wise to consider moving to a location elsewhere in this country or abroad where the cost of living could easily be supported by your expected income. Or perhaps you should look for cheaper living quarters in your present area and find a part-time job to cover the shortfall.

Bear in mind that a number of costs go down. Such items as life insurance and annuities no longer have to be paid for, but instead start producing a lifetime income. Social Security deductions will no longer be made from your income. Instead, you will be receiving Social Security and payments have for some time been raised annually to reflect the cost of living. That has had a great deal to do with the fact that relatively few of those over 65 are destitute. The U.S. Bureau of the Census reported that the average income of families headed by individuals over 65 grew from about $3,000 per year in 1950 to about $21,000 in 1983—about twice the amount needed to keep up with inflation. In the 33 years between 1950 and 1983, many more company pension programs were instituted, and a wider selection of financial instruments in which to place savings have been developed.

Once you have a clear picture as to just what kind of life your retirement income will support, you and your spouse can decide whether early retirement is "out" and whether even regular retirement will be comfortable.

A HINDSIGHT VIEW OF RETIREMENT STRESS

There are clearly a number of potentially stressful factors in the retirement process (Table 1). These include lifestyle and location factors, spousal factors, financial factors, and health factors. Depending on individual circumstances, these factors can play a role at any point in the retirement process, whether planning for retirement, deciding to retire, or living in retirement. For example, my wife's concerns about our financial well-being were greatest during

Table 1

Retirement Stressors

LIFESTYLE AND LOCATION FACTORS

o   vocational and avocation decisions: retirement job, volunteer
    work, leisure activities

o   relocation decisions: cost; proximity to children, friends,
    leisure activities; development of new social relationships

o   death of friends, family members, former work associates

SPOUSE FACTORS

o   impact on spouse's life-style

o   dual career considerations

o   spouse concerns and anxieties

FINANCIAL FACTORS

o   income uncertainty: Social Security, pension funds, investments

o   expense uncertainty: rising health care needs, inflation, leisure activity expenses, relocation expenses

o   balance of income and expenses: changes in standard of living, expectations of retirement living

HEALTH FACTORS

o   declining physical capacity: endurance, vision, hearing, musculoskeletal condition

o   onset of major illness

o   time and effort for health care

o   insurability

the planning stages for my retirement and have eased during the retirement. Such concerns should not be taken lightly, as illustrated by the case of the former Texas Governor, John Connally, who risked and lost a fortune in the later stages of life. Retirement time is probably the time to be more conservative with regard to financial planning and investments.

There are a number of good books which may be of assistance in thinking about lifestyle, spousal, financial, and health factors which can create stress in retirement (Adler, 1975; Anonymous, 1975; Dickinson, 1976; Sunshine, 1975; Willing, 1981). In addition, one may want to join the American Association of Retired Persons.[1]

Considering the stress involved in any retirement, and the financial risks to be assumed, why retire before the oldest age at which you can work? I suggest that only health bad enough to warrant early retirement, or a strong desire for leisure to pursue other activities, coupled with the financial means necessary to provide an acceptable standard of living, are sufficient reasons for early retirement. Early retirement can be pleasant to contemplate if the remaining years to the legal age limit of 70 promise to be dull or uninviting, compared with what is planned for retirement.

NOTE

1. American Association of Retired Persons (AARP), Membership Processing Center, PO Box 199, Long Beach, CA 90801-9989.

REFERENCES

Adler, J. (1975). *The retirement book*. New York: William Morrow.
Anonymous (1978). *Plan your retirement now*. Washington, DC: U.S. News & World Report Books.
Dickinson, P. A. (1976). *The complete retirement planning book*. New York: E. P. Dutton.
Sunshine, J. (1975). *How to enjoy your retirement*. New York: Amacom.
Willing, J. Z. (1981). *The reality of retirement*. New York: William Morrow.

Career Stress in Changing Times:
Some Final Observations

Edgar H. Schein

Massachusetts Institute of Technology

The papers in this volume make an important set of observations about the changing nature of the world and the implications of those changes for career management. Several of these observations need to be underlined before I make some of my own comments.

Paid work, whether conceived in career terms or not, is created by the economic institutions of society. One of the persistent and troubling observations made repeatedly by career researchers is that the economic, political, technological, and socio-cultural environments of our economic institutions are becoming increasingly turbulent, as pointed out by Wheeler in the current volume. The effect of this is more rapid change on all fronts causing organizations to have to become more flexible and responsive to globalization, technological changes that create product obsolescence, political turmoil that makes markets uncertain, and socio-cultural changes in the needs and attitudes of people entering the work force.

Economic institutions cannot fulfill their functions if they do not survive as viable entities. If they cannot survive in their present form, they must metamorphose into other forms through mergers, acquisitions, and joint ventures. These are the subject of Matteson and Ivancevich's chapter. The complexity of tasks and the possibilities opened up by advances in information technology and "net-

Reprints may be obtained from Edgar H. Schein, Alfred P. Sloan School of Management, 50 Memorial Drive, E52-583, Massachusetts Institute of Technology, Cambridge, MA 02139.

working'' may even create brand new non-hierarchical forms of organization (Malone, 1987; Schein, 1989).

As organizations cope with increasingly turbulent environments, career stresses mount, but they do not impact all sectors of the labor market equally, and the stresses are different at different career stages, as the Quicks have pointed out in their opening chapter. Indeed, one of the more important contributions of this entire volume is the analysis of stresses at different stages and in different populations.

Furthermore, a number of the papers point out that stressors do not necessarily produce negative consequences. Under some conditions they provide opportunities for growth and redirection that are viewed positively both by career occupants and employing organizations. In thinking about preventive and ameliorative activities, we must not lose sight of the positive consequences of certain stressors, and figure out how to heighten the probability that such positive consequences will indeed follow.

As we contemplate the consequences of these changing times it is necessary, however, to focus on the primary *negative* consequences and to think in terms of preventive measures. How can the negative impacts of stressors be reduced, and whose responsibility should it be to worry about such issues? In the observations I will make below, I will try to sort out both what can be done and who should do it.

Unemployment

All of the major changes noted above have the common feature that they will create career stress. The most severe form of that stress is temporary or permanent unemployment, which has been studied extensively by Louis Ferman (1981). His research has identified a variety of patterns associated with unemployment. As many of the papers point out, unemployment has much more severe effects on some parts of the labor market — those who are financially less secure in the first place, those who are not professionalized or whose level of skill does not make them readily re-employable or trainable, and those who by personality are more vulnerable to the devastating effect that the loss of a job can have on one's self-image.

When one examines the forces acting on companies, it is clear that we cannot expect them to solve the problem of unemployment, or they simply will not survive economically. For the disadvantaged unemployed, therefore, we need preventive and ameliorative measures that will have to be created, funded, and administered either by industry consortia, unions, and/or government.

The nature of those preventive measures should take into account that the rate of change will not decrease. The only genuine preventive strategy, therefore, is to create mechanisms for better initial education and training to make people employable in the first place, and better mechanisms for retraining as technological changes make some skills obsolete. Someone other than the unemployed worker will have to finance the period of retraining, but such support should not be defined as "welfare" or unemployment compensation. Instead, it should be defined as an "educational or training expense" to keep the labor force technologically current.

We must figure out a way to define temporary unemployment as an *inevitable* and *normal* condition of modern, technologically sophisticated, global society. And we must find a way to insure that unemployment is indeed temporary; that there is always some avenue for reemployment or retraining, unless the person is financially secure and voluntarily unemployed, as in early retirement.

It is important to note the finding in this volume that retirement, especially when it is early, does not have all of the negative consequences that popular literature has emphasized. This emerges from the findings of McGoldrick and Cooper concerning their study of British workers. If people have financial security and do not feel that their self-esteem has been damaged by leaving work, they can successfully retire without negative physical or psychological consequences.

In other words, being unemployed has many meanings and facets, and it is the *consequences* that are the primary stressors. For those who need the economic returns and the self-esteem of work and who cannot find either, it can be totally devastating. For those who see it as an opportunity to develop other aspects of their lives and who feel economically secure, it can be a welcome state.

Entry, Reality Shock, and Socialization

The second major area of stress occurs around entry into the career. Specifically, the process of entry into work organizations is stressful, as Long and Nelson have discussed in their chapters. The reality shock that comes with the transition from school to work seems to occur in every occupation, and, as the rate of change of type of work increases, one can expect that the stresses of entry into the career will increase as well.

Here I think the companies must take more responsibility for reducing or preventing such stress by more realistic job/role planning and better communication during the recruitment and socialization process. This area has been extensively studied and the means are available to management to insure that the people hired will become productive and creative in the shortest possible time (see Nelson's chapter).

It is also the case that the individual career aspirant will have to take more responsibility for searching out the right kind of organization and job. Schools and training institutions have not done a good enough job in giving future employees the necessary self-insight and skill to manage their own job search and entry process better, but the knowledge base is there to do it. And many companies have instituted career development programs that emphasize self-insight, self-development, and greater taking of responsibility for the career by the career occupant.

Midlife and Midcareer

The impact of changing times on midcareer is complicated by the fact that in this stage people vary greatly in how much they are involved in career versus personal and family issues, and how much negative impact career problems will have (see, for example, the chapters by Bhagat; Davis & Kodella; Hurrell, McLaney, & Murphy). It is also a fact that some of the organizational changes, especially mergers and acquisitions may have their most severe impact on the mid-career person, as Matteson and Ivancevich and Pliner have pointed out in their chapters. To be redundant in mid-career permits neither the option of starting all over again in another company nor early retirement. Hence, not surprisingly, tensions in mid-career employees run high when companies restructure. Whose problem is this? As some of the papers imply, this is a shared problem between the individual career occupant and the employing organization. The individual must anticipate the possibility of being redundant at some point in his or her career and make contingency plans for this possibility. The company must provide as much information as possible to enable people to plan and cope with what may be ahead, and must provide counseling and reemployment services if needed (Gray, Gault, Meyers, & Walther). If such services become too expensive for a given company, one might again have to think in terms of industry consortia or public sector help.

For some people, midcareer shifts will involve potentially expensive periods of reeducation or retraining. This is especially true for those who have found in the early career that their own talents and interests are mismatched with the occupations they entered (Schein, 1978, 1985a, 1987). Providing mechanisms and funding for new education and entry into new careers that are a better match is in everyone's interest in order to maximize the productivity of society as a whole.

The midcareer group can also benefit most from various kinds of internal and external support, the importance of which is discussed by Gerpott in his study of British/American and West German research and development professionals. Support groups or mutual aid associations, often composed of peers who have had similar experiences, can have a powerful ameliorative effect and can provide ideas and resources to help people with problems to cope more effectively. Such groups work best when they are self-generated, and one may anticipate that if midcareer stress increases in the next decade, we will see more such groups springing up.

Retirement and Alternate Employment Forms

The meaning of retirement has changed in the last few decades as more companies have created programs of early retirement as a way of dealing with obsolete and excess human resources. McGoldrick and Cooper and J. F. Quick have discussed these issues earlier. By far the biggest problem of retirement appears to be whether or not the person is and feels financially secure. A secondary issue is the change in life routine when one switches from full involvement in a job and organization to a less structured situation at home. But it is clearly not the case that retirement always produces psychological and physical ill health. In fact, many voluntary early retirees appear to be very content with their decision.

For retirement to be minimally stressful, therefore, both the individual and the employing organization have to plan for the financial well being of the retiree, and the retiree has to plan for his or her psychological disengagement from the company. The company can help here by having pre-retirement seminars and sponsoring support groups to help people to make plans. It apparently does not work well to retire first and then think about what to do next.

The meaning of retirement, whether early or late, is probably also very much a function of the culture of the country and the organization (Schein, 1985b). For example, a large Mexican brewery that employed primarily members of extended families found that retirement was very stressful because the retiree had nothing to do but hang around with his children, which both the children and the retiree hated. The company diagnosed this problem and decided that the retiree had to be able to be useful; he had to have a role to play. They instituted an elaborate pre-retirement training program to teach common house maintenance skills such as plumbing, painting, electrical repair, and gardening. Now the retiree was welcomed by his busy children and could feel useful when he visited them.

Many organizations in the United States deal with such issues by phasing people out slowly, allowing part-time work or consulting and contract work following formal retirement from full-time duties. As company restructuring becomes more common and as more people are forced into early retirement, it will become essential to examine these non full-time options as transitional forms of employment.

It should also be noted that one of the major changes in the labor market is the growing number of dual career families. In such situations it becomes possible and often desirable during child rearing years for both members to work less than full time. Thus new kinds of employment contracts and part-time work should be factored into our thinking about so called "early" retirement.

One particular example that may become more common is work at home, not in addition to the normal office routine, but as a substitute for it (Bailyn, 1988). As we shift toward more of a service economy, and as information technology makes networking more feasible, it may well be that more work will be done from home. Cultural concepts of how home and work should be separated and managerial assumptions about how to exercise authority and control presently stand in the way of more widespread use of this form of work, but one may anticipate that we will see major changes in this area (Perin, 1987; Schein, 1989).

Career Anchors, the Internal Career, and Career Management

Possibly the most troubling forecast is that with organizations changing and restructuring constantly, the very concept of a career will be undermined. In other words, we will not be able to specify with respect to organizations what a typical technical, professional, or managerial career will look like. There will be fewer predictable steps, and it will be harder than ever to figure out how to prepare oneself because one will not know which skills and knowledge bases will be needed in the future. Employees may, over the course of their life, end up working for a number of companies in possibly unconnected kinds of jobs, being retrained each time they make a shift.

All of this suggests a shift in focus toward what I have called the "internal career" (Schein, 1985a, 1987). The "external" career can be thought of as the steps that one goes through in getting into and traversing a given occupation, the kinds of things one typically puts into a resume. In contrast, the "internal" career is the themes and concepts one develops that make sense out of one's own occupational pursuits. So it is perfectly possible to have an external career that looks disjointed and random, yet have a very clear concept of what one is looking for that causes one to shift so much.

As the external environment becomes more turbulent, it becomes more and more important to develop and become aware of a self-concept that provides the stability, consistency, and sense of direction that is increasingly lacking in the external environment. One of the most important stress prevention mechanisms available to us is our ability to predict what is ahead and to prepare for it. If we have a clear sense of ourselves and our options and if we have the ability to decipher what is happening in our environment, we can make better choices.

Longitudinal research has revealed (Schein, 1978; 1987) that, as we enter the career, we have a very broad view of our talents and what we are looking for. The internal career is not very well articulated, even if we have taken tests and received career counseling, because we do not have actual experience to tell us what we are good at and what we want. As we acquire work experience we gradually begin to get a clearer self-image of:

1. Our *talents and abilities* — what we are good at and what we are not good at;
2. Our *needs and motives* — what we really want out of our career and life; and
3. Our *values* — what kind of organization we want to work in and what kind of work we want to be associated with.

As we develop clarity in each of these three domains over the first three to ten years of the career we develop a self-image of who we are, what we want to do, and more importantly, what we do not want to do. This self-image I have called a "career anchor" because it functions as a guide and constraint on our career choices. Career anchors form and clarify throughout the career as a function of actual work experiences and are thus our reality test of how our inner needs can best be matched with external possibilities. Whereas our initial aspirations may be out of line with possibilities, the anchor is the evolving self-concept that takes actual work experiences into account. Anchors thus do not exist and, therefore, cannot be accurately assessed until the person has accumulated a number of years of work experience.

In our original research (1978) we found that graduates of our Masters Program in Management fell into five major clusters when interviewed 10 to 13 years following graduation:

1. *Security*: for people anchored here the overriding concern was to get work that would allow the person to feel economically secure and stable;
2. *Autonomy*: for people anchored here the overriding concern was to be the master of one's own fate, free of organizational constraints and rules;
3. *Technical or functional competence*: people in this group built their entire self-image around the particular skill or area of work in which they excelled and which they enjoyed, and for them the most important aspect of their work was to be ever more challenged in this area;
4. *Entrepreneurial creativity*: for people in this group the overriding concern was to build an organization of their own, to create a product or service that was clearly identified with their own creativity;
5. *General management competence*: these people discovered that they really wanted a position of high responsibility where their decisions would really make the difference, and that they had the analytical, interpersonal, and emotional skills to function in high level integrative jobs.

In subsequent research (1987) we found that there were at least three more types of anchors:

6. *Service/dedication to a cause*: these are people who pursue a career that is meaningful to them because of the values that it permits them to express, such as making the world a better place, helping people, and curing disease.
7. *Pure challenge*: some people enjoy their work and build their career around pure competition and challenge, either against other people, or over impossible obstacles, or against impossible odds; it is the winning, the solving of problems, the overcoming of obstacles that is more important than the area of work;
8. *Lifestyle*: with the increasing number of dual careers, and with the changing values in society around the importance of work relative to other aspects of life, a growing number of people define their career in terms of its total fit into their lifestyle, choosing the content and location of their work in terms of considerations of family and personal needs.

Though these data were originally gathered with management graduates, we have since studied other occupations and have looked at various other socio-economic groups. In each occupation we find that the people within it vary in terms of their anchors, and if the occupation is too constraining, as in assembly line work, we find that the anchors show up in the activities of the person off the job.

We are continuing to study people in different occupations and it is quite conceivable that we will uncover other anchors, but so far we have found that these eight cover most people in most occupations. The career anchor should not be confused with general motives or concerns. Most people want some aspects of each of the above, but the anchor is intended to describe that aspect of the self that a person will not give up if life circumstances force him or her to make a choice. It is the stabilizing core of the inner career, and our data so far suggest that this core gets stronger with age. So I would not expect dramatic changes in career anchors in mid or later life, though one certainly sees dramatic changes in the external career of some people, such as businessmen becoming opera singers or successful managers suddenly dropping out and deciding to sail around the world with their family.

Though these dramatic changes appear to reflect changing anchors, I have found when I am able to interview the person in depth that these changes usually reflect powerful themes that have been there all along but have been thwarted by various kinds of life circumstances such as lack of money or family obligations of various sorts. In other words, the person's dramatic shift *externally* is often the result of his or her trying to work out some aspect of their *internal* self-image that has been thwarted or held in check, but has always been there.

Many kinds of job situations permit a person to fulfill a variety of needs, motives, and values, and permit the exercise of a variety of talents. It may thus appear that the person has many anchors. However, if one poses forced choice questions to oneself, one usually discovers that if one had to make a choice, our priorities are quite clear and there are some things we would not give up. It is those things that are the anchor.

I believe that it is extremely important for people to discover what their own career anchors are so that they do not make mistakes when they find themselves in career choice situations, possibly end-ing up in a job that they are no good at or do not enjoy. Increasingly, people will have to learn to manage their career in terms of their anchor and other priorities they may have.

Such self-insight and self-management will apply not only to the occupations normally considered "careers," but will apply to all levels of employees. And that will mean a very different concept of high school and college career counseling. Instead of broad occupational choice as the focus, counselors may have to put more emphasis on trying out many different options, developing all of one's skills (since one cannot predict which ones will be most relevant in the future), being prepared for a longer period of trial and error in getting into one's work life, and being prepared for periodic stints of retraining and shifting one's area of work even as one's anchor remains stable.

In other words, if some of the things discussed in this book come to pass, the responsibility for career management will fall even more on the individual employee at every level, and we must begin to build the institutions to make such self-management possible into our educational system. Only if the employee of the future enters the labor market psychologically prepared for the turbulence he or she will find there can he or she cope effectively with its realities and turn stressors into opportunities for growth.

REFERENCES

Bailyn, L. (1988). Freeing work from the constraints of location and time. *New Technology, Work, and Employment, 3*, (in press).

Ferman, L. (1981). *Plant closing and economic dislocation*. Kalamazoo, MI: W. E. Upjohn.

Malone, T. W. (1987). Modelling coordination in organizations and markets. *Management Science, 33*, 1317-1332.

Perin, C. (1987). Working together across space and time. *Management in the 1990's*. Cambridge, MA: Sloan School of Management, MIT.

Schein, E. H. (1978). *Career dynamics*. Reading, MA: Addison-Wesley.

Schein, E. H. (1985a). *Career anchors*. San Diego: University Associates.

Schein, E. H. (1985b). *Organizational culture and leadership*. San Francisco: Jossey Bass.

Schein, E. H. (1987). Individuals and careers. In J. Lorsch (Ed.), *Handbook of organizational behavior*. Englewood Cliffs, NJ: Prentice-Hall, 155-171.

Schein, E. H. (1989). Reassessing the "divine rights" managers. *Sloan Management Review, 10* (Winter), 63-68.

T - #0035 - 230425 - C0 - 212/152/15 [17] - CB - 9780866569569 - Gloss Lamination